Social Entrepreneurship and Social Innovation

T0358896

This book provides comprehensive and advanced analysis of the characteristics of social entrepreneurship in Europe. It offers innovative, up-to-date research on the ecosystems of social entrepreneurship, the behavior of social entrepreneurs, their ability to produce social innovation, social capital and social inclusion, and the role of stakeholders in fostering socially oriented businesses. Moreover, it addresses the diversity of the European social enterprise sector from an evolutionary perspective, with particular reference to the rise of social entrepreneurship and the role of new-generation social entrepreneurs throughout Europe. Multidisciplinary contributions authored by experts from business and accounting, economics, and sociology serve the purpose of delivering a holistic study of social entrepreneurship, also providing the necessary data for delivering policy implications on the features of the most effective enabling social and institutional ecosystems.

The broad approach, based on different theoretical frameworks and methodologies across numerous disciplines, enables the authors to tackle all of the complex research issues connected to social entrepreneurship in the region. The book builds on the results of the European Union 7FP (European Union's Research and Innovation funding program for 2007–2013)-funded "EFESEIIS – Enabling the flourishing and evolution of social entrepreneurship for innovative and inclusive societies" research project.

The central theme of the book is an evolutionary perspective on the dynamics and the rise of the social enterprise in Europe. This evolutionary perspective can be used in an economic as well as a social longitudinal analysis of changing contexts and entrepreneurial practices. The evolutionary perspective will be used as a tool to account for the specificity of developmental pathways in different contexts and countries.

Mario Biggeri is Associate Professor in Development Economics at the Department of Economics and Management of University of Florence, and Scientific Director of ARCO (Action Research for CO-development) research center, Italy.

Enrico Testi did his PhD in Economics at the University of Florence on Enabling Eco-systems for Social Enterprises. Since 2009, he has been the executive director of ARCO (Action Research for CO-development) research centre, Italy. Since 2011, he has been director of the Yunus Social Business Centre at the University of Florence.

Marco Bellucci is Postdoctoral Research Fellow in Accounting at the University of Florence, Italy. His research interests include corporate social responsibility, sustainability reporting, third-sector organizations, and social enterprises.

Roel During is coordinator of the Social Innovation for Value Creation Programme of Wageningen University and Research, the Netherlands. Although educated as a biologist, much of his work is dedicated to social and governance studies.

H. Thomas R. Persson is Associate Professor at the Department of Work Science and the Director of the Research Platform of Business Collaboration of Kristianstad University, Sweden. His research interests include governance, social responsibility, and social enterprises.

RIOT!

Routledge Studies in Innovation, Organizations and Technology

The New Production of Users
Changing Innovation Collectives and Involvement Strategies
*Edited by Sampsa Hyysalo, Torben Elgaard Jensen,
and Nelly Oudshoorn*

Foundations of Information Systems
Research and Practice
Andrew Basden

Social Inclusion and Usability of ICT-Enabled Services
Edited by Jyoti Choudrie, Panayiota Tsatsou and Sherah Kurnia

Strategic Marketing for High Technology Products
An Integrated Approach
Thomas Fotiadis

Responsible Research and Innovation
From Concepts to Practices
Edited by Robert Gianni, John Pearson and Bernard Reber

Technology Offsets in International Defence Procurement
Kogila Balakrishnan

Social Entrepreneurship and Social Innovation
Ecosystems for Inclusion in Europe
*Edited by Mario Biggeri, Enrico Testi, Marco Bellucci,
Roel During and H. Thomas R. Persson*

For more information about the series, please visit www.routledge.com/
Routledge-Studies-in-Innovation-Organizations-and-Technology/book-
series/RIOT

Social Entrepreneurship and Social Innovation

Ecosystems for Inclusion in Europe

Edited by Mario Biggeri, Enrico Testi,
Marco Bellucci, Roel During and
H. Thomas R. Persson

LONDON AND NEW YORK

First published 2019
by Routledge
2 Park Square, Milton Park, Abingdon, Oxon OX14 4RN

and by Routledge
52 Vanderbilt Avenue, New York, NY 10017, USA

First issued in paperback 2020

Routledge is an imprint of the Taylor & Francis Group, an informa business

British Library Cataloguing-in-Publication Data
A catalogue record for this book is available from the British Library

Library of Congress Cataloging-in-Publication Data
A catalog record has been requested for this book

ISBN 13: 978-0-367-58574-7 (pbk)
ISBN 13: 978-0-8153-7579-1 (hbk)

Typeset in Sabon
by codeMantra

We dedicate this volume to the memory of Pat van der Jagt, member of the Dutch team of EFESEIIS, who inspired the project with her cultural curiosity and creativity.

Contents

List of figures   xi
List of tables   xii
Contributors   xiv

1 An introduction to social entrepreneurship in Europe   1
   ENRICO TESTI, MARIO BIGGERI, MARCO BELLUCCI,
   ROEL DURING, AND H. THOMAS R. PERSSON

2 Research background, theoretical frameworks, and
   methodologies for social entrepreneurship   13
   ROEL DURING, H. THOMAS R. PERSSON, MARIO BIGGERI,
   ENRICO TESTI, AND MARCO BELLUCCI

3 The rise of social enterprises and social entrepreneurship
   in Western Europe   24
   SIMONE BAGLIONI, DIDIER CHABANET,
   AND H. THOMAS R. PERSSON

4 The diversity of European social enterprises:
   an evolutionary perspective   38
   ROEL DURING AND ROSALIE VAN DAM

5 Emerging managerial aspects of social entrepreneurship
   in Europe   54
   MARCO BELLUCCI, ENRICO TESTI, SERENA FRANCHI,
   AND MARIO BIGGERI

6 Are decision makers in Social Enterprises more
   pro-social than their peers? An analysis of production
   and consumption choices   69
   ENRICO TESTI, MARIO BIGGERI, DOMENICO COLUCCI,
   NICOLA DONI, AND VINCENZO VALORI

 7 Social capital in social enterprises   96
    AGATA ZABŁOCKA, RYSZARD PRASZKIER,
    MARTA KACPRZYK-MURAWSKA, AND EWA PETRUSHAK

 8 The role of stakeholder networks in shaping the development
    of social enterprise ecosystems   110
    RICHARD HAZENBERG, MEANU BAJWA-PATEL,
    AND TOA GIROLETTI

 9 Understanding the innovative behavior of social enterprises   127
    ANA ALEKSIĆ MIRIĆ, MARINA PETROVIĆ, AND
    ZORICA ANIČIĆ

10 Social innovation in niches   145
    CHRISTINA GRABBE, KATHARINA OBUCH, AND
    ANNETTE ZIMMER

11 The in-between space of new generation social enterprises   164
    MARA BENADUSI AND ROSARIO SAPIENZA

12 A framework to understand enabling ecosystems
    for social enterprises   179
    MARIO BIGGERI, ENRICO TESTI, AND ANDREA FERRANNINI

13 Concluding remarks on social entrepreneurship in Europe   200
    H. THOMAS R. PERSSON, MARIO BIGGERI,
    ENRICO TESTI, MARCO BELLUCCI, AND ROEL DURING

    Index   209

Figures

1.1 The relationship between social entrepreneurship, social enterprises, and social innovation   7

4.1 Fitness in social entrepreneurship   48

4.2 An overview of the evolutionary process   49

6.1 Personal, enterprise, and contextual features that influence decision-making   74

6.2 Interpretative framework and variables   79

7.1 Trust levels by relation (average number of contacts)   102

7.2 Trust levels by type of organization (average number of contacts)   102

7.3 Trust levels by age of organization (average number of contacts)   103

7.4 Sense of support levels from social networks by relation (average number of contacts)   103

7.5 Sense of support levels from social networks by type of organization (average number of contacts)   104

7.6 Sense of support levels from social networks by age of the organization (average number of contacts)   104

7.7 Cooperation levels by perceived closeness of relations (average number of contacts)   105

8.1 Comparative development of the Scottish and English ecosystems   113

8.2 Social enterprise ecosystem typologies   121

12.1 A framework to analyze social enterprises in the ecosystem   185

Tables

2.1	Focus, theoretical framework, and methods for each strand of research	17
3.1	Paid employment in the social economy in relation to total paid employment (in thousands)	29
3.2	Paid employment in cooperatives, mutuals, and associations	29
4.1	Evolutionary concepts and social enterprises	41
6.1	Variable definitions and descriptive statistics	80
6.2	Regression between "Social Value of Consumption" (a dependent variable) and several independent variables	82
6.3	Regression between dependent variable Social Value of Consumption and independent variables including positioning	82
6.4	Regression between dependent variable Social Value of Consumption and independent variables including positioning, using multiple imputation for missing data	83
6.5	Ordered logit regression between "Social Value of product" (a dependent variable) and several independent variables with imputed values	84
6.6	Ordered logit regression between dependent variable Social Value of product and independent variables including positioning	85
6.7	Ordered logit regression between dependent variable Social Value of product and independent variables, including positioning with imputed values	86
9.1	Problem solving and innovativeness	132
9.2	Importance of innovation during different stages of the life cycle—testing equality of means	132
9.3	Importance of growth and innovativeness	133
9.4	Size of enterprises and innovativeness	133
9.5	Turnover and innovativeness	134
9.6	Education and innovativeness	135
9.7	Age and innovativeness	135
9.8	Previous founding and/or managing experience	136
9.9	Motivations and innovativeness	137

9.10	Satisfaction with professional life and innovativeness testing equality of means	137
9.11	Paid staff involvement	138
9.12	Team characteristics and innovativeness—testing equality of means	138
9.13	Impact of the external environment on organizational innovativeness	138
9.14	Starter funds and innovativeness	139
9.15	Actual funds and innovativeness	139
9.16	Stakeholder influence and innovativeness—testing equality of means	140
9.17	Stakeholder engagement practices and innovativeness	140
9.18	Summary table	141
10.1	Cases (overview)	158
12.1	The main features of an enabling ecosystem	192

Contributors

Ana Aleksić Mirić is an Associate Professor in the Faculty of Economics at the University of Belgrade. She holds a MSci and PhD from the Faculty of Economics at the University of Belgrade. She has been a visiting scholar at Duke University's Fuqua School of Business (USA) and Carnegie Mellon University (USA). She has been involved in research projects financed by the European Union, the World Bank Institute, and the Serbian government. These projects emphasized the effects reforms to the Serbian economy have had on growth, employment, competitive market structure, and the competitiveness of firms. Ana has served as a consultant for both private and public organizations. She also has a rich publishing history, producing individual chapters and articles in several edited collections and scholarly journals.

Zorica Aničić is a Teaching Assistant in the Faculty of Economics at the University of Belgrade. She holds a MSc. from the Faculty of Economics at the University of Belgrade. While working on her MSc., she was hired as a regional pricing analyst by a multinational pharmaceutical company. She is currently a doctoral student in the Faculty of Economics at the University of Belgrade. She has been involved in research projects financed by the European Union, the Serbian government, and several private companies in Serbia. Her research focused on entrepreneurship, corporate government, financial analysis, and facilities studies. She has served as a consultant for both private- and public-sector organizations, and has had her work published in several scholarly journals.

Simone Baglioni is Professor of politics in the Yunus Centre for Social Business and Health, Glasgow Caledonian University, the UK. His research interests include social innovation and the social economy, civil society and social movements. On these topics he has extensively published. Currently he is the principal investigator and coordinator of the EU Horizon 2020 project SIRIUS (Skills and Integration of Migrants, Refugees and Asylum Applicants in European Labour Markets) and the principal investigator for Glasgow Caledonian University in the EU Horizon 2020 projects Fab-Move (For a Better Tomorrow: Social Enterprise on the Move) and TransSOL (Transnational Solidarity at Times of Crisis).

Meanu Bajwa-Patel is a Senior Researcher in the Institute for Social Innovation and Impact (ISII) at the University of Northamton. She is currently engaged with a range of projects, both national and European, looking at social impact, social innovation, and social enterprise. Meanu has taught trainee teachers and modules on an MA in Special Educational Needs (SEN) and Inclusion. She is a member of the British Educational Research Association (BERA). Her research interests include education and disadvantaged young people, pupil premium, SEN and inclusion, social impact and innovation, gender and equality, and research methods.

Marco Bellucci is Postdoctoral Research Fellow in Accounting at the University of Florence. He holds a PhD with distinction in Business Administration and Management from the University of Pisa. His research interests include corporate social responsibility, sustainability reporting, social enterprises and third sector organizations. He is Social Economy Unit Coordinator at Action Research for CO-development (ARCO) and Project Manager of the Yunus Social Business Centre of the University of Florence under the patronage of Nobel laureate Muhammad Yunus. He was Visiting Scholar at the Schulich School of Business at York University in Toronto. He is the author of many articles in a host of respected scholarly journals and a book on *Sustainability Reporting and Stakeholder Engagement* published by Routledge. He is Associated Editor for *Business Ethics: A European Review*.

Mara Benadusi is Associate Professor in Anthropology at the Department of Political and Social Sciences, University of Catania (Italy). Her main research interests focus on the theme of vulnerability, resilience, and risk related to natural disasters and environmental crises, and the social and political consequences of the processes of deindustrialization and "green grabbing." She has served as scientific supervisor for the IMPACT HUB network in the EFESEIIS Project. Most recently, she was involved as local coordinator in the European project "For a Better Tomorrow: Social Enterprises on the Move (FAB-Move)" and became president of the Italian Society for Applied Anthropology (SIAA).

Mario Biggeri is Associate Professor in Development Economics at the Department of Economics and Management at the University of Florence, Italy. He is the Academic Director of the BA in Economic Development, International Social and Health Cooperation and Conflict Management at the University of Florence, Italy. His research interests include sustainable human development, international cooperation, capability approach, social innovation, impact evaluation, local development, social economy, social enterprises, clusters of small and medium enterprises, informal activities, child labor, children and youths' well-being, and persons with disabilities' well-being. He has also acquired relevant experiences coordinating as the scientific director of many international and national research groups in financed research projects (such as EuropeAid and the 7thFP research projects EFESEIIS and DISCIT – Making Persons with Disabilities Full Citizens), field researches, and projects' impact eva luations. He has worked for UNICEF Innocenti Research Centre (IRC), for the ILO/UNICEF/World Bank Project Understanding Children Work, and for UNDP on territorial human development. He is Scientific Director of the university research center ARCO and Director of the Scientific and Ethical Committee of the Yunus Social Business Center, University of Florence. He has been a Fellow of the Human Development Capability Association (HDCA) since 2010, and since 2016, he has been member of the Executive Committee. He is the co-author and/or co-editor of twenty books (including three for Routledge) and has published extensively in a broad range of international academic journals.

Didier Chabanet is Senior Lecturer at IDRAC Business School in Lyon and at TRIANGLE (University of Lyon). He is also Research Associate at CEVIPOF-Sciences Po. He has established himself as a well-known international scholar in the field of social movements, social exclusion, and social economy.

Domenico Colucci holds a PhD in Mathematics for Economic Decisions at Pisa University, with a thesis on "Limits to computational ability in economic models: some mathematical foundations with economic applications." He is Tenured Researcher at the Department of Economics and Management, University of Florence. His research interests include experimental, behavioral, and computational economics: expectation formation, heterogeneous agents, and stability of rational expectations equilibria.

Nicola Doni is a Professor in Economics at the University of Florence. He studied in Pisa, Torino, and Siena. His research interests include Auctions Theory, Industrial Organization, and Environmental Economics. Since 2006, he has been teaching Environmental Economics. He has managed many research reports on issues related to procurement for many national institutions such as the Italian Ministry of Environmental Policy and GSE (Gestore servizi elettrici). He has published in international journals, including *Journal of Economics*, *Resource and Energy Economics*, *Journal of Economics and Management Strategy*, *Economics Letters*, *Journal of Regulatory Economics*, *Energy Policy*, and *Annals of Public and Cooperative Economics*.

Roel During is coordinator of the Social Innovation for Value Creation Programme of Wageningen University and Research. Although educated as a biologist, much of his work is dedicated to social and governance studies. He did his PhD on cultural heritage in Europe. He specializes in social systems analysis. He prefers to work in a political context and did so in various assignments from the Dutch Parliament and Senate. He has a broad interest in public policy making, addressing bottom-up environmental, cultural, and economic issues at all policy levels. He worked on trends and transitions in society related to the so-called participation or do-it-yourself society.

Andrea Ferrannini is senior researcher at ARCO (Action Research for CO-development) and coordinator of the Strategic Unit on Local Development since 2012. He is also Lecturer of Development Economics in the School of Economics and Management at the University of Florence, as well as member of the Executive Board of ILS LEDA – International Links and Services for Local Economic Development Agencies. He has conducted and coordinated several research projects in Armenia, Bolivia, Cape Verde, Colombia, Dominican Republic, Ethiopia, Italy, Mauritius, Palestine, and Uganda. His research activities focus on sustainable human development at the local level, international cooperation, industrial policies, local economic development, and participatory methods, on which he has published several articles, books, and chapters. He holds a MSc in Local Economic Development from the London School of Economics and Political Science and he is currently PhD student in Economics and Management of Innovation and Sustainability at the University of Ferrara.

Serena Franchi obtained the MA degree in Local and Regional Development Analysis and Policies at the University of Florence with honors in 2015. Since January 2014, she has worked as Research Assistant at ARCO lab under the unit "Social Economy and Responsible Businesses." Her research fields are local development and social inclusion policies.

Toa Giroletti is a Researcher at the Institute for Social Innovation and Impact at the University of Northampton. She has a bachelor's degree and MSc from the University of Pavia (Italy). In 2017, she obtained her PhD in Quantitative Models for Policy Analysis from the Catholic University of the Sacred Heart of Piacenza (Italy). She is currently working on several local and international projects focusing on social impact. Toa's current research interests are focused on individual perceptions of poverty and well-being, applied to the study of social innovations. Furthermore, she is interested in the collection of primary data and the methodological issues that arise when an individual's perspective are investigated using subjective evaluation.

Christina Grabbe is a master's student in Political Science at the University of Münster and graduated with a double bachelor's degree in Public Administration and European Studies from the University of Münster and the University of Twente in the Netherlands. She worked as a student research assistant in the European research project "EFESEIIS" (2013–2016) and was a visiting student at the China Academy of

Social Governance at the Beijing Normal University. Her research interests span welfare states and civil society in Europe and China.

Richard Hazenberg is a Principal Researcher and Research Leader of the Institute for Social Innovation and Impact at the University of Northampton. Since joining the University of Northampton in 2009, he has completed a PhD that explored the evaluation of outcome benefits in social enterprises in the work-integration sector. He also has research interests in the areas of social innovation, social finance, social enterprise governance, and social impact measurement. He also contributed a book chapter to the Routledge book *Social enterprise: Accountability & evaluation around the world*, which explored international perspectives of social enterprise. He is one of the University of Northampton's leading academic researchers in the field of social innovation, social entrepreneurship, and social impact.

Marta Kacprzyk-Murawska is a sociologist whose main research interests focus on applications of complex systems theory to social science but also on policy modelling, social influence, trust, phenomena of coherence, and Alternative Dispute Resolution. Since 2010, she has been working in the area of policy modelling, gaining expertise in transferring the narratives provided by stakeholders into simulation models. She has extensive experience in the development and realization of international as well as national projects.

Katharina Obuch is project manager of the European research project "FAB-Move." She studied Political Science, English, and Romance Philology, and holds a PhD in Political Science from the University of Münster. She worked as a Research Assistant in a project on "Gender Relations in Authoritarian Regimes" (2013–2015) at the Center for European Gender Studies (ZEUGS) and on the European research project "EFESEIIS" (2013–2016). Her research interests include civil society, gender relations, and democratization, with a focus on Latin American countries.

H. Thomas R. Persson is Associate Professor at the Department of Work Science and the Director of the Research Platform of Business Collaboration of Kristianstad University, Sweden. His research interests include governance, social responsibility, and social enterprises.

Marina Petrović is a Teaching Assistant in the Faculty of Economics at the University of Belgrade. She holds an MSci from the Faculty of Economics at the University of Belgrade. She is currently pursuing a PhD in statistics from the Faculty of Economics at the University of Belgrade. She has taken part in research projects financed by USAID, the World Bank, and the Serbian government. These projects involved statistical analysis on the effects reforms to the Serbian economy have had on economic growth, the labor market, and education. Her primary research interests are statistics, market research, and online surveys. She has contributed individual chapters and articles to several edited collections and scholarly journals.

Ewa Petrushak, psychologist, is a Research Assistant in the Robert B. Zajonc Institute for Social Studies and an instructor at Warsaw International Studies in Psychology, University of Warsaw. Her scientific interests circle around social entrepreneurship and forensic psychology. She works as a probation officer and an educator for minors and their families.

Ryszard Praszkier, PhD, hab., is an Assistant Professor at the Institute for Social Studies, University of Warsaw (www.iss.uw.edu.pl), and is a Professor at the International Institute for Social & European Studies in Hungary (ISES). As an academic researcher, he studies the dynamics of social change, specifically the mechanisms that make change durable and irreversible. Dr. Praszkier worked for Ashoka, Innovators for the Public (www.ashoka.org), for over 16 years, joining in 1994 as a Country Director to launch Ashoka Poland; since 2000, he has been an international staff training director and, until now, a second-opinion reviewer, chairing, in many countries, the selection process to Ashoka Fellowship. He authored and co-authored several articles and book chapters, co-authored the Cambridge University Press book *Social Entrepreneurship: Theory and Practice* (2012), and authored the book *Empowering Leadership of Tomorrow* (Cambridge University Press, 2018).

Rosario Sapienza is an anthropologist with more than 20 years of experience in the field of social sciences. He carried out and coordinated several research projects on immigration, criminality, trafficking of human beings, and different youth-related issues. He also monitored, evaluated, planned, and managed projects and programs in the field of International Cooperation and Humanitarian Aid. Among the principal organizations to which he provided his services are the EC, the Italian Cooperation, IFAD, UNDP, UNICEF, and USAID. Since 2010, Rosario has been cofounder of Impact HUB Siracusa within the Impact HUB Network. In recent years, for the Impact HUB Network, he has been the scientific coordinator of the projects EFESEIIS and FAB-MOVE.

Enrico Testi has a PhD in Economics at the University of Florence. Since 2009, he has been the executive director of ARCO research centre. In 2011, he cofounded and started managing, as Director of International Relations, the Yunus Social Business Centre University of Florence (www.sbflorence.org) in partnership with Nobel Peace Prize winner Muhammad Yunus, the founder of Grameen Bank. In 2012, he started a pilot program to create an enabling ecosystem for Social Entrepreneurship and Social Innovation in Pistoia (2012) called "Social

Business City Program." The program was scaled to Barcelona (Spain) in 2015. In 2013, *Vita Non-Profit Magazine* included him in the list of the top 100 Social Innovators in Italy. Between 2013 and 2016, he has been the project manager of the FP7 EFESEIIS research project financed by the EU Commission.

Vincenzo Valori is Professor of Economics at the University of Florence, Italy. He is also cofounder and coordinator of BEELab, the Behavioural and Experimental Economics Lab of the University of Florence. His research interests presently span from bounded rationality and expectations formation to reputation building and feedback mechanisms in online markets. Further details are available at http://vincenzovalori.altervista.org/.

Rosalie van Dam did her PhD on self-organizing communities and governmental responses to them. She was educated as a policy analyst, and most of her work involves fieldwork on active citizenship and the various forms of cultural and social capital involved. Recently, she works on citizens' science.

Agata Zabłocka, PhD, psychologist, is a Dean's plenipotentiary for quality evaluation and a deputy director of the Institute for the Foundation of Psychology at the SWPS University of Social Sciences and Humanities. Her scientific interests concern social entrepreneurship, specifically the role of social innovators in the accumulation of social capital and positive social change in Polish education. She participated in various EU and Polish academic grants in the field of social psychology. She is teaching the methodology of psychosocial studies and is an expert in data analysis. Dr. Zabłocka co-authored several articles and book chapters.

Annette Zimmer, Professor of Social Policy and Comparative Politics at Muenster University, was affiliated with the Program on Non-profit-Organizations at Yale University (USA) and with the John Hopkins Project. She served as the DAAD Visiting Professor at the University of Toronto (Canada) and as a visiting scholar at the American Institute for Contemporary Germany Studies (AICGS) in Washington D.C. Currently, she is a member of the Advisory Board of the German Survey on Volunteering (Freiwilligensurvey), which is funded by the federal government. She is the author of numerous books and articles, and she served as President of the International Society for Third Sector Research (ISTR).

1 An introduction to social entrepreneurship in Europe

Enrico Testi, Mario Biggeri, Marco Bellucci, Roel During, and H. Thomas R. Persson

A worldwide phenomenon

In recent years, the search for alternative and more sustainable models of economic and human development has increased significantly (Anand & Sen, 1994; Stiglitz et al., 2009; Crane & Matten, 2016). The traditional idea of enterprises as mere profit-maximizing organizations, as well as the notion that entrepreneurs are interested only in maximizing their personal gains, has also been questioned (Freeman, 1984; Elkington, 1998; Bagnoli, 2004; Bellucci & Manetti, 2018). Enterprises set up for social purposes rather than profit maximization or personal gain have a long history in Europe, especially in Italy and the United Kingdom (Bellucci et al., 2012; Testi et al., 2017). However, the advocacy activities of Nobel Peace Prize winner Prof. Muhammad Yunus, the founder of the Grameen Bank, have had the greatest impact in changing the perception of enterprises among the general public. According to Muhammad Yunus (2003), "Personal gains is not the only possible fuel for free enterprise. Social goals can replace greed as a powerful motivational force. Social-consciousness-driven enterprises can be formidable competitors for the greed-based enterprises" (p. 149).

The 2008 economic crisis, in tandem with growing concern for sustainability issues, has resulted in a widespread awakening of consciousness (Becattini, 2015). For this reason, social entrepreneurship, social innovation, and social enterprises (SEs) have received a great deal of attention. The exact meanings of these concepts and how they relate to one another has, at various times, been the subject of intense debate, particularly as their relevance and popularity in policy circles has ebbed and flowed. All three concepts are capable of facilitating positive social change, including tackling problems associated with aging populations, widening access to education, and promoting a gender-balanced and just society. These concepts are also seen as measures to foster policy innovation by engaging both policy makers and citizens.

SEs are often perceived as being able to satisfy the growing need for social services in a context of decreased public spending while also creating greater employment opportunities, especially for people who have been excluded from the labor market (Defourny & Nyssen, 2006; Borzaga et al., 2008).

In Europe, for instance, SEs started to assume greater importance after the Social Business Initiative (SBI) was launched by the EU Commission in 2011. The SBI aimed to create a favorable financial, administrative, and legal environment for SEs, thereby allowing them to operate on equal footing with other types of enterprises.

The SBI drew attention to the relationship between SEs and the larger economic environment in which they are set while also emphasizing how various features of the system influence the overall development and performance of SEs. Since SEs are often seen as having a positive impact on society and contributing to human and economic development (Scarlato, 2012), many countries have tried to pinpoint the best methods to promote their establishment and success. This strategy had already been emphasized in academic circles for several years, but policy makers lagged behind. In her seminal paper on creating a workable research agenda for SEs, Helen Haugh (2005) claimed that the environmental context in which SEs operate deserved further research, an argument that has also been put forth by Peattie and Morley (2008). Moreover, given the increasingly relevant role of SEs across much of Europe, many research strands require new scientific contributions, including how to assess the impact generated by these organizations and/or the best way to promote accountability and sustainability reporting from a triple bottom line perspective (Elkington, 1998; Manetti et al., 2015; Bellucci et al., 2012; Bellucci & Manetti, 2018; Manetti & Bellucci, 2016).

European policy has also focused on the related concept of social innovation (Ilie & During, 2012). For instance, in 2010, the European Commission published a set of recommendations (EU, 2010) on how member states can achieve innovation in all policy fields. The Commission expressed the need to foster innovation by adopting a more strategic approach. "Innovation," it argued,

> is the overarching policy objective where we take a medium – to longer – term perspective, where all policy instruments measures and funding are designed to contribute to innovation, where EU and national/regional policies are closely aligned and mutually reinforcing, and last but not least, where the highest political level sets a strategic agenda, regularly monitors progress and tackles delays.
>
> (EU, 2010)

Social innovation is, of course, a pivotal part of this strategy, and specific recommendations have been devoted to it. For example, social innovation policies (Biggeri et al., 2017) have been drawn up to help member states modernize their education systems; deal with the challenge of aging populations; and "develop a better understanding of public sector innovation, identify and give visibility to successful initiatives, and benchmark progress" (EU, 2010).

SEs are often regarded as vectors of social innovation. Looking at how SEs and the concept of social innovation have developed in several different countries allows us to discuss the differences that have emerged in national, regional, and urban contexts. A multitude of practices have been highlighted in our study, some of which are embedded in local economies, while others are embedded in social and cultural initiatives. Different approaches to value creation, competition, and revenues can be found all across Europe and will be presented in this volume. And yet, despite these differences, a few common "coordination" mechanisms can also be detected. For instance, when an SE and/or social innovation complements/operationalizes a specific policy, affects change in social relationships, or empowers vulnerable groups, a "coordination" mechanism has been employed. This, in turn, allows the government, private groups, and individuals (e.g. social entrepreneurs and social innovators) to come together, often with positive results.

Coordination mechanisms are products of various types of interactions, including exchanges of information, ideas, and commitment. Studying them requires a bottom-up evolutionary perspective, one that goes beyond the scope of recently developed governance models—most notably multi-level and multi-stakeholder governance. In fact, these two models overestimate the role of governmental actors and underestimate other sources of innovation (Van Assche et al., 2013). Moreover, understanding what actually constitutes an enabling ecosystem for SEs (and assessing its influence) requires new analytical frameworks that take into account dynamic developmental processes that shape both ecosystems and the SEs that operate in those ecosystems (Biggeri et al., 2017).

Enabling the Flourishing and Evolution of Social Entrepreneurship for Innovative and Inclusive Societies (EFESEIIS project)

The various chapters in this edited volume discuss the main results of the EFESEIIS project, an initiative that had four main objectives. The first objective was to construct an evolutionary theory that can explain how social entrepreneurship developed differently in various European countries. The researchers examined the history and evolution of social entrepreneurship; its operational and organizational forms; and how social entrepreneurship was often shaped by communities, cultures, traditions, social innovation, and dialogue between the state and its citizens.

The second objective involved identifying the various features of an enabling ecosystem for social entrepreneurship. This objective is especially important to policy makers who want to better understand how to promote social entrepreneurship in their particular countries. The project partners agreed that social entrepreneurship is a mainly local phenomenon, meaning that its activities are usually performed at the local level and focus on local problems. Social entrepreneurship is thus expressed through relationships with consumers and producers, the financial sector, support services, and policy makers operating at the local level. Of course, it is also influenced by the broader context in which it takes place, including the dominant discourses and ideologies that often define any given historical moment and the various cultural, legal, and institutional features of the jurisdiction itself. As a result, our research had to consider all of these components when building a framework capable of analyzing ecosystems and how they may or may not support SEs.

The third objective was to identify the New Generation of Social Entrepreneurs (NGSEs). Social entrepreneurs have faced unique conditions in the past decade or so. On the one hand, the 2008 economic crisis precipitated drastic welfare cuts in the name of austerity, which reduced the incomes of some social entrepreneurs, created new social problems that had to be addressed, and spurred innovative approaches. On the other hand, significant attention has been placed on social entrepreneurship by citizens, governments, and financial institutions, which has had a profound impact on NGSEs. Likewise, the EFESEIIS project made an effort to examine the various features, needs, constraints, and contributions to social innovation that often characterize NGSEs, which will, in turn, help policy makers, financial institutions, and support organizations harness their potential.

The final objective of this study was to provide advice to stakeholders on how to draft policies and services that will foster social entrepreneurship and social innovation. All in all, this volume hopes to provide new theoretical and empirical contributions that can address all four research objectives.

In order to meet these research objectives, a large European consortium was formed. The group was led by PIN S.c.r.l. Servizi didattici e scientifici per l'Università di Firenze (Italy); its research center ARCO (Action Research for CO-development); and research institutions from several different European countries, including Glasgow Caledonian University (Scotland), Fondacija Za Razvoj Ekonomske Nauke (Serbia), Impact Hub Vienna (Austria), Nxitja e Biznesit Social Sha (Albania), Science Po – Fondation Nationale des Sciences Politiques Paris (France), Stichting Dienst Landbou wkundig Onderzoek – Alterra (the Netherlands), and Syddansk Universitet (Denmark). Our researchers examined SEs in 11 countries—Albania, Austria, England, France, Germany, Italy, Poland, Serbia, Scotland, Sweden, and the Netherlands—and received funding from the European Union's Seventh Framework Programme.

The researchers implemented a complex research design that was built on both qualitative and quantitative methodologies. The findings were used to determine how social entrepreneurship and SEs emerged in various countries, placing special emphasis on their coevolution with major institutions, their reciprocal relationship with their ecosystems, and how people who have recently founded SEs differ from older generations of social entrepreneurs. All of the project partners created in-depth case studies on NGSEs. They also surveyed representatives from several SEs and presided over focus groups and one-on-one interviews with stakeholders. All in all, more than 1,500 social entrepreneurs and stakeholders were involved in the three-year project.

Data analysis has been done at a micro, meso, and macro level. Our micro-level analysis focuses on the internal features of social entrepreneurship, such as the background of entrepreneurs, behavioral issues, management techniques, business design, social value creation, sustainability, market orientation, and innovation. Our meso-level analysis, meanwhile, focuses on how social entrepreneurs and SEs interact with their surrounding environments—most notably customers, policy makers, financial institutions, support services, other social entrepreneurs/enterprises, and citizens—and the extent to which they rely on social capital. Lastly, our macro-level analysis focuses on national and international trends, paying special attention to various legal, historical, and cultural contexts. Thanks to the passion, knowledge, and experience of social entrepreneurs and their stakeholders, the EFESEIIS project was able to examine and assess many of the issues related to SEs in several European countries.

The "glossary controversy": basic definitions of social entrepreneurship and social innovation

The scholarly literature has not been able to reach a consensus in terms of how SEs ought to be defined or classified (Nicholls, 2006; Hockerts, 2006; Jones & Keogh, 2006). Some of the difficulties in defining SEs stem from the interchangeable use of terms such as social business (Yunus & Weber 2008) and social entrepreneurship. According to Borzaga and his colleagues (2012), the terms social entrepreneurship, social business, and SE tend to overlap because all of them refer

> to initiatives which have the explicit aim to generate social value through the private use and management of human and financial resources that are partially generated by market and quasi-market exchanges. As such, these initiatives are not designed to pursue the maximization of profits, but rather to use market mechanisms to underwrite the provision of goods and services that have a social impact.
>
> (p. 400)

The EMES network defines SEs as

> not-for-profit private organizations providing goods or services directly related to their explicit aim to benefit the community. They rely on collective dynamics involving various types of stakeholders in their governing bodies, they place a high value on their autonomy and they bear economic risks linked to their activity.
>
> (Defourny & Nyssen, 2008, p. 204)

Using ideas that were initially formulated by both Borzaga and Defourny (2001) and Defourny and Nyssens (2010, 2012), the EMES envisioned an ideal type of SE that is based on a set of indicators covering economic/entre-preneurial and social/participatory governance dimensions. The economic/entrepreneurial dimension includes the following indicators: a continuous activity producing goods and/or selling services, a significant level of economic risk, and a minimum amount of paid work. The social dimension includes an explicit aim to benefit the community, an initiative launched by a group of citizens or civil society organizations, and limited profit distribution. The participatory governance dimension includes a high degree of autonomy, decision-making power that is not based on capital ownership, and a participatory approach to governance that involves various parties affected by the activity (Defourny & Nyssens, 2012).

Social entrepreneurship is a broad term that has many different meanings (Zahra et al., 2009). It encompasses not only entrepreneurial activities but also activities that create social value, such as entrepreneurial attitudes in public entities and NGOs. Social entrepreneurship is therefore an umbrella concept that also includes social business. According to Mair and Martí (2006), "definitions of social entrepreneurship typically refer to a process or behavior; definitions of social entrepreneurs focus instead on the founder of the initiative; and definitions of social enterprises refer to the tangible outcome of social entrepreneurship" (p. 37).

The growing use of the term social innovation has only made matters more complicated. The concept of social innovation, which was first introduced by Weber (1978) and supported by Schumpeter (2001, 2002), has become a key topic in both social scientific circles and the political sphere (Moulaert et al., 2005). Social innovation acknowledges the role of civil society in post-modern processes of societal transformation (Chambon et al., 1982; Moulaert et al., 2005; Swyngedouw, 2005) and has been a focus of study in several disciplines. For instance, scholars working in the fields of management science and business administration use social innovation to study organizational efficiency. Economic theorists, however, tend to emphasize the importance of accompanying technological innovation with advancements in social planning, while political scientists and public policy experts use social innovation to explain the horizontal models of decision-making that have emerged in recent years. Scholars from the fine arts, meanwhile, focus on how social innovation affects intellectual and social creativity (Moulaert et al., 2005; Mumford, 2002).

The European Commission's "Guide to Social Innovation" (EU, 2013) defines social innovation as the development and implementation of new ideas (products, services, and models) to meet social needs and create new social relationships or collaborations. Social innovation offers novel responses to pressing social demands, which, in turn, affect social interaction processes. In short, it aims to improve the well-being of humanity. Social innovations are social in nature in terms of both their ends and their means. They are not only good for society but also enhance an individual's capacity to act. As Figure 1.1 illustrates, all of the concepts mentioned earlier are

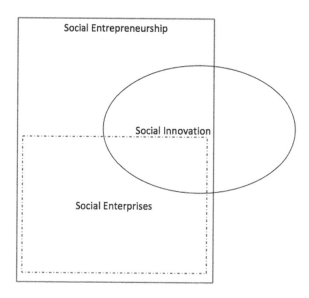

Figure 1.1 The relationship between social entrepreneurship, social enterprises, and social innovation.

related to each other. Though not all social innovations are associated with SEs—or even fall inside the domain of social entrepreneurship—SEs are definitely key components of social entrepreneurship.

The road map behind this book

Although this book discusses some of the EFESEIIS project's main findings, it shouldn't necessarily be seen as an exhaustive account. It should instead be seen as an overview of the EFESEIIS project's most important topics while also offering inspiration for policy makers and future research. In some cases, topics are addressed using new, stimulating, or provocative perspectives.

Chapter 2, entitled "Research background, theoretical frameworks, and methodologies for social entrepreneurship", discusses the multidisciplinary approach that was adopted in the EFESEIIS project as well as the different methodologies and theoretical frameworks that were used to answer the project's main research questions. Theoretically speaking, this chapter uses evolutionary economic theories alongside evolutionary sociological concepts (e.g. social learning and social capital) while also examining the main differences in SE ecosystems on a nation-to-nation basis.

Chapters 3 and 4 address the history and evolution of both social entrepreneurship and SEs in Europe. Chapter 3 is authored by Simone Baglioni, Didier Chabanet, and H. Thomas R. Persson, and is entitled "The rise of the social entrepreneurship in Europe." The authors adopt a cross-temporal approach in order to investigate the evolution of SEs in Western Europe, starting with the creation of national welfare states in the nineteenth century. The authors discuss a range of organized activities involving both the state and market forces, paying special attention to various features that mark current SEs, such as emphasizing the common good and the capacity to provide services to people in need. These earlier social organizations are treated as predecessors of SEs, and their evolution in the years following World War II is discussed in great detail.

Chapter 4, written by Roel During and Rosalie Van Dam, is entitled "The diversity of the European social enterprise sector: an evolutionary perspective." During and Van Dam use analogy, grounded theory, and design in their chapter. Their use of analogy involves applying evolutionary concepts to an analysis of social entrepreneurship. Grounded theory analysis, meanwhile, is used to reveal different pathways of development, while design is used to systematize these observations and put them in an encompassing framework that accounts for the succession of an SE and its ecosystem.

Chapters 5 and 6 focus on the various features and behaviors of SEs and social entrepreneurs. Chapter 5 was authored by Marco Bellucci, Enrico Testi, Serena Franchi, and Mario Biggeri, and is entitled "Emerging managerial aspects of social entrepreneurship in Europe." It discusses the entrepreneurial, social, and innovative nature of social entrepreneurs, focusing on their needs, motivations, and difficulties as well as stakeholder engagement practices and the innovation capacities of SEs. The authors identify some salient features of social entrepreneurs and SEs, the most common challenges and obstacles faced by these types of organizations during their life cycle, and the constraining factors that prevent European social entrepreneurs and SEs from having a more inclusive and innovative impact on the communities they serve.

Authored by Enrico Testi, Mario Biggeri, Domenico Colucci, Nicola Doni, and Vincenzo Valori, Chapter 6 is entitled "Are decision makers in Social Enterprises more pro-social than their peers? An analysis of production and consumption choices." It examines the behavior and choices of decision-makers in SEs and the social impact they generate. This has been accomplished by focusing on two questions:

- Do decision-makers in SEs make more pro-social choices than other decision-makers?
- What can be done to increase the amount of pro-social choices made by decision-makers?

To answer these questions, the authors surveyed 36 decision-makers from SEs and 38 decision-makers from traditional enterprises in Northeast Tuscany.

Chapters 7 and 8 apply ideas on networks and social capital to SEs and their ecosystems. Chapter 7 was authored by Agata Zabłocka, Ryszard

Praszkier, Marta Kacprzyk-Murawska, and Ewa Petrushak, and is entitled "Social capital in the social economy." It discusses the ways in which social capital is built. The authors focus on three basic characteristics that help foster social capital: trust, cooperation, and sense of support (i.e. social connectivity). The main focus of the chapter is on understanding how these three variables, all of which determine an individual's ability to foster social capital, manifest themselves in different types of organizations.

Chapter 8 is entitled "The role of stakeholder networks in shaping the development of social enterprise ecosystems" and was written by Richard Hazemberg, Meanu Bajwa-Patel, and Toa Giroletti. It explores the role of stakeholder and institutional networks in shaping the development of SE ecosystems in various European countries. This chapter draws on evolutionary theory, social network theory, and network pluralism in order to create a typology of SE ecosystems. The creation of this typology was based on qualitative data that was collected across 11 European countries from focus groups and interviews with 258 key stakeholders as well as an analysis of the historical, political, social, legal, and economic conditions in each country. The emergence of four SE ecosystem types—Statist-macro, Statist-micro, Private-macro, and Private-micro—are identified.

Innovation and social innovation are discussed in Chapters 9 and 10. Chapter 9 is authored by Ana Aleksić Mirić, Marina Petrović, and Zorica Aničić, and is entitled "Understanding the innovative behaviour of social enterprises." The authors explore the role of organizational and external factors in shaping innovative behavior among SEs. Their research offers useful insights into how entrepreneurs, organizations, and their surrounding environment can increase innovative behavior in Social Enterprises.

Chapter 10 is entitled "Social innovation in niches." Its authors—Christina Grabbe, Katharina Obuch, and Annette Zimmer—use two case studies from Germany to show how NGSEs tend to occupy "niches" in developed welfare states while also discussing the various features that allowed these organizations to establish themselves as drivers of social innovation in well-established fields.

Chapter 11, entitled "The in-between space of new generation social enterprises," focuses on whether or not a new generation of SEs actually exists. Authored by Mara Benadusi and Rosario Sapienza, this chapter provides an overview of the main organizational characteristics, forms of diffusion, and various identity-based features that shape NGSEs in Europe. The authors adopt a critical perspective to assess whether these can actually be identified as such, adopting behavior—i.e. forms of governance, use of networks, models of enterprise, values, motivations, and work styles—and needs that differ from previous conceptualizations.

Enabling ecosystems, a hotly debated topic in the scholarly literature, is addressed in Chapter 12, "Enabling ecosystems for social enterprises: a capability approach perspective." Written by Mario Biggeri, Enrico Testi, and Andre Ferrannini, this chapter offers a dynamic analytical framework that will allow scholars and practitioners to better understand the ecosystem in which SEs are set while also identifying whether or not these ecosystems act as an enabling force. The framework proposed by the authors uses the capability approach of Sen (1998) to highlight the processes through which a particular ecosystem enables SEs to pursue their goals as well as the various factors that help SEs contribute to human development within that ecosystem.

The final chapter of the volume, "Remarks and policy implications on social entrepreneurship in Europe," was written by H. Thomas R. Persson, Mario Biggeri, Enrico Testi, Marco Bellucci, and Roel During. It sums up the main findings of our research, discusses their policy implications, and identifies future avenues for research.

Final remarks

This book offers an overview of the research that was undertaken over a four-year period under the aegis of the EFESEIIS project while also highlighting the vast amount of time and expertise offered by numerous stakeholders. One of the main strengths of our edited volume is that we collected several different multidisciplinary contributions in a single book. Every chapter, authored by experts in the fields of management, accounting, economics, and sociology, delivers a holistic study of social entrepreneurship and social innovation in Europe while also providing the necessary data for improving policy options among organizations and individuals who seek to better understand enabling social and institutional ecosystems. We also feel that our book is strengthened by the wide variety of topics that are addressed and the decision to discuss these trends from a Pan-European perspective.

An undertaking as large as the EFESEIIS project cannot be fully summarized in a single volume. Unfortunately, many interesting issues and ideas had to be set aside, including at least fifty-five case studies that could have shed further light on the activities of social entrepreneurs across Europe. Indeed, many of the chapters in this study deserved a book of their own. At the same time, however, we opted for a concise approach so that our findings are presented in a clear and efficient manner, thus ensuring that the finished product will serve as a practical source for scholars from several different disciplines. We leave it up to the reader to determine if our efforts make a valuable contribution to the literature on SEs, social entrepreneurship, and social innovation in Europe.

We would like to express our gratitude to the various individuals—from all across Europe—who shared their expertise and knowledge with us. Unfortunately, it would be impossible to list them all here, as approximately 1,500 social entrepreneurs, government officials, consultants, bankers, and academics participated in our research. Last but not least, we would like to thank the European Commission for believing in our project and providing us with the funds to implement it. We hope that the reader will enjoy reading this book and appreciate our attempts to challenge some commonly held beliefs on SEs and social innovation in Europe.

References

Anand, S., & Sen, A. (1994). *Sustainable human development: Concepts and priorities.* UNDP Human Development Report Office 1994 Occasional Papers. New York.

Bagnoli, L. (2004). *Quale responsabilità sociale per l'impresa?* (Vol. 21). Milano: Franco Angeli.

Becattini, G. (2015). *La coscienza dei luoghi.* Roma: Donzelli.

Bellucci, M., Bagnoli, L., Biggeri, M., & Rinaldi, V. (2012). Performance measurement in solidarity economy organizations: The case of fair trade shops in Italy. *Annals of Public and Cooperative Economics, 83*(1), 25–59.

Bellucci, M., & Manetti, G. (2018). *Stakeholder engagement and sustainability reporting.* London: Routledge.

Biggeri, M., Testi, E., & Bellucci, M. (2017). Enabling ecosystems for social enterprises and social innovation: A capability approach perspective. *Journal of Human Development and Capabilities, 18*(2), 299–306.

Borzaga, C., & Defourny, J. (2001). L'impresa sociale in prospettiva europea. *Trento, Edizioni, 31,* 29–32.

Borzaga, C., Defourny, J., Galera, G., Les, E., Nogales, R., Nyssens, M., & Spear, R. (2008). *Social enterprise: A new model for poverty reduction and employment generation.* New York: UNDP.

Borzaga, C., Depedri, S., & Galera, G. (2012). Interpreting social enterprises. *Revista de Administração (São Paulo), 47*(3), 398–409.

Chambon, J.-L., David, A., Devevey, J.-M. (1982). *Les innovations sociales.* Paris: Presses Universitaires de France.

Crane, A., & Matten, D. (2016). Engagement required: The changing role of the corporation in society. In D. Barton, D. Horvath, & M. Kipping (Eds.), *Reimagining Capitalism: Building a Responsible, Long-Term Model.* Oxford University Press.

Defourny, J., & Nyssens, M. (2006). Defining social enterprise. In M. Nyssens (Ed.), *Social enterprise. At the crossroads of market, public policies and civil society* (pp. 3–26). London: Routledge.

Defourny, J., & Nyssens, M. (2008). Social enterprise in Europe: Recent trends and developments. *Social Enterprise Journal, 4*(3), 202–228.

Defourny, J., & Nyssens, M. (2010). Social enterprise in Europe: At the crossroads of market, public policies and third sector. *Policy and Society, 29*(3), 231–242.

Defourny, J., & Nyssens, M. (2012). *The EMES Approach of Social Enterprises in a Comparative Perspective* (EMES WP n. 12/03). Liege, Belgium.

Elkington, J. (1998). Partnerships from cannibals with forks: The triple bottom line of 21st-century business. *Environmental Quality Management, 8*(1), 37–51.

EU (2010). Communication from the commission to the European parliament, the council, the European economic and social committee and the committee of the Regions Europe 2020 Flagship Initiative Innovation Union SEC (2010) 1161. Brussels.

EU (2013). *Guide to social innovation.* Brussels: Regional and Urban Policies.

European Commission. (2010). https://eur-lex.europa.eu/procedure/EN/199719

Freeman, R.E. (1984). *Strategic management: A stakeholder approach.* Boston, MA: Pitman.

Haugh, H. (2005). A research agenda for social entrepreneurship? *Social Enterprise Journal, 2,* 346–357.

Hockerts, K. (2006). Entrepreneurial opportunity in social purpose ventures. In J. Mair, J. Robinson, & K. Hockerts (Eds.), *Social entrepreneurship* (pp. 142–154). Basingstoke: Palgrave Macmillan.

Ilie, E.G., & During, R. (2012). *An analysis of social innovation discourses in Europe concepts and strategies of social innovation.* Wageningen: WUR. http://edepot.wur.nl/197565.

Jones, D., & Keogh, W. (2006). Social enterprise: A case of terminological ambiguity and complexity. *Social Enterprise Journal, 1*(1), 11–26.

Mair, J., & Marti, I. (2006). Social entrepreneurship research: A source of explanation, prediction, and delight. *Journal of World Business, 41*(1), 36–44.

Manetti, G., & Bellucci, M. (2016). The use of social media for engaging stakeholders in sustainability reporting. *Accounting, Auditing & Accountability Journal, 29*(6), 985–1011.

Manetti, G., Bellucci, M., Como, E., & Bagnoli, L. (2015). Investing in volunteering: measuring social returns of volunteer recruitment, training and management. *Voluntas, 26*(5), 2104–2129. doi:10.1007/s11266-014-9497-3.

Moulaert, F., Martinelli, F., Swyngedouw, E., & Gonzalez, S. (2005). Towards alternative model(s) of local innovation. *Urban Studies, 42*(11), 1969–1990.

Mumford, M. D. (2002). Social innovation: Ten cases from Benjamin Franklin. *Creativity Research Journal, 14*(2), 253–266.

Nicholls, A. (2006). *Social entrepreneurship: New models of sustainable social change.* Oxford: Oxford University Press.

Peattie, K., & Morley, A. (2008). Eight paradoxes of the social enterprise research agenda. *Social Enterprise Journal, 4*(2), 91–107.

Scarlato, M. (2012). Social enterprise and development policy: Evidence from Italy. *Journal of Social Entrepreneurship, 3*(1), 24–49.

Schumpeter, J.A. (2001). *Capitalismo, Socialismo e Democrazia (1942).* Milano: ETAS.

Schumpeter, J.A. (2002). *Teoria dello sviluppo economico (1911).* Milano: ETAS.

Sen, A.K. (1998). The possibility of social choice. *American Economic Review, 89*(3), 349–378.

Stiglitz, J., Sen, A., & Fitoussi, J.P. (2009). *The measurement of economic performance and social progress revisited.* Reflections and Overview. Commission on the Measurement of Economic Performance and Social Progress, Paris.

Swyngedouw, E. (2005). Governance innovation and the citizen: The Janus face of governance-beyond-the-state. *Urban Studies, 42*(11), 1991–2006.

Testi, E., Bellucci, M., Franchi, S., & Biggeri, M. (2017). Italian social enterprises at the crossroads: Their role in the evolution of the welfare state. *VOLUNTAS: International Journal of Voluntary and Nonprofit Organizations, 28*(6), 2403–2422.

Van Assche, K., Beunen, R., & Duineveld, M. (2013). *Evolutionary governance theory: An introduction.* Basel: Springer Science & Business Media.

Weber, M. (1978). *Economy and society: An outline of interpretive sociology* (Vol. 1). Berkeley: University of California Press.

Yunus, M. (2003). *Banker to the poor.*

Yunus, M., & Weber, K. (2008). *A world without poverty. Social Business and the Future of Capitalism.* New York: Public Affairs.

Zahra, S. A., Gedajlovic, E., Neubaum, D. O., Shulman, J. M. (2009). A typology of social entrepreneurs: Motives, search processes and ethical challenges. *Journal of Business Venturing, 24*(5), 519–532.

2 Research background, theoretical frameworks, and methodologies for social entrepreneurship

Roel During, H. Thomas R. Persson, Mario Biggeri, Enrico Testi, and Marco Bellucci

Research context

European welfare systems play an important role in improving the living conditions of its citizens, most notably in the areas of childcare, health prevention services, employment services, and benefits for the elderly. In other words, social policies are put in place to meet the growing needs of citizens. In 2013 Europe launched the Social Investment Package as a response to major social challenges—including unemployment, poverty, and social exclusion—brought about by the 2008 economic crisis and an ageing population (Brancati et al., 2017). According to the OECD, economic and industrial innovation often leads to an increase in inequality, as benefits predominantly accrue to innovators and their customers (OECD, 2016). Made worse by an ageing populace and a decline in the total working population, these types of societal challenges may be well beyond the scope of existing social policy aims (Misuraca et al., 2017). As a result, social entrepreneurs and representatives from the private sector are expected to play a pivotal role in encouraging innovative social policies (European Commission, 2015).

The EU and most European countries face difficult problems, particularly long-term unemployment (while unemployment might be going down in several EU countries, long-term unemployment is not) and the refugee crisis (which has a profound impact on the welfare system and on Work Integration Social Enterprise, WISEs). Social policy in Europe aims at building a more resilient society, with social services and institutions playing a key role (Misuraca et al., 2016). Many observers acknowledge that addressing problems associated with an ageing population and varying welfare standards should come from below. Resilience gains more weight at the cost of the actual *acquis* (European Commission Joint Research Centre, 2015). Thus, social enterprises (SEs) are of greater significance in this particular context (OECD Local Economic and Employment Development, 2013), as they might be able to act as powerful instruments to tackle inequality and social exclusion in various cultural contexts. Indeed, some scholars believe that they can assist in building a European welfare union that is capable of overshadowing the European union of welfare states (Manca et al., 2017).

The EFESEIIS project was created in an attempt to produce new knowledge that will enable member states, non-member states, and the European Union as a whole to fully understand the conditions under which social entrepreneurship starts, develops, and contributes to solving societal challenges in an effective, efficient, and sustainable manner. In many respects, the EFESEIIS project is a response to the challenges identified in Europe 2020: Strategy for Smart, Sustainable and Inclusive Growth and HORIZON 2020, both of which call for the creation of inclusive, innovative, and secure societies. The EFESEIIS project addressed several Innovation Union priorities on smart, sustainable and inclusive growth, which shows that it is serious about drawing up a wide range of policies relating to social entrepreneurship (EFESEIIS, 2013). Its ambitions require a combination of reflective and performative research (Beunen et al., 2012), and a complex, multifaceted, and multilayered methodology. Qualitative and quantitative data were gathered at all levels—continental, national, regional, and municipal—addressing social policy innovation, social investment strategies, institutional context analysis, and stakeholder interaction. This last point about stakeholders (e.g. local authorities, banks, and other financial institutions) is important because it allows us to better understand how to draw greater attention to social entrepreneurship while also explaining why some SEs have problems accessing resources and how their various cultural and legal environments have evolved over time. In the end, our methodology focuses on the importance of communities, cultures, traditions; the various discourses on social entrepreneurship that have emerged among relevant stakeholders; and the coevolution of social entrepreneurship and the institutions that emerge in its wake.

Legal, political, and cultural differences are just a few of the problems our methodologies have to tackle. For instance, there is no consensus on how to legally define SEs (Defourny & Nyssens, 2010). In some countries SEs are poorly defined, while others treat it as a mere label that allows enterprises to rename and reframe their activities in order to gain access to specific programs that promote social entrepreneurship. Enterprises that do not have any specific social means or ends are thought to engage in mimicry.

Of course, the problems the EFESEIIS project encountered while trying to arrive at a clear definition of SE created a pressing ontological problem. Basically, the SE concept is often defined by ideology, some of which is local in nature. However, the methodological approach adopted in the EFESEIIS project was created by scholars whose views on social entrepreneurship were already well developed, which means that there is a risk of ideological bias. This, in turn, leads us to the question that will be discussed throughout the remainder of the chapter: how can one benefit from methodological and contextual pluralism while avoiding unproductive controversies?

Partnership and methodological consensus

Description of the partnership

Since social entrepreneurship is a relatively new phenomenon, building both a partnership and a methodology required a great deal of attention. Fortunately, our team was made up of scholars and practitioners who brought in their own unique skill sets, their diverse cultural backgrounds and history, and a vast knowledge of different legal frameworks, cultures, traditions, stages of development, and trajectories of social entrepreneurship. Ten European countries are involved: Albania, Austria, Denmark, France, Germany, Italy, Poland, Serbia, England, Scotland, and the Netherlands. The social entrepreneurial sector in each of these countries has reached different stages of development and has different resources and infrastructure (e.g. banking and funding) available to them. In fact, in some countries (e.g. Italy) the sector is well established and academic debate is flourishing. Meanwhile, in other countries (e.g. Albania), social entrepreneurship (and the academic debates that emerge in its wake) are in a nascent state. Each country also has different legal frameworks regulating social entrepreneurship and SEs, an aspect of this project that had to be overcome in order to provide a proper analysis of the evolution of social entrepreneurship in each country.

The partnership also made an attempt to balance theory and practice. Indeed, some of the partners have strong links with practitioners in the SE sector, which means that their scholarly expertise is often complemented by more practical forms of knowledge. This is especially true among the scholars who are affiliated with the project's lead partner, PIN Polo Universitario Città di Prato, an organization that is strongly connected to the Yunus Social Business Centre of the University of Florence. Founded by Muhammad Yunus, a 2006 Nobel Prize winner, the Yunus Social Business Centre is an international network of research centers, universities, business incubators, practitioners, and consultants. Two other partners in this project—Glasgow Caledonian University (GCU) and the Yunus Centre for Social Business and Health—also try to balance theory and practice, while the Impact HUB, a global network of social innovation and social entrepreneurship centers, tends to emphasize practical concerns, placing special attention on the emergence of the most recent generation of social entrepreneurs. Meanwhile, our Albanian partner, Promoting Social Business, emphasizes practical matters by promoting the virtues of SE and building an enabling ecosystem. With its close links to the Yunus Centre and its emphasis on development problems in developing nations, the PIN Polo Universitario Città di Prato focuses primarily on developmental economics and business/management studies. Glasgow Caledonian University, by contrast, focuses on health and social issues, which means that their disciplinary interests tend to gravitate towards social policy analysis and social science in general. The Institute of Political Science in the Faculty of

Social Sciences and Humanity at the University of Münster is also part of the consortium. Its activities focus on social policy and comparative political studies. The Centre of Political Research at the Fondation Nationale des Science Politiques in France, meanwhile, specializes in socioeconomic issues and the humanities.

Political science and economics are just two fields of study represented in our project. For instance, our Serbian partner (FREN) specializes in labor markets, while the Department of Marketing and Management at the University of Southern Denmark specializes in business and the social sciences. Both the University of Northampton and the Institute for Social Innovation and Impact (ISII) stress institutional and holistic learning, and preside over educational programs for students who wish to become social entrepreneurs. The University of Warsaw and its Centre for Complex Systems, by contrast, favor cross-disciplinary research and teaching. They conduct empirical studies of social and psychological processes while also performing research on biology and natural science. Lastly, Alterra, a research institute in the Netherlands, specializes in systems analysis and evolutionary pathways.

The multidisciplinary approach adopted in this study will allow us to achieve our objectives. In fact, our partnership consists of economists (many of whom specialize in development, business administration, and behavioral economics), financial experts, sociologists, evolutionists, anthropologists, and practitioners with experience in social entrepreneurship and social innovation.

The partnership is also geographically balanced, featuring two partners from Western Europe (France and the Netherlands), two partners from the German-speaking states of Central Europe (Germany and Austria), one partner from Northern Europe (Denmark), two partners from the United Kingdom (England and Scotland), one partner from southern Europe (Italy), and three partners from post-communist nations (Poland, Serbia, and Albania). This allows us to determine how different welfare systems, income levels, educational systems, culture, and history have shaped the evolution of social entrepreneurship in each country.

Mixed methods and multi-disciplinary approach

The EFESEIIS research project was based on a mixed method approach that included interviews and focus groups with 164 stakeholders, a survey of representatives from 850 SEs in 11 EU countries, and behavioral experiments with decision-makers. The research has been organized into nine work packages (WPs), each of which was presided over by one of the partners. In practice, this allowed us to create a measure of consensus in terms of the methodology that was used by each partner. Disciplinary divergence had to be solved through a consensus-based approach. The most significant obstacles emerged during discussions on the validity of the outcomes, which came about because standards often vary between qualitative and quantitative research traditions. Moreover, the data in most of the work packages required varying levels of interpretation, which also became a significant point of discussion. As always, these discussions took place when the work packages were being assigned. All of these issues are explained in the following table (WPs involving administration and communication have been omitted). In the end, we found that many of the debates that emerged only served to strengthen our methodology (Table 2.1).

Table 2.1 Focus, theoretical framework, and methods for each strand of research

Work package	Focus	Theoretical frameworks	Methods
Comparative historical perspective on social inclusion, social innovation (SI), and social entrepreneurship (SE)	Assessing the role of institutions in generating a specific pattern of SE and SI	Welfare models/ regimes, social economy, historical institutionalism	Review of scholarly literature and policy documents, Internet-based research (websites, grey literature, policy and public documents) Stakeholder workshops
Analysis of social entrepreneurs	Data collection and analysis on the role of communities, cultures, and traditions	Structuralism, social capital	Surveying, experiments, multilevel data analysis, social network analysis
Understanding stakeholder perspectives	Stakeholder engagement and relationships at the national and European level	Advocacy, stakeholder theory	Stakeholder focus groups, in-depth interviews, stakeholder analysis (key actors, levels, and impact)
New generation of social entrepreneurs	Mapping experiences (learning, ecosystem problems, approaches to social value deliverance)	Use of metaphors in signification; organizational identity	Case studies, narrative methods (via in-depth individual and group interviews, focus groups) Document analysis Stakeholder analysis Participative observation
The role of primary institutions, with specific focus on welfare and education	Institutional changes in education and welfare since 1945	Welfare models/ regimes, social economy, historical institutionalism	Internet research, document analysis (policy and public documents, grey literature), interviews
Evolutionary theory	Disclosure of evolutionary pathways in specific national contexts	Evolutionary theory, actor-network-theory, system theory	Grounded theory approach on previous WPs and Discourse analysis
Enabling eco-system	Find conditions that are present in enabling ecosystems	Sustainable human development paradigm and capability approach	Case studies, collecting examples from enabling ecosystems

Theoretical pluralism: asset or constraint?

Having discussed the structure of the partnership and the design of the project, we will now focus on how the various partners and fields of study affected its findings. We will discuss some ambivalences, divergences, convergences, and unifying concepts.

Ambivalences

Previous work on social entrepreneurship in Europe reveals that its development differs significantly from country to country (Hazenberg et al., 2016). The analytical reports produced by the EFESEIIS project reinforce this notion, as do the findings from similar projects, including SIMPACT (Debref et al., 2015) and SEFORIS (SEFORIS, 2016). In many cases, trends that are specific to certain countries are explained by referring to contextual differences (Svensson, 2015), especially differences in resources, institutions, economic objectives, social needs, political objectives, and governance (Terstriep et al., 2015). Indeed, Terstriep and her peers (2015) state that very few projects use network analysis as a theoretical tool, which is often used in Social Innovation Biographies and narrative approaches. Thus, little weight is given to the interaction between SEs and their environments from a system analysis perspective. However, we believe that employing an evolutionary perspective in the EFESEIIS project can help us better understand how the success of a SE depends on its ecosystem.

But how does one clearly pinpoint the rise of SE? From a social scientific perspective, the study of SEs is a recent phenomenon that emphasizes social networks, biographies, social capital, and social learning, all of which are examined via discourse analysis, grounded theory, and historical institutionalism (Andersen, 2003; Gasson, 2004; Roy et al., 2015). The field of economics, however, sees SE as a "thing in itself" whose essence—which is often seen through the eyes of the state (Scott, 1998)—should be described thoroughly. The state often focuses on how different institutional contexts produce different SEs, but it doesn't take into account how SEs reshape their institutional context, or how they often emerge as an idea.

These paradigmatic differences often collide when discussing the internal structure of the sector and its position in society. Economists see SEs as innovative businesses, oftentimes implying that they work according to the rules of the neoliberal market. These rules presuppose competition to be the pivotal shaping power of an economy, leading it to the survival of only those who are fit and well adapted. Social scientists, meanwhile, claim that SEs function as a network—a sort of humus layer representing the mushrooming of numerous connected entrepreneurial activities in society—that stresses the creating capacity of collaborative internal structures. Their identities are situational: an organization that is seen as a SE may actually be an informal partnership. Indeed, informal structures may be much more important than formal structures. Both of these views were raised by members of the partnership, which, in turn, led to tension and ambivalence. One dispute emerged over whether SE should be understood as a next step in economic development (Granovetter, 2005) or as a societal innovation that transcends traditional approaches to business.

Divergences

A further constraint involves the qualitative and quantitative research traditions that shaped the partnership. This resulted in several discussions on how to best incorporate case studies and data from questionnaires into our findings. Qualitative researchers, for instance, tend to focus on in-depth case studies and have doubts that a series of predefined questions can lead to useful information. However, after more than a year of discussions, a compromise was reached: the creation of a lengthy and elaborate questionnaire. Although the new questionnaire allowed us to reach some solid conclusions, there were also some drawbacks that need to be considered. To no one's surprise, the number of respondents varied significantly between participating countries, which undermined the empirical basis of the EFE-SEIIS project. Fortunately, these problems have been solved via statistical techniques.

An interesting divergence occurred at the crossroads of management and research. As the project unfolded, our partners began to focus on the motivations of social entrepreneurs—they began to ask, "what's in it for them?" Unfortunately, the rather vague promise of influencing the European Commission agenda was not concrete enough, which pushed us towards adopting more practice-oriented research strategies. On one occasion, this helped us overcome differences sprouting from different epistemological ideas that emerged in the behavioral experiment—a discussion about the relationship between social outcomes and creating profit for social entrepreneurs. The rules of the experiment forced social entrepreneurs to make a choice between taking out a sum of money as a form of profit or reinvesting it in their enterprise in order to increase its social impact, which led to a theoretical dispute about the relevance of such a dichotomy. Some researchers, in short, wondered whether it was realistic to frame this issue in such an oppositional manner. In the end, the practitioners in the partnership convinced the others that creating profit and achieving significant social impact were not mutually exclusive concepts.

Convergences

The partnership fully agreed that developmental pathways are shaped by context and can vary from nation to nation. This led us to agree that evolutionary theory can help us better understand specific aspects of development pathways. The researchers also agreed that cities are relevant and interesting ecosystems that demand significant attention. Although the eco-system concept has not been defined in a clear and specific manner, it did not invoke any controversy in the partnership itself. In fact, the wider use of various evolutionary concepts and metaphors enabled the partnership to deal with the elusive and intangible object of our study. It did so by using some unifying concepts, which will be elaborated later.

Unifying concepts

Several evolutionary concepts were used to unify the results of the project. For instance, a document was circulated, outlining the relevant concepts of Darwin's theory of evolution and their applicability for understanding the emergence of social entrepreneurship in several different contexts. This was used as inspiration for the overall historic and institutional analysis, using ideas associated with historical institutionalism as guides (Thelen, 1999). Existing evolutionary concepts that have been adopted in several different disciplines were also used to assess processes of change. Evolutionary con-cepts from the field economics, for instance, were used to discuss the extent to which altruistic behavior determined the success of an enterprise, while the social capital approach—a sociological concept—was used to discuss social learning and cultural evolution. Both approaches were used success-fully in the EFESEIIS project.

The most difficult aspect of applying evolutionary theory to the study of SEs involves how to precisely describe pathways of change that are specific to each partner's country of origin. This issue pushed us to adopt a vari-ation on the grounded theory approach that applies evolutionary theory to the study of SE. All but one of the partners succeeded in offering this type of analysis. However, due to the richness of our empirical data, this approach couldn't be mainstreamed in a precise or comparable manner; it merely reiterated the idea that social entrepreneurship is a purely institu-tional phenomenon.

The cooperative methodology employed by the partnership inspired controversy, consensus, and ambivalence. Although the overall methodo-logical approach was discussed during the application stage, the practical details required greater deliberation. Nonetheless, the project benefitted immensely from these discussions because a host of theoretical perspectives were considered while these problems were being sorted out. Methodologi-cal expertise came from partners who studied SE sectors that were already well on the way to maturity. This favored the "through the eyes of the state" perspective discussed earlier in which SEs are seen as distinct objects that ought to be supported through an enabling ecosystem policy (Biggeri et al., 2017). Although this perspective would end up playing a positive role in the project, it also hampered our ability to determine how the sector evolved in different cultural and political contexts, and how it emerged as a social construction—a product of specific economic trends. After all, a methodology that works well in Scotland—with its elaborate ecosystem and complex urban/rural divide—might not be applicable in countries such as Poland or Albania. The evolution of SE varies from country to country and is often affected by context-dependent political ideologies and the institutional landscapes found in each country. If the political, cultural, and social contexts vary significantly, any imposed methodology will inevitably generate a loss of information. Suffice it to say that generalized approaches are popular among some disciplines (e.g. economics), while generating skepticism from others (e.g. anthropology).

Conclusions

From a methodological point of view, the EFESEIIS project is full of interesting tensions and ambivalences. Indeed, the diverse nature of the partnership means that a certain amount of conflict was inevitable. For instance, tensions emerged regarding the difficulties in balancing practical and theoretical considerations. These tensions not only affected our basic analysis, but also how we looked at peripheral concepts (e.g. impact and target groups). Fortunately, pluralism is an important part of the research traditions used in this study, which is why we ultimately adopted a multidisciplinary approach.

Getting our design up and running required a lot of negotiation and deliberation. Partners who have studied more mature forms of social entrepreneurship have played the biggest role in settling methodological differences. This resulted in a more theoretical/essentialist methodology, which, in turn, led to an overall approach that emphasized treating SEs as distinct objects. Thus, an institutional analysis of SEs and their ecosystems prevailed, at the expense of crisis-oriented theories that focus on migration of concepts from one discursive context to another and how ideas evolve alongside social relationships. The good news is that the findings of the EFESEIIS project are quite relevant to governmental actors; the bad news is that this has been achieved by downplaying the impact of these findings on the sector itself.

We set out in this chapter to determine whether or not a pluralistic approach to the study of SE can pay off. Did EFESEIIS manage to profit from it? If so, why did this happen? Based on the basic make-up of the partnership, the methodologies we adopted, and the various ambivalences, controversies, and convergences that were identified in our research, we can say that the multidisciplinary approach produced prolonged periods of negotiation as the project unfolded. This was especially true near the end of the project, when path dependencies were being analyzed using various ideas associated with evolutionary theory. These discussions on the need of a similar methodology across all cases, dominated by those partners with a longer tradition of social entrepreneurship that focus on institutional frameworks and relationships (the eyes of a state), caused the conclusions to remain in the safe zone of historical institutionalism, overlooking the finesses of micro path dependencies and pathways of emerging practices in various cultural and political contexts. Nevertheless, the most important questions to emerge from the EFESEIIS project—what an enabling ecosystem looks like and how it can be put in place—have been answered with substantive evidence, a positive outcome that was aided greatly by the project's multidisciplinary nature.

Ultimately, we conclude that a multidisciplinary approach is the best way to address some of the complex research questions posed by the EFESEIIS project. Nonetheless, efforts need to be made to ensure that multidisciplinarity isn't turned into theoretical and methodological "bricolage." The EFESEIIS project proved that using a wide variety of disciplines to answer challenging research questions is certainly doable, even though several methodological countermeasures are required to make it work.

References

Andersen, N. A. (2003). *Discursive analytical strategies. Understanding Foucault, Laclau, Luhmann.* Bristol: The Policy Press.

Beunen, R., Duineveld, M., During, R., Straver, G., & Aalvanger, A. (2012). Reflexivity in performative science shop projects. *Gateways: International Journal of Community Research and Engagement, 5*, 135–151.

Biggeri, M., Testi, E., & Bellucci, M. (2017). Enabling ecosystems for social enterprises and social innovation: A capability approach perspective. *Journal of Human Development and Capabilities, 18*(2), 299–306.

Brancati, C. U., Kucsera, C., & Misuraca, G. (2017). *ICT-enabled social innovation for active and healthy ageing. Redesigning long-term care and independent living in Europe* (No. JRC107828). Brussels: Joint Research Centre (Seville site).

Debref, R., Alijani, S., Thomas, L., Boudes, M., & Mangalagui, D. (2015). *Meta-analysis of social innovation across Europe.* Deliverable D3.1 of the project "Boosting the Impact of SI in Europe through Economic Underpinnings." (SIMPACT), European Commission – 7th Framework Programme. Brussels: European Commission DG Research and Innovation.

Defourny, J., & Nyssens, M. (2010). Conceptions of social enterprise and social entrepreneurship in Europe and the United States: Convergences and divergences. *Journal of Social Entrepreneurship, 1*(1), 32–53.

EFESEIIS. (2013). Project Proposal No 613179 – EFESEIIS.

European Commission. (2015). *Social Policy Innovation. Meeting the needs of citizens.* Retrieved from https://ec.europa.eu/eip/ageing/library/social-policy-innovation-meeting-social-needs-citizens_en.

European Commission Joint Research Centre. (2015). *The challenge of resilience in a globalised world.* Retrieved from https://ec.europa.eu/jrc/en/publication/challenge-resilience-globalised-world.

Gasson, S. (2004). Rigor in grounded theory research: An interpretive perspective on generating theory from qualitative field studies. In M. E. Whitman & A. B. Woszczynski (Eds.), *The handbook of information systems research* (pp. 79–102). Hershey, PA: Idea Group.

Granovetter, M. (2005). The impact of social structure on economic outcomes. *Journal of Economic Perspectives, 19*(1), 33–50.

Hazenberg, R., Bajwa-Patel, M., Mazzei, M., Roy, M. J., & Baglioni, S. (2016). The role of institutional and stakeholder networks in shaping social enterprise ecosystems in Europe. *Social Enterprise Journal, 12*(3), 205–222.

Manca, A. R., Benczur, P., & Giovannini, E. (2017). *Building a scientific narrative towards a more resilient EU society.* Retrieved from https://ec.europa.eu/jrc/en/publication/eur-scientific-and-technical-research-reports/building-scientific-narrative-towards-more-resilient-eu-society-part-1-conceptual-framework.

Misuraca, G., Kucsera, C., Pasi, G., Gagliardi, D., & Abadie, F. (2016). *ICT-enabled social innovation to support the implementation of the social investment package: Mapping and analysis of ICT-enabled social innovation initiatives promoting social investment across the EU: IESI Knowledge Map 2016.* Retrieved from https://ec.europa.eu/jrc/en/publication/eur-scientific-and-technical-research-reports/ict-enabled-social-innovation-support-implementation-social-investment-package-mapping-and-0.

Misuraca, G., Pasi, G., & Abadie, F. (2017). *Innovating EU social protection systems through ICTs. Findings from analysis of case studies in fourteen Member States.* Retrieved from https://ec.europa.eu/jrc/en/publication/eur-scientific-and-technical-research-reports/jrc-insights-social-policy-innovation-series-innovating-eu-social-protection-systems-through.

OECD. (2016). *OECD science, technology and innovation Outlook 2016.* OECD. Retrieved from www.oecd.org/sti/Megatrends%20affecting%20science, %20technology%20and%20innovation.pdf.

OECD Local Economic and Employment Development (Ed.). (2013). *Policy brief on social entrepreneurship – Entrepreneurial activities in Europe.* Retrieved from http://ec.europa.eu/social/main.jsp?catId=738&langId=en&pubId=7552&furtherPubs=yes.

Roy, M., McHugh, N. A., Huckfield, L., Kay, A., & Donaldson, C. (2015). "The most supportive environment in the world"? Tracing the development of an institutional 'ecosystem' for social enterprise. *Voluntas, 26*(3), 777–800. DOI:10.1007/s11266-014-9459-9.

Scott, J. C. (1998). *Seeing like a state. How certain schemes to improve the human condition have failed.* New Haven, CT and London: Yale University Press.

SEFORIS. (2016). Cross Country Report. A first cross-country analysis and profiling of social enterprises prepared by the SEFORIS research consortium (p. 36). Brussels: Oksigen Lab.

Svensson, C. F. (2015). *Contextualisation matters: Aligning social enterprises nation-state diversity.* Retrieved from https://emesphdnetwork.wordpress.com/2015/02/26/contextualisation-matters-aligning-social-enterprises-to-nation-state-diversity/.

Terstriep, J., Kleverbeck, M., Deserti, A., & Rizzo, F. (2015). *Comparative report on social innovation across Europe.* Deliverable D3.2 of the project Boosting the Impact of SI in Europe through Economic Underpinnings (SIMPACT). European Commission, 7th Framework Programme. Brussels: European Commission DG Research and Innovation.

Thelen, K. (1999). Historical institutionalism in comparative politics. *Annual Review of Political Science, 2*(1), 369–404.

3 The rise of social enterprises and social entrepreneurship in Western Europe

Simone Baglioni, Didier Chabanet, and H. Thomas R. Persson

Introduction

Social enterprises (SEs) in Western Europe have emerged as powerful actors that engage in activities that rely on both market forces and the state. By either sharing social risk or acting as innovative, business-like organizations that offer employment opportunities to vulnerable people, SEs have become pivotal and complementary actors in public systems of social protection and service provision, especially in the fields of health care, employment, disability, education, leisure, and many others.

The largest expansion of the welfare state—the so-called *"trente glorieuses"*—took place between 1945 and 1975. During this period, SEs enjoyed a supportive social climate, as they offered to complement welfare provisions through service innovation or by reaching out to people who weren't being served by the welfare state. By the late 1970s, however, the welfare state started to shrink due to the growing popularity of Thatcherite policies. In this context, SEs became important actors in addressing various social problems. Their capacity to combine social and profit-making aims transformed SEs into a "quick and cheap" means of balancing the needs of the market with pressing social justice issues while also addressing the social costs of a shrinking public sector. SEs, in short, started to play a much larger role in shaping major public policies, partnering up with public authorities during both the design and implementation phases.

These structural shifts were also accompanied by a semantic shift. The "social enterprise" discourse was replaced by a discourse emphasizing "social entrepreneurship" and/or "social entrepreneurs." This semantic shift emphasized the heroic social entrepreneur/change-maker who creates wealth for both the company and community, thus replacing the cooperative ideals that often marked earlier periods of history. Perhaps not surprisingly, this new approach stressed marketization and professionalization, thereby transforming SEs into social *businesses*.

The transformation of SEs into market-based institutions has been nurtured by ad hoc political, social, and economic environments at the local, national, and supranational level. Indeed, this chapter places emphasis on all three levels, discussing the mutual interests of SEs/social entrepreneurs and neo-liberal policy-makers/stakeholders.

The first section of this chapter offers a brief historical discussion of the evolution of SEs in Western Europe from the nineteenth century to the 1970s; the second section, meanwhile, focuses on how these institutions changed from 1980 to the present; the third section sheds light on the role political institutions at all levels played in reshaping the sector; the fourth section discusses the connections between SEs and market forces, and how these connections produced dramatic changes in the past 40 years; and the final section addresses how our cross-temporal analysis can help us understand contemporary SEs and welfare regimes.

Caught between the welfare state and market forces: an historical evolution of social enterprises

When the idea of a SE—a business that has social purposes—first emerged, it originally developed as a socio-economic phenomenon that combined business activities with social solidarity (Borzaga & Santuari, 2003). Mixing economic goals with social goals allowed SEs to increase their usefulness to the welfare state, especially programs that addressed work-related injuries, health care, unemployment, and old age (Ferrera, 2005). European welfare regimes have undergone sweeping changes over the past 120+ years (the earliest welfare state was created in Bismarck's Germany during the late nineteenth century). Small programs that addressed work-related injuries eventually evolved into life-long programs that shielded all citizens from the ups and downs of modern capitalist society. Early welfare policies also differed from country to country. According to Esping-Andersen (1990), some states created liberal welfare regimes, while others opted for conservative-corporatist or social democratic approaches. Other researchers, meanwhile, have pointed towards the creation of residual or sub-protective welfare states in parts of Southern Europe (Ferrera, 1996; Gallie & Paugam, 2000; Ritter, 2003).

SEs have also evolved in a similarly sweeping manner. Indeed, by discussing the activities of SEs vis-a-vis the welfare state, we can trace current forms of SEs back to earlier eras of history, when equivalent forms of support were put in place by church-related or charity-driven organizations, some of which are still active today.

Up until the nineteenth century, during the early phases of the industrial revolution, social services were provided by private organizations, primarily churches and religious groups. Individuals were not yet seen as citizens, which means that the state encouraged a patron-based approach to the provision of social services. In Germany, for instance, religious organizations and early capitalist philanthropists often coalesced to create associations supporting the poor (Zimmer & Obuch, 2017). However, in secular France, which was already in the early phases of industrialization and urbanization, the "mutuelles" system first emerged when workers established cooperatives and emergency funds that could be used during times of need (Chabanet, 2017). The insurance-based approaches that would eventually come to characterize modern welfare strategies were not prevalent during this era of history, as most social services were based on a simple assistance model. Early forms of SE were essentially private organizations that provided assistance on the basis of compassion, solidarity, and, occasionally, altruism.

In the early twentieth century, when the relationship between the individual and the state first started to be defined by ideas on citizenship, the patron-based approach was replaced by a more active caregiver approach that was based on rights and entitlements. This is also when many European countries began to shift away from assistance-based schemes to insurance-based schemes. In this new policy environment, the predecessors of SEs did not necessarily stop delivering welfare-type services. Instead, they often reinforced their status by becoming the state's primary partners in delivering publicly-subsidized welfare services and taking part in activities that complemented the welfare state. For instance, some cooperatives in France and Italy, and a few large charities in Germany (e.g. Caritas and Diakonie), expanded their activities by partnering up with the state. Meanwhile, welfare regimes in some Nordic countries commonly adopted initiatives that were originally created by charity-driven organizations.

After World War II, when the relationship between state and the individual was based entirely on principles of citizenship—including areas of Europe that embraced Communism—the welfare state reached its peak in terms of the breadth and scope of public provisions. Once again, civil society and charity-based welfare activities continued to increase in importance, as the state established itself as an interested caregiver that was actively engaged in protecting the rights of its citizens. The role of SEs in this particular phase depended on whether they offered services in a corporatist, pluralist, or socialist economy. In neo-corporatist countries, such as Germany and Italy, a range of well-articulated religious or secular organizations (e.g. cooperatives) acted alongside government entities, forming a multifaceted, yet integrated, constellation of actors in a regulated system of capitalism.

In pluralistic market economies, meanwhile, a range of private organizations also worked alongside public entities, but these private organizations were less likely to mutualize risk and coverage, and more likely to act like independent, business-oriented organizations. This is how things worked in the United Kingdom, for example, although it must be noted that Scotland's approach differed significantly from England's (Mazzei & Roy, 2017). Although they were considered part of the British welfare state, many Scottish communities—especially ones in remote areas—have continued using SE predecessors that emphasize essential care, well-being, and other services that a distant and politically distracted centralized public entity would not usually offer. Reliance on older SEs in Scotland took on increasing important years later, even when the welfare state was reorganized to better accommodate remote areas (Alcock 2012; Mooney & Williams 2006).

A third economic system grew in importance during the years following World War II: the planned economies of the Soviet Union and its satellites. Although certain aspects of civil society were nonexistent in these countries, some welfare activities continued on via cooperatives devoted to supporting disabled people—most notably disabled veterans (Zarkovic Rakic et al., 2017). In Poland, moreover, the emergence of the Solidarity movement helped keep civil society alive during the era of Communist rule, when any form of private organization or collective action that happened outside the imprimatur of state and/or the party was deemed illegal (Praszkier et al., 2017). In fact, the civic vigor that marked the Solidarity movement was key in maintaining a vibrant "zeitgeist" that would later lead to the creation of numerous SEs.

SEs have developed in a host of different ways in Europe, according to the cultural, economic and political context of each country. As a result, there is no common definition that allow us to embrace the plurality of conceptions and practices associated with social entrepreneurship. Nonetheless, two conceptions of SEs can be distinguished (European Commission, 2013). One is based on the legal status of organizations. This is the case, for instance, in France, where cooperatives, mutual societies, associations, and foundations form the legal foundation of the social economy. The other conception emphasizes the outcomes of organizations—that is to say the values and principles that make them different from traditional enterprises. According to this perspective, social entrepreneurship is not necessarily defined by a specific legal status, but rather by a project or a capacity to articulate economic and social goals. This tradition dominates among European Union (EU) member states, of which the United Kingdom is undoubtedly the leader (European Commission, 2015). Countries that stress legal designations usually feature a strong, interventionist state that focuses on the social economy's impact on the "general interest." Countries that stress outcomes, by contrast, are often defined by a liberal tradition that sees all economic actors as being better able to play a role in society when the state leaves them to their own devices.

Evolution of the sector since 1980

The idea that any kind of organization can fulfill a social purpose began to spread throughout Europe during the early 1980s. Supporters of this idea think that the state is unable to (or simply shouldn't) take on the full financial burden of social assistance policies that, in a context of growing inequality and social exclusion, add to the government's fiscal deficit (Dubetz, 2014). Civil society must therefore step in and design new projects by working with state services, shouldering some of their responsibilities, or setting up networks with organizations that are both financially viable and socially useful. This approach, which seeks to combine entrepreneurial drive with limited profit-making, is in line with the neoliberal theories of Friedrich Hayek and various members of the Chicago School of Economics, including

Milton Friedman, Robert E. Lucas, and Gary Becker (Clarke, 1988). Their work influenced the neoliberal turn that took place in most industrialized countries following the rise of Margaret Thatcher in the United Kingdom in 1979, and the election of Ronald Reagan in the United States in 1980 (Jobert, 1994). Even countries that aren't defined as much by liberal traditions (e.g. France) became more familiar with social entrepreneurship by drawing inspiration from the Anglo-Saxon experience (Chabanet, 2017).

The fall of the Berlin wall in 1989, followed by the collapse of the communist bloc, prompted some commentators to proclaim the End of History (Fukuyama, 1992), an era marked by the final and unavoidable victory of capitalism. This was the context in which social entrepreneurship began to fully emerge, replacing older traditions associated with the social economy. The concepts was promoted by its advocates as a new means to combine economic efficiency and social value, by relying on the methods and organizational principles of management theory. This was a global phenomenon that was partly inspired by American and British precedents, including Ashoka International, an organization launched by Bill Drayton in India in 1980, whose programs spread to the rest of the world during the following decade. Prestigious business schools followed suit, including the Harvard Business School, which started its own social initiative in 1993. Europe, of course, did not lag far behind. For instance, the Schwab Foundation for Social Entrepreneurship was set up in Geneva in 1998. In 1991, Italy granted special legal status to social solidarity cooperatives, explicitly mentioning social entrepreneurship, while Belgium passed a law regulating commercial ventures set up for social ends in 1995. The United Kingdom, meanwhile, championed a form of social entrepreneurship that combined patronage and social philanthropy by setting up the Coalition for Social Enterprise in 2002, the Big Society project in 2010, and, more recently, the Social Values Act in 2013 (Nicholls & Teasdale, 2016).

The enlargement of the EU to ten new members in 2014—most of them former communist countries with deep suspicions of state interference in economic matters—represents another fertile breeding ground for social entrepreneurship. In Poland, Hungary, and Romania, in particular, small-scale voluntary initiatives started to slowly grow (Monzón & Chaves, 2012). Advocates of an interventionist model found themselves increasingly sidelined in Europe, even as the European Commission launched the European Alliance for Corporate Social Responsibility, a forum open to all European companies, which was designed to encourage social initiatives (Kinderman, 2013). At the same time, the Commission also began to scrutinize the legal statuses of SEs at the national level in order to ensure that their privileges did not violate European rules on free and fair competition. It also granted financial support to the EMES (Emergence of Social Enterprises in Europe) network, which works to promote an institutional environment that favors a shared vision of social entrepreneurship.

The European Commission's definition of SEs, which is based on nine specific socioeconomic markers, has been adopted by academics and policy-makers alike. Four of these markers are economic: a constant output of goods or services; a high level of autonomy; a significant level of economic risk; and a certain level of reliance on paid employees. The remaining five markers are based on social criteria: a project started by a group of citizens; the adoption of a decision process that is not based on the amount of contributed capital; a dynamic form of governance involving all concerned parties; a cap on the proportion of profits that can be redistributed; and a stated aim of providing a form of community service (Defourny & Nyssens, 2010). Even if this definition does not take into account social entrepreneurship as such, this aspect of the social economy has indirectly benefited from this type of research. However, the EMES definition does not take into account legal status or the importance of openly political goals, such as the promotion of solidarity, social justice, or the fight against inequality. It instead focuses on a number of practices and norms that should be implemented so that broader social goals can be achieved by civil society actors and social entrepreneurs.

Nowadays, despite all the statistical difficulties associated with defining and quantifying the social economy, the sector is estimated to account for around 6.5 percent of paid employment in the EU27, and 7.5 percent of paid employment in the EU15 (Rosenblatt, 2013, p. 10). Not surprisingly, the social economy is more developed in older member states than in newer ones. Thus, the rate of paid employment in the social economy varies between 9 percent and 11 percent of the working population in Belgium, France, Italy, and the Netherlands, while Sweden is the only EU country that exceeds the 11 percent mark (Rosenblatt, 2013, p. 10) (Table 3.1).

Associations—including foundations and other similar organizations—constitute the biggest portion of the social economy, representing 65 percent of paid employment (Table 3.2).

Table 3.1 Paid employment in the social economy in relation to total paid employment (in thousands)

	Employment in the social economy	Total employment	%
EU15	12,806.4	172,790.4	7.4
EU27	14,128.1	216,397.8	6.53

Source: Rosenblatt (2013, p. 10).

Table 3.2 Paid employment in cooperatives, mutuals, and associations

Cooperatives	Mutuals	Associations	Total
4,548,394	362,632	9,217,088	1,412,813
32.2%	2.6%	65.2%	100%

Source: Rosenblatt (2013, p. 9).

The role of national, international, and supranational institutions

Despite contrasting experiences, social entrepreneurship has become an area of priority for some European countries and the EU in a matter of a few short years. The 2008 economic crisis played an important role in this trend, obliging national and EU authorities to focus on the social economy sector as a means of creating or saving jobs, especially among marginalized and vulnerable groups (Demoustier & Colletis, 2012). However, job creation is not the social economy's only objective. In most countries the social economy seeks to promote a wide range of initiatives, such as facilitating viable economic development, fighting against discrimination, promoting the inclusion of people with disabilities, and supporting cultural, educational, and health-related initiatives (Osborne, 2014). Several EU countries have proposed framework legislation to address these concerns in recent years, including Spain and Greece in 2011 (Cadic, 2013, 2014), Portugal in 2013 (Gire, 2014), and France in 2014. Social economy legislation was also adopted in three regions of Belgium in 2012 (Chorum, 2014). Although not officially enacted into law, various initiatives undertaken by regional/national public authorities, civil society actors, and social entrepreneurs indicate that there has been growing interest in the social economy in recent years (Morel et al., 2012).

Nonetheless, the development of a general legal framework is far from complete in Europe, as only five countries currently have a law defining and regulating the social economy sector. Moreover, all of these laws have been drawn up in recent years, and most of them are quite concise. For instance, the Spanish law features 6 articles, while the Portuguese and Greek laws include 14 and 20 articles (respectively). France, however, has adopted an exceedingly complex statute that features 98 articles and an especially technical text (Stokkink & Perard, 2016, p. 7). In many respects, the development of the social economy sector has relied on specific measures that either focus on cooperatives, mutual societies, associations, and foundations, or general policies that fight poverty and social exclusion. Indeed, one wonders whether the difficulties encountered by the sector are based on its struggles to gain full political recognition in several jurisdictions. There are three main reasons for this: the fragmentation and dispersal of the field, which hinders its recognition among political figures and institutions; its lack of interest among political parties and trade unions; and the view among public authorities that social entrepreneurship and SEs tend to focus on reparation issues, which reduces their significance when the economy is strong (thus explaining the lack of continuity and funding for public policies that are meant to support the social economy).

International and supranational organizations—especially the EU— have also sought to promote the social economy (Pezzini & Pflüger, 2013). The institutional recognition of the social economy and the formulation of specific European policies began in the 1980s, culminating in 1989 with the Communication of the Commission on "Businesses in the social economy sector – Europe's frontier-free market" (European Commission, 1989), which suggested providing cooperatives, associations, and mutual societies with legal recognition through the creation of a specific statute. The creation of the Social Economy Unit by the Directorate-General XXIII of the European Commission (which at that time was chaired by Jacques Delors) is also evidence of a strong desire to promote the sector. During the 1980s, moreover, two institutions—the European Parliament and the European Economic and Social Committee (EESC)—published a multitude of reports, proposals, and resolutions highlighting the social value brought about by various actors in the social economy.

After much procrastination, the European Commission launched the Social Business Initiative in 2011 (European Commission, 2011). It was created as a means of encouraging the growth of SEs by expanding their access to funding. To this end, the Commission established an Expert Group on Social Entrepreneurship (GECES) in February 2012 that consisted of one representative from each member state and 43 representatives from the social economy sector, the banking sector, and academia. A subgroup in charge of social impact measurement was set up a few months later to develop a methodology that could measure the socioeconomic impact of SEs, while the Commission outlined new mechanisms—most notably the European Structural Fund—to improve financing opportunities. Even though its recommendations were only treated as voluntary guidelines, the GECES should be seen as an epistemic community, "a network of professionals with recognized expertise and competence in a particular domain or issue area and an authoritative claim to policy-relevant knowledge within that domain or issue-area" (Haas, 1992, p. 3). It represents a wide variety of opinions, sensitivities, and priorities, but most of the experts support a market-oriented form of social entrepreneurship, and those who are critical of free-market approaches are entirely unrepresented.

Social entrepreneurship is now considered a mainstay of the Europe 2020 initiative, a project that promotes full employment, economic growth, and a sustainable and inclusive economy. Developments in Europe have been reproduced in other parts of the world. The United Nations, for example, recently indicated that social entrepreneurship was of vital importance in ensuring sustainable economic development (Masquelin, 2014). A G8 Task Force was also established in June 2013 with a view towards focusing on the social impact of investments. Under the chairmanship of British Prime Minister David Cameron, it was given the task of developing a set of general guidelines that would help impact measurement become a fundamental part of social impact investing. These trends suggest that support for social entrepreneurship has begun to emerge across much of the world.

Nonetheless, enthusiasm for the social economy seems to have diminished in recent years. Member states that were most eager to develop the social economy under the Barroso Commission—most notably Belgium, France, Spain, Italy, Luxembourg, and Portugal—are now in the minority. Indeed, the Juncker Commission has decided to "clean up the table"—that is, ignore all issues where there is no unanimity among member states (Interview with Ariane Roder, Vice-President of the EESC Group III, June 27, 2016). This is what happened, for example, with the European Status of Foundations and Mutuals. Perhaps more importantly, the European Commission did not cite the social economy at all in its 2015 work program. Weakened by the general European political context, the Commission now considers that the work carried out by the GECES should convince the stakeholders, and therefore the representatives of the Member States, without taking any particular initiative. Despite pressure from the European Economic and Social Council, the European Parliament, and some NGOs (e.g. Social Economy Europe), interest in the social economy continues to lag due to a lack of commitment from the European Commission and the leaders of most member states.

Towards a takeover of the market

As the EFESEIIS project (Enabling the Flourishing and Evolution of Social Entrepreneurship for Innovative and Inclusive Societies) confirmed, social entrepreneurship, SEs, and innovation vary greatly within and between countries. Much of this variation comes about due to the nature and level of development of the national/territorial ecosystems in which SEs are situated. SEs operate in different sectors, take on different legal forms, differ in their capacity to remain in the market, and depend on external financing to varying degrees. They also differ in terms of their overall income, how they use their profits, and the number of employees and volunteers. Nevertheless, in spite of strong and persistent differences between European countries, we argue that social entrepreneurship tends to be more and more market-oriented as times goes on. This is not to say that there are SEs acting outside of their specific market. Being market-oriented is neither one-dimensional nor always a preferred approach. Instead, SEs are being forced to become more market-oriented due to growing competition from both the private sector and other nonprofit organizations (Doherty et al., 2014).

SEs have gone from complementing the public sector to filling the numerous gaps that have emerged in contemporary welfare systems. Examples are found within most sectors, but due to the last year's asylum crises and together with increasing numbers of long-term unemployed across Europe those examples are frequently found amongst work integration social enterprises (WISEs). Other examples are found within the public health sector as elderly care or home care, the education sector (schools with specific pedagogical approaches or for pupils with special needs) and the housing sector (such as specific housing for homeless people). However, the growing reliance on neo-liberal policies in the public sector have resulted in a more competitive environment where SEs compete with for-profit enterprises and other SEs (Cooney et al., 2016). This is especially noticeable in England, Italy, and Scotland (Brookes et al., 2011; EFESEIIS, n.d.). Despite the obvious differences between SEs and for-profit enterprises—the emphasis on solving social or environment issues among the former, and the importance of profits among the latter—their organizational behavior and objectives are often similar (Borzaga et al., 2010). This continuum, together with the aforementioned increasing market competition, may be of more importance when analyzing the market situation, than addressing the market in form of growth or degrowth economy made up of not-for-profit and not-only-for profit organizations (Johanisova et al., 2013).

Nevertheless, despite attempts to acclimatize themselves to market rules, SEs clearly struggle when they compete for procurements. The most common explanation provided by social entrepreneurs is that procurements are dominated by market-based assumptions in which monetary concerns triumph over social value (Focus group interview with Swedish social entrepreneurs, January 14, 2015; see also, Loosemore, 2016). According to Pirvu and Clipici (2016), this is the result of a lack of knowledge among public employees about the importance of drawing up public procurement processes that enable active participation from SEs. Fortunately, Italy, Germany, and France seem to be exceptions to the rule.

There seem to be two dominant approaches among SEs in terms of how they deal with market forces: the grant approach and the business approach. The former approach emphasizes grants that focus on specific social issues. The latter approach, meanwhile, involves competing with for-profit enterprises via traditional, market-based strategies. Although SEs tend to prefer the market-driven approach, their income and employee/volunteer ratios vary significantly. Moreover, many SEs have to combine the different approaches in order to be successful, a trend that clearly emerges in the EFESEIIS project (EFESEIIS, n.d.). Organizations that emphasize market activities employ a larger portion of paid staff than grant dependent SEs (many of which rely mostly on volunteers). The types of customers these SEs attract often depend on both the sector and the market in which they operate, as well as how the welfare state is organized in their specific jurisdiction. However, the findings of the EFESEIIS project indicate that the degree of collaboration between SEs and the welfare sector—most notably in the fields of social services and health care—vary significantly from country to country, even in jurisdictions that have decentralized welfare systems. As a result, the shrinking budgets and higher standards required by public authorities while awarding public tenders may both help and hinder SEs. The praxis between different municipalities, counties, or regions in one country may vary and not uncommonly is it as in the case of the aforementioned procurement dilemma down to the knowledge and abilities of individuals to influence the systems.

Conclusion

To both understand the present and predict the future, one must look at the past. This chapter has looked at the evolution of SEs from a historical perspective, using the nineteenth century as a starting point. We have described the historical evolution of solidarity in the context of the sweeping changes that have been made to various welfare regimes. We tried to provide a fair assessment of the evolution and growth of the welfare sector across Europe, as well as how these predecessors have affected current SEs. We talked about how SEs (and their predecessors) complemented traditional welfare systems, and how current SEs have stepped in to fill the many gaps that have emerged in recent years due to the growing popularity of neoliberal policies. Furthermore, we were able to distinguish two main types of SEs: one based on legal status and another based on outcomes. We then discussed how these new SEs are different from traditional or mainstream economic actors. We then looked at the overall evolution of SEs since the 1980s, an era in which traditional approaches to welfare were seen as being incapable of solving various social problems, a trend that was further reinforced due to the fall of the Berlin Wall and the triumph of capitalism over communism. It is in this context that current trends in the SE sector first started to emerge. As the public sector began to shrink, civil society was given the task of shouldering some of the responsibilities of the welfare state by setting up networks of flexible, financially viable, and socially useful organizations. Despite the difficulties scholars and practitioners have faced in agreeing on a clear definition of SEs, the sector has grown exponentially in recent years due to the fact that former communist countries have embraced free market principles.

We then paid attention to the multilevel governance situation in which the concept and praxis of SEs take place by looking at the role of the national, European and international institutions. While social entrepreneurship is a mainstay of the Europe 2020 initiative, enthusiasm among political leaders seems to have waned in recent years. This may be due to the victory of free market principles, the lack of a common agenda, or just a natural result of the neo-liberal approaches to social welfare—all of which are certainly worth investigating. Regardless, our research suggests that the first factor—the victory of free market principles—is reflected in the heightened competition between for-profit enterprises and other types of SEs, an issue that can be addressed by simply revising pre-existing procurement processes. Nevertheless, for a sector that works hand in hand with welfare regimes—which are shaped by various political ideologies—it is difficult to determine what the future will bring.

References

Alcock, P. (2012). New policy spaces: The impact of devolution on third sector policy in the UK. *Social Policy & Administration, 46*(2), 219–238.

Borzaga, C., Depedri, S., & Tortia, E. (2010), *The growth of Organizational Variety in Market Economies: The case of Social Enterprises*, Euricse Working Papers, N. 003|10.

Borzaga, C., & Santuari, A. (2003). New trends in the non-profit sector in Europe: The emergence of social entrepreneurship. In OECD (Eds.), *The non-profit sector in a changing economy* (pp. 31–56). Paris: OECD Publications Service.

Brookes, N., Kendall, J., & Mitton, L. (2011). *Local welfare in the United Kingdom: Housing, employment and child care* (WILCO Publication no. 01). Canterbury: University of Kent.

Cadic, P. (2013). *L'économie sociale en Espagne: un bilan de la législation nationale et régionale.* Think Tank européen Pour la Solidarité. Retrieved from www.pourlasolidarite.eu/sites/default/files/publications/files/7es_essenespagne_bilanlegislationnationaleetregionale.pdf.

Cadic, P. (2014). *L'économie sociale en Grèce.* Think Tank européen Pour la Solidarité. Retrieved from www.pourlasolidarite.eu/sites/default/files/publications/files/2014_05_economie_sociale_grece.pdf.

Chabanet, D. (2017). The social economy sector and the welfare State in France: Toward a takeover of the market? *Voluntas: International Journal of Voluntary and Nonprofit Organizations, 28*(6), 2360–2382.

Chorum – Note d'actualité. (2014). *La législation relative à l'économie sociale et solidaire: analyse comparée France/Europe.* Retrieved from http://rtes.fr/IMG/pdf/2014-04_Note_d_actu_4_Legislation_ESS.pdf.

Clarke, S. (1988). *Keynesianism, monetarism and the crisis of the state.* Aldershot: Edward Elgar.

Cooney, K., Nyssens, M., O'Shaughnessy, M., & Defourny, J. (2016). Public policies and work integration social enterprises: The challenge of institutionalization in a neoliberal era. *Nonprofit Policy Forum, 7*(4), 415–433.

Defourny, J., & Nyssens, M. (2010). Conceptions of social enterprise and social entrepreneurship in Europe and the United States: Convergences and divergences. *Journal of Social Entrepreneurship, 1*(1), 32–53.

Demoustier, D., & Colletis, G. (2012). L'économie sociale et solidaire face à la crise: simple résistance ou participation au changement. *Revue internationale de l'économie sociale, 325,* 21–33.

Doherty, B., Haugh, H., & Lyon, F. (2014). Social enterprises as hybrid organizations: A review and research agenda. *International Journal of Management Reviews, 16*(4), 417–436.

Dubetz, E. (2014). *Économie sociale et Europe: quel(s) dialogue(s)?* Think Tank européen pour la Solidarité. Retrieved from http://base.socioeco.org/docs/2014_07_economie_sociale_eu.pdf.

EFESEIIS. (n.d.). Thematic focus #4: Financial resources. Retrieved from www.fp7-efeseiis.eu/results/thematic-survey-focus/.

Esping-Andersen, G. (1990). *The three worlds of welfare capitalism.* Cambridge: Polity Press.

European Commission. (1989). Communication from the Commission to the Council, *Businesses in the social economy sector – Europe's frontier-free market'.* Brussels: Commission of the European Communities, SEC (89) 2187 final.

European Commission. (2011). Communication from the Commission to the European Parliament, the Council, the European Economic and Social Committee and the Committee of the Regions, *Social Business Initiative. Creating a favourable climate for social enterprises, key stakeholders in the social economy and innovation.* Brussels: Commission of the European Communities, SEC (2011) 1278 final.

European Commission. (2013). *Social economy and social entrepreneurship, Social Europe guide, Volume 4.* Directorate-General for Employment, Social Affairs and Inclusion. Luxembourg: Publications Office of the European Union. Retrieved from www.igfse.pt/upload/docs/2013/DGEMPL_Social_Europe_Guide_Vol.4_EN_Accessible.pdf.

European Commission. (2015). *A map of social enterprises and their eco-systems in Europe.* Synthesis Report. Directorate-General for Employment, Social Affairs and Inclusion. Luxembourg: Publications Office of the European Union. Retrieved from ec.europa.eu/social/BlobServlet?docId=12987&langId=en

Ferrera, M. (1996). The "southern model" of social Europe. *Journal of European Social Policy,* 6(1), 17–37.

Ferrera, M. (2005). *The boundaries of welfare.* Oxford: Oxford University Press.

Fukuyama, F. (1992). *The end of history and the last man.* New York: The Free Press.

Gallie, D., & Paugam, S. (2000). *Welfare regimes and the experience of unemployment in Europe.* Oxford: Oxford University Press.

Gire, H. (2014). *L'économie sociale au Portugal.* Think Tank européen Pour la Solidarité. Retrieved from www.pourlasolidarite.eu/sites/default/files/publications/files/wp2014_1_es_ess_portugal.pdf.

Haas, P. (1992). Epistemic communities and international policy coordination. *International Organization,* 46(1), 1–35.

Jobert, B. (1994). *Le tournant néo-libéral en Europe.* Paris: L'Harmattan.

Johanisova, N., Crabtree, T., & Fraňková, E. (2013). Social enterprises and non-market capitals: A path to degrowth? *Journal of Cleaner Production, 38,* 7–16.

Kinderman, D. (2013). Corporate social responsibility in the EU, 1993–2013: Institutional ambiguity, economic crises, business legitimacy and bureaucratic politics. *Journal of Common Market Studies,* 51(4), 701–720.

Loosemore, M. (2016). Social procurement in UK construction projects. *International Journal of Project Management,* 34(2), 133–144.

Masquelin, A. (2014). *Economie sociale et solidaire et Nations-Unies. Un rapprochement récent.* Think Tank européen Pour la Solidarité. Retrieved from www.pourlasolidarite.eu/sites/default/files/publications/files/na-2014-ess-onu_0.pdf.

Mazzei, M., & Roy, M. (2017) From policy to practice: Exploring practitioners' perspectives on social enterprise policy claims. *Voluntas, International Journal of Voluntary and Nonprofit Organizations,* 28(6), 2449–2468.

Monzón, J. L., & Chaves, R. (2012). *The Social Economy in the European Union.* Report drawn up for the European Economic and Social Committee by the International Centre of Research and Information on the Public, Social and Cooperative Economy. Brussels: European Economic and Social Committee. Retrieved from www.eesc.europa.eu/resources/docs/qe-30-12-790-en-c.pdf.

Mooney, G., & Williams, C. (2006). Forging new 'ways of life'? Social policy and nation building in devolved Scotland and Wales. *Critical Social Policy,* 26(3), 608–629.

Morel, N., Palier, B., & Palme, J. (2012). *Towards a social investment welfare state?* Bristol and Chicago, IL: The Policy Press.

Nicholls, A., & Teasdale, S. (2017). Neoliberalism by stealth? Exploring continuity and change within the UK social enterprise policy paradigm. *Policy & Politics, 45*(3), 323–341.

Osborne, S. P. (2014). *The third sector in Europe: Prospects and challenges.* London: Routledge.

Pezzini, E., & Pflüger, K. (2013). Economie sociale et politiques publiques européennes. Un long parcours inachevé, des visions plurielles. In D. Demoustier & R. Chaves (Eds.), *L'émergence de l'Economie sociale dans les politiques publiques* (pp. 73–110). Brussels: Peter Lang.

Pirvu, D., & Clipici, E. (2016). Social enterprises and the EU's public procurement market. *Voluntas, International Journal of Voluntary and Nonprofit Organizations, 27*(4), 1611–1637.

Praszkier, R., Petrushak, E., Kacprzyk-Murawska, M., & Zablocka, A. (2017) The polish social enterprise sector Vis-a`-Vis the welfare regime: Following on the solidarity movement? *Voluntas, International Journal of Voluntary and Nonprofit Organizations, 28*(6), 2383–2402.

Ritter, G. A. (2003). *Storia dello Stato Sociale*, Roma-Bari: Laterza (Original ed. 1991, *Der Sozialstaat.* [The welfare state] Munchen: R. Oldenbourg Verlag).

Rosenblatt, C. (2013). Quelle place pour l'économie sociale en Europe? Think Tank européen pour la solidarité.

Stokkink, D., & Perard, P. (2016). *L'économie sociale et solidaire en Europe.* Think Tank européen Pour la Solidarité. Retrieved from www.pourlasolidarite.eu/sites/default/files/publications/files/na-2016-ess-europe.pdf.

Zarkovic Rakic, J., Aleksic Miric, A., Lebedinski, L., & Vladisavljevic, M. (2017) Welfare state and social enterprise in transition: Evidence from Serbia. *Voluntas, International Journal of Voluntary and Nonprofit Organizations, 28*(6), 2423–2448.

Zimmer, A., & Obuch, K. (2017) A matter of context? Understanding social enterprises in changing environments: The case of Germany. *Voluntas, International Journal of Voluntary and Nonprofit Organizations, 28*(6), 2339–2359.

4 The diversity of European social enterprises

An evolutionary perspective

Roel During and Rosalie van Dam

Why adopt an evolutionary perspective?

Several in-depth analyses of social entrepreneurship in Europe reveal significant differences in the way it has developed (Hazenberg et al., 2016). The EFESEIIS project supports this notion, as do other European projects, such as SIMPACT (Debref et al., 2015) and SEFORIS (SEFORIS, 2016). In many cases, national differences are explained by referring to contextual information (Svensson, 2015), including resources, institutions, economic objectives, social needs, political objectives, and governance (Terstriep et al., 2015). Indeed, Terstriep and his peers (2015) state that very few projects engage in network analysis, which is often a significant part of Social Innovation Biographies or narrative approaches. Until now, the system analysis perspective has not been used as a means of analyzing the interaction between social enterprises (SEs) and their environments.

Obviously, a SE is conceived of as a *thing in itself* whose essence, as it is seen through the eyes of the state, should be described thoroughly (Scott, 1998). After all, different institutional contexts produce different SEs, but the state doesn't always see how SEs reshape their institutional context or how they emerged as an idea from nothing. Analyses are often done in a prestructured way, using directly applicable science, based on the distinction between the actor and the structure or institution. The study of social entrepreneurship, however, can also be based on the idea that science is always evolving (Latour, 1987). According to this notion, the object of social entrepreneurship itself is rapidly changing, leaving scientists with no consensus on how to observe and classify it (Debref et al., 2015). This is why an evolutionary approach might be helpful amidst the confusion and calls for clear definitions.

This chapter discusses evolutionary theory in order to increase our understanding of several phenomena:

- the start and (initial) growth of social entrepreneurship;
- the relationship between social entrepreneurs and their ecosystems;

- the path dependencies that lead to diversity, context specificity, radiation, and other forms of pluralism;
- societal embedding of social entrepreneurship as an evolutionary process.

Using evolutionary theory in this manner can also help overcome the gap between the evolutionary principles that are often associated with the study of economics (Constanza et al., 2007; Foster, 2003; Kamimura et al., 2011; Nelson & Winter, 2002; Pelikan, 2011) and the behavioral approaches associated with the social sciences (Cavalli-Sforza, 2001; Chantarat & Barrett, 2012; Granovetter, 2005; Tan, 2005; Tata & Prasad, 2010).

Methodology

Evolutionary theory can help us find the mechanisms of path dependencies that lead to radiation and diversity in the coevolution of SEs and their ecosystems while also accounting for contextual issues that tend to affect these mechanisms (During et al., 2016a; During, 2017). This theory was combined with Causal Process Tracing in the EFESEIIS project, an approach that is often used to reconstruct pathways of development (Blatter & Haverland, 2012). Evolutionary theory can help us understand the various processes of institutionalization that are found in a specific ecosystem. Participants in the EFESEIIS project, for instance, were initially encouraged to adopt an evolutionary perspective via inspiration papers. When the project drew to a close, however, participants were asked to discuss relevant developments that emerged in their countries over time. This was done by means of Process Tracing. The results have been analyzed in terms of micro-, meso-, and macro-evolutionary processes. Our analysis revealed contextual specificities in pathways of development, which were then used to discuss the velocity and direction of the evolutionary process. This part of the analysis provided us with a more in-depth understanding of both enabling and inhibiting factors. Using grounded theory as a guide, a theoretical framework has been designed that may assist future research on the coevolution of SEs and their ecosystems (see, for example, During & van Dam, 2016).

Our specific methodology has been chosen in order to bridge different paradigmatic views. Mixing the approaches used by economists and social scientists will improve our understanding of contextual influences and path dependencies that can lead to embedding or disembedding processes in the social economy (Granovetter, 2005; Polanyi, 2001). Rather than simply comparing the experiences of SEs in several European countries, this chapter uses data from the EFESEIIS project to highlight the importance of the evolutionary perspective.

Evolutionary analogy

In 1859 Charles Darwin presented his ideas on evolution in *On the Origin of Species by Means of Natural Selection, or the Preservation of Favoured Races in the Struggle for Life*. He argued that all species emerged from other species by descent, which undermined some of the more pastoral views that saw nature as a harmonious creation. As a consequence, it became obvious that species can change over time. Darwin postulated that the success of an individual's offspring depends on the way its characteristics fit into its environment, and that only the best traits will be passed on to the next generation. His theory is based on three principles: variation, selection, and heredity. Variation describes how individual animals and populations differ from one another. The differences may be small and seemingly insignificant, but they are very important for the process of evolution. If all individual creatures from a certain species were exactly the same, then change might be stymied. Variation is often the source of selection, depending on the individual species' environment. Some characteristics are favorable and others are problematic. A population with predominantly favorable characteristics (relative to other populations of the same species) has a greater chance of producing offspring than a population with less favorable characteristics. This approach to selection—a central part of Darwin's larger theory—was called *survival of the fittest*, as Darwin knew that plants and animals pass on their characteristics to the next generation.

Several scientists have added to Darwin's theories. For instance, in recent years, supporters of memetic theory have argued that genes may be selfish in nature and influence specific behavior, thereby acting as a driver of evolution (Dawkins, 1976). Other scientists, moreover, have argued that genes that can be activated or deactivated (Verhoeven & Preite, 2013), while the role of social learning has become apparent among various species of fish (Mesoudi et al., 2016). These concepts should be applied when using evolutionary theory to examine social entrepreneurship as well. Indeed, social learning may increase the competitiveness of a SE (Åmo, 2013). Those who learn together may be fitter than those who are muddling along in solitude. Social learning within an ecosystem may also contribute to the emergence of radiation as a strategy to avoid competition.

Table 4.1 lists the various evolutionary concepts that will be used to analyze social entrepreneurship.

If we try to apply Darwin's theory to our new species of SE, we are immediately confronted with misfits and choices to be made about ontologies. We see SEs not as static objects in a collection of institutions (e.g. an ecosystem), but rather as organisms that are viable and capable of producing good ideas that provide a competitive advantage in the struggle for economic success. Their environment, in short, is based on social relationships that infringe upon the institutional environment.

It is important to note that species are always defined by sexual reproduction in evolutionary theory. If reproduction is still possible in a certain

Table 4.1 Evolutionary concepts and social enterprises

Evolutionary concept	Application to social enterprise
Species	Social enterprise (nascent state)
Fit	Economically viable (including low rating of productive hours inherent to small enterprises); capable of managing many social relationships and social capital
Meme	Idea that competes with other ideas for social impact
Genotype	Legal status
Phenotype	Organizational structure
Epigenotype	Expertise, including business models and value propositions
Mutation	Change in legal structure
Variation	Inherent diversity in organizational structure and business models
Selection	Environmental pressure on organizational structure
Heredity	Using experiences to grow, scale up, and multiply
Adaptation	Ability to address social needs in a social economy marked by de-institutionalization
Radiation	One specific SE may develop into various other distinct legal or organizational forms
Co-evolution	Mutually influenced change of characteristics between species and/or ecosystems, resulting in highly specialized relationships and or niches
Stepping stone	Presence of a transitional situation that enables SEs to proliferate in unprofitable (in evolution: remote) areas
Tipping point	Small changes invoking big effects on the structure of an ecosystem
Succession	The complexity of ecosystems over time

species, despite all sorts of variety, it is still referred to as either a single species or a subspecies (the latter is used whenever striking differences emerge). According to Darwin, separate species emerge only when reproduction does not occur between two populations that have common ancestors.

SEs can currently be understood as varieties of profit or nonprofit enterprises. Up until now, there have been no clear legal or organizational distinctions that prevent them from merging with a traditional company. If organizations differ to such an extent that they are unable to merge, then a new species is born: the SE. For example, most traditional enterprises claim to produce social value for society, which blurs the distinctions between their activities and the activities of SEs. We have not yet reached the point where a separate species that cannot reproduce with traditional enterprises has been born, and yet SEs are growing and becoming much more varied, which suggests that they are taking part in a process of institutionalization. In evolutionary terms, the SE should be seen as a subspecies, or a collection of different subspecies, that is adjusting to its environment. It is just a matter of time before these subspecies turn into a unique species that is capable of generating a fertile environment of its own, thereby producing new niches for other subspecies and species. If a species proliferates, it must conquer the next best niche or other niches that feature harsh living conditions. It is in these niches that genetic modifications often lead to new species. If identical SEs coexist within a certain social context, they will tend to specialize and avoid competition in a similar manner. This is similar to the specialization and differentiation that takes place in an evolutionary pathway.

Succession is understood as the ways in which ecosystems and communities of entrepreneurs evolve over time, thus profoundly changing ecosystems and the rules governing them. Coevolution can be seen as the intertwined processes of change that crisscross the boundaries of SEs and their ecosystems. There may also be coevolution within ecosystems and communities of social entrepreneurs that is based on social learning and creating interdependencies. This view of succession and coevolution is more elaborate than earlier theories in which SEs were seen as clearly defined objects in society that need to be fostered and regulated. It combines anti-essentialism (Fuchs, 2001), actor-network theory (Latour, 1987), and social system theory (Even Zohar, 1990; Luhmann, 1995) with evolutionary theory. Hereafter, these concepts will be used to account for various pathways of evolution in specific national contexts.

Pathways of evolution

This section sheds light on the evolution of social entrepreneurship in Europe, and how these processes differ in various national and local contexts and different periods of history.

A protohistoric view on pathways of change

The rise of social entrepreneurship cannot be easily located in time. What should we look at when considering its origins? Should we look for the very first SE? Or is the evolution of ideas more important as a driver of change (Hull, 1982)? It is obvious that SEs existed long before the concept of social entrepreneurship had been invented. For instance, a cooperative social movement emerged as a result of the urbanization and industrialization of society in nineteenth-century England. Indeed, one can see the establishment of the Rochdale Pioneers in 1834 as a starting point. In Austria, meanwhile, the founding of the Erste Bank in 1819 to provide working class people with savings accounts also represents a notable example of an early social business. The Erste Bank serves as an important point of reference because it helped contribute to the rise of social entrepreneurship. Social cooperatives—predecessors of SEs—first emerged in Italy in the nineteenth century. For example, the Magazzino di previdenza, a prominent mutual aid society, was established in Turin in 1854 as a means of taking care of the needs of citizens during periods of famine. The first cooperatives had a family structure and strong internal bonds, a tradition that remains to this day. Despite the introduction of cooperatives in nineteenth-century Poland, many of which helped consolidate agricultural production and local supply issues, debates over SE were influenced by communist doctrine and the legacy of state agricultural farms—the idea that everything should be taken care of by the state and that individual initiatives are either unnecessary or worthy of persecution. Indeed, SEs would only emerge in Poland after the collapse of the Berlin Wall in 1989. In fact, the forerunners of the solidarity movement initiated the rise of SEs in recent decades.

While modernization processes have unfolded gradually in some countries, Serbia has witnessed some truly disruptive transformations. During the communist period after World War II, workers were supposed to, in theory, serve as co-owners of enterprises. In practice, however, they had no say in how most organizations were run. Nonetheless, cooperatives were an integral part of the political system, which affected ideas on citizenship and how Yugoslavians understood various social and economic issues. After the overthrow of Slobodan Milosevic's government in 2000, the nation's understanding of both "social" and "entrepreneurship" had to be re-invented.

In Sweden, a strong and well-developed welfare state emerged between 1880 and World War I, during a period that has become known as the Liberal Reform Era. Their ideas on sickness benefits, injury insurance, and pensions were heavily influenced by Bismarck's reforms in Germany, many of which led to the creation of a strong welfare state in which the emergence of a new generation of social entrepreneurs was not readily apparent. Although social entrepreneurship can be traced back to the nineteenth century, it was affected in some cases by disruptive events such as revolutions.

A historic view on pathways of change

The full emergence of social entrepreneurship is a recent phenomenon. For instance, Muhammad Yunus's Nobel Prize in 2006 compelled many Austrian entrepreneurs to include social values in their businesses. This was followed by the creation of a new generation of social entrepreneurs that were almost exclusively located in Vienna, becoming an integral part of the city culture. In Poland, meanwhile, social entrepreneurship was shaped by members of the Solidarity movement who developed a specific form of cooperation that combined innovation, self-organization, and trust in others. In many respects, SEs became contemporary spin-offs of the Solidarity movement. Whereas the origins of social entrepreneurship in Austria were inspired by alternative business traditions, the Polish example originated in a movement that fought communism and favored economic modernization.

Germany and Italy also has diverse pathways of change. For instance, Germany has several civil society organizations that are firmly connected to both the church and the state. The nonprofit sector, moreover, has increasingly adopted a business attitude. Similarly, Italy has a strong social cooperative tradition, featuring social service providers that are defined by law and inspired by socialist and religious ideas, featuring red cooperatives that are connected to communist ideology and white cooperatives that are connected to the Catholic Church. Other third-sector organizations have also emerged after the creation of a new law in 2006. In many cases, however, they have to compete with well-established social cooperatives.

In some countries, the establishment of SE sectors came about without taking economic traditions into account. In Serbia, for instance, the ecosystem developed over a short period of time and was heavily influenced by external ideologies. The legacy of the SE before 2000 has been left aside, unused. This led to networks that emerged in a top-down manner, thereby inhibiting growth. In France, however, major changes occurred after SEs were clearly defined in a legal sense. Many private companies were allowed to operate as part of the Social and Solidarity Economy, which caused an instant break with the past. This is an example of a tipping point, after which evolutionary processes began to accelerate.

Recent trends

If we focus on the recent history of social entrepreneurship, we can see that complex ecosystem relationships emerged alongside simple ones, occupying space within regulatory frameworks that were still in their infancies. In England, for instance, the sector initially built on notions of Corporate Social Responsibility and Fair Trade practices, new public management theory, and the marketization of welfare. The sector gained substantial momentum after the establishment of the Community Interest Company as a new legal form. Evolutionary processes were similarly accelerated as a result of the Right to Request and Right to Provide framework, the Mutual Pathfinder Support Programme, and the Social Value Act. A complex supportive ecosystem evolved in due time.

In Sweden, as in England, health care was opened up to non-public providers, followed by intermediate funding organizations such as the Social Economy Network. However, the pace of change was slow because SEs found it difficult to compete with bigger companies that had already secured contracts with the government. These differences show that funding alone doesn't solve problems associated with competition. As the English example illustrates, regulatory and legal provisions, when combined with stimulation programs, can play a vital role in mitigating these types of problems. Indeed, supportive ecosystems and complexity go hand in hand, as complexity often plays a supportive role. In the Netherlands, for example, ecosystem support is boosted by granting philanthropic organizations a greater role. This involves extending tax privileges (which is normally restricted to donating money) to impact investment areas with a return on investment. These types of tax provisions can be seen as a stepping stone towards a more complex and receptive ecosystem.

Cities also play a key role in the development of SEs. The sector often operates in tight-knit networks in urban areas, featuring structures that enable social learning. In Vienna, Amsterdam, and Glasgow, for example, city development contributed to the evolution of their respective ecosystems. We see a connection between municipal policies and smart city initiatives, including digital service provisions and severe austerity programs. Indeed, Glasgow claims to have the most supportive ecosystem in the world (Roy et al., 2015).

Inhibiting and enabling evolutionary factors

Grounded theory analysis has yielded interesting data on the coevolution and path dependencies of SEs and their ecosystems (During, 2017). This approach will be used to address the most important issue that has emerged from the EFESEIIS project—namely the extent to which ecosystems enable social entrepreneurship. This involves the relationship between social entrepreneurs who have ideas on how social value-creation acts as a starting point in the coevolutionary process, and the responses they receive from the ecosystem. Although an entrepreneur might have a brilliant idea and be well-equipped to launch a SE, this does not guarantee success. As in biology, the environment decides which ideas and social entrepreneurs are fit enough to settle into a niche, and whether or not these environments are hostile or receptive towards SE. Attitudes toward SEs are, of course, multilayered, pluriform, and full of ambiguities, which is why it is important to describe how a positive attitude can help build basic infrastructure, and how complications can spoil an otherwise positive atmosphere.

An important positive indicator is a country's willingness to adjust the rules for public procurement. If attitudes are positive, the government can create both educational programs for entrepreneurs and infrastructure that helps forge connections between funders, end users, and entrepreneurs. Another pathway of development involves the creation of programs in which SEs are designated as experiments and innovations. Governments can also develop specific privileges for funders and/or social entrepreneurs, and create a regulatory framework that enables a social economy to emerge. This includes tax privileges or the use of local currencies. Moreover, an enabling ecosystem allows individuals and organizations to voice their needs, expectations, and ideals while also creating and implementing joint actions. A high level of trust and social capital between different actors in the ecosystem positively influences the capacity of social entrepreneurs to introduce social innovation. Moreover, social innovation processes are often bottom-up and deinstitutionalized, especially in their initial phases (Biggeri et al., 2017).

A negative environment often emerges whenever there is public denial of added value-creation by the SE sector. Few opportunities will arise under such conditions, thus ensuring that public procurement is limited to larger, well-established social welfare institutions. This makes it quite difficult to start an enterprise because the bureaucracy prohibits newer forms of competition that might encroach on the turf of older social welfare entities. In many cases, people with social needs (e.g. migrants) are forbidden from engaging in social projects because they aren't permitted to receive public services or, in the case of programs aimed at inclusion, engagement is framed as *work that should be paid for*. As a result, nepotistic structures may emerge that force social entrepreneurs to engage with groups and individuals who have procurement powers in order to secure funding. This may end up bringing things to a standstill or even lead to devolution.

A widely-accepted definition of SE is valuable, but it doesn't guarantee success. Although the SE sector often pleads for clear legal definitions, other organizations tend to use mimicry to meet these definitions and change is stifled. Discursive mechanisms of identification, counter-identification, and disidentification shed light on the various pathways that helped social entrepreneurship enter the third sector in England (Dey & Teasdale, 2013). A set of principles giving access to a label as deployed in Scotland seems to become more beneficial to the evolution of the sector. The lesson here is that gradual coevolution in a sector and its ecosystem works better than an ecosystem that is instantly designed to promote and provide privileges to those who fit the legal definition (which is what happened in Croatia).

Towards an evolutionary theory of social enterprise

The following section features a theoretical framework that is based on three of Darwin's most important concepts: variation, selection, and heredity. In order to provide a more complete overview of the evolutionary process among SEs, we also added the concepts of succession and evolutionary pathways to our analysis.

Variation

Obviously, variation is significant in the SE sector. The first type of variation is caused by a decision to adopt social inclusion principles (the input of social resources), strive for social impact, or try to achieve both. A second type of variation emerges whenever an organization decides to address one or several different social impact areas. In evolutionary terms, this type of diversification would be seen as a form of radiation. A third type of variation develops due to a unique combination of aims and resources—some of which are the products of social reciprocity mechanisms, while others are the products of crowd sourcing, social impact bonds, or impact investors. Internet resources and social media create huge differences in the way resources are obtained and managed. A fourth type of variation is caused by the institutional predecessors of a SE. Did the SE emerge from a business, an NGO, or a governmental institute? Or did it start from scratch? A fifth type of variation is caused by a social entrepreneur's previous experiences. Some have a lifetime of business development behind them, while others rely on ideological motivations rather than experience. All of the variations discussed earlier are connected to each other and to various features of the ecosystem (e.g. financing).

Despite strong pluralization, some societal problems remain unaddressed by the SE sector, including, most notably, the challenge of tackling the debt levels of poor people. No organization has been able to draw up a business model that solves the financial problems of the poorest segments of society in a profitable manner (although someone might argue that microcredits perform this type of task).

This pluralizing tendency should be treated as a set of practices that may or may not succeed in establishing a well-functioning SE (During et al., 2016b). Ideas migrate easily from one context to another. It has been noted that the diversity and quality of ideas are enhanced in cities or regions that have creative reputations (van Dam et al., 2015). Which ideas survive, however, is a matter of selection.

Selection

Regardless of which country social entrepreneurs start their businesses in, the quality of their ideas is very important to achieve success. In the early stages of an enterprise, pitching and testing the idea is crucial. If social entrepreneurs operate within a livable and vibrant network of colleagues, they will have a competitive advantage (During & van Dam, 2016). The quality of an idea is based on the following dimensions:

- Adds social value
- Avoids direct competition with other social service institutions
- Based on both a good business plan and social start-up capital

Social entrepreneurs are fit if they manage to create synergy between social impact, social capital, and investment (see Figure 4.1). Social impact contributes to their reputation and status, thus attracting more funders to their enterprises (Saeed & Arshad, 2012). With more money at their disposal, social entrepreneurs can achieve greater impact and their social capital will grow. The ability to create social capital is therefore a vital trait for social entrepreneurs (Praszkier et al., 2009).

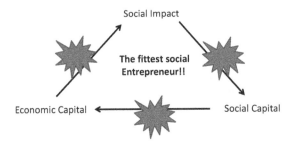

Figure 4.1 Fitness in social entrepreneurship.

Although an entrepreneur might have a brilliant idea and be well equipped to launch a SE, this is not a guarantee for success. Just as in biology, it is the environment that decides which part of the whole repertoire is fit enough to settle into what could be classed as a niche. Environments can be hostile or receptive towards a SE. How the SE perceives itself and its environment is key, which leads to an important question: what determines the basic attitude of an environment towards a SE?

Heredity

Heredity defines how traits that are important for the survival and adaptability of social entrepreneurs are passed from one generation to the next. This process depends on both the larger cultural context and the internal structures upon which learning is organized. If a society is defined by an emphasis on planning—where ideas and implementation schemes are always written down and preserved—beneficial traits are more likely to be learned and passed on. Meanwhile, if a society has a strong family tradition, other learning paths will probably be taken. Heredity is therefore a product of both macro- and micro-evolutionary processes. The temporal boundaries of micro-level processes are approximately 30 years, but this is flexible (During & van Dam, 2016). It is important to note, however, that while social entrepreneurs can pass on various traits to their successors, the ecosystem itself also undergoes a process of learning that influences the next generation's traits. This can be seen as a form of coevolution. Both the entrepreneur and the ecosystem learn, in various social contexts, how to deal with all sorts of challenges. When an ecosystem begins to undertake a learning process, its interior complexity increases—a process known as succession.

Succession

The pathways of change discussed earlier clearly show that complexity increases as a consequence of a coevolutionary process in the SE sector and its ecosystem. In the nineteenth century, this relationship was simple, as it most often involved a certain charity's relationship with the church. In more recent decades, a regulatory framework has emerged as a result of greater specialization, which, in turn, came about due to growing interest from outside actors and other sources of funding. Social entrepreneurs are now connected to each other in a rather thorough manner, and the set of relationships with their institutional environment is expanding. In evolutionary terms, this can be described as succession. If for instance we look at funders, it can be observed that its landscape becomes more attached and diverse. Funding strategies are diversifying. Some seek quick return on investments, while others seek a boost to their reputation or have opted for long-term goals. Social entrepreneurs may seek out funding from a wide variety of sources in order to minimize risk. This is when succession becomes truly beneficial.

Evolutionary pathways

Enabling or disabling environments are the products of public opinion (e.g. views of the EU, reactions to austerity measures, and repetition of historical events or identity discourses), defensive reactions from established social service institutions, and various political debates on the merits of socialism and liberalism. Ambiguity dominates in this type environment, serving as a driver of innovation. In the evolutionary process, these factors function as tipping points on the path to stagnation or progress—or even evolution or devolution. Managing these ambiguities is seen as a form of social learning, a means of creating a competitive environment. Figure 4.2 nicely illustrates this type of evolutionary pathway by emphasizing both stepping stones and tipping points.

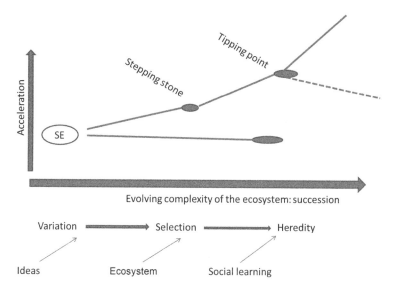

Figure 4.2 An overview of the evolutionary process.

A multitude of ideas are developed by entrepreneurs and discussed in the ecosystem in order to ensure that the best ideas are put into practice. Both entrepreneurs and the ecosystem influence this selection process by treating some of these ideas as innovations. The speed with which social entrepreneurship evolves is dependent on tipping points, which are often ambiguities and dilemmas that must be overcome and stepping stones that result in new pathways. This process is rather blind and has its own situational logic.

Discussion and avenues for further research

Drafting an evolutionary theory of social entrepreneurship has been an interesting challenge for a number of reasons. To begin with, it has been quite challenging to apply Causal Process Tracing in an exceedingly complex context, which hampered the discovery of causal relationships that can better our understanding of how these ecosystems evolve. On a national level, it is almost impossible to adequately separate speed from direction in the evolutionary process. Moreover, there is a significant discrepancy between grounded theory and the basic design of our research. Grounded theory is rich in descriptions of the various mechanisms and drivers of change that actually shape the evolutionary process. Unfortunately, we couldn't mention all of these mechanisms in our study without creating the type of theoretical chaos that would necessitate merging an evolutionary and cybernetic approach. Moreover, our decision to combine theoretical approaches highlights the importance of contextualization and the limits of generalization. Given these circumstances, we felt it was more appropriate to adopt a simpler approach that was more adaptive to fundamental differences in evolutionary contexts.

Our work on evolutionary theory deviates from the ecology approach, opting instead to build on ideas associated with Darwinism (Aldrich et al., 2008; Hodgson, 2013) and cultural evolution (Binder et al., 2013). The cultural approach provides tools for synthesizing various social and economic theories, thereby bridging the paradigm gap (Mesoudi, 2011). Whereas many socioeconomic studies use a smattering evolutionary concepts as theoretical guides, our research was based on both the core precepts of Darwinian thought and recent insights on evolutionary processes. Given the preliminary nature of our theory, we recommend using it alongside other theoretical approaches, as was done during the EFESEIIS project. We believe that our theory allows us to better analyze the diversity and evolution of social entrepreneurship in Europe while also helping us examine related issues in a longitudinal perspective, provide new insight into longstanding theoretical disputes, produce innovative policy frameworks, and inform monitoring and evaluation programs. Perhaps most importantly, it might be able to provide solutions for the disembedded economy that came about with the ascendency of neoliberalism.

References

Aldrich, H. E., Hodgson, G. M., Hull, D. L., Knudsen, T., Mokyr, J., & Vanberg, V. J. (2008). In defence of generalized Darwinism. *Journal of Evolutionary Economics, 18*(5), 577–596. doi:10.1007/s00191-008-0110-z.

Åmo, B. W. (2013). Linking network, human capital and the extended competence network to business start-up: A multilevel approach. *International Journal of Entrepreneurial Venturing, 5*(2), 105–119.

Biggeri, M., Testi, E., & M. Bellucci. (2017). Enabling ecosystems for social enterprises and social innovation: A capability approach perspective. *Journal of Human Development and Capabilities, 18*(2), 299–306.

Binder, C. R., Hinkel, J., Bots, P. W. G., & Pahl-Wostl, C. (2013). Comparison of frameworks for analyzing social-ecological systems. *Ecology and Society, 18*(4), 26. doi:10.5751/es-05551-180426.

Blatter, J., & Haverland, M. (2012). *Designing case studies: Explanatory approaches in small-N research.* London: Palgrave Macmillan UK.

Cavalli-Sforza, L. L. (2001). *Genes, peoples and languages.* London: Penguin Books.

Chantarat, S., & Barrett, C. B. (2012). Social network capital, economic mobility and poverty traps. *Journal of Economic Inequality, 10*(3), 299–342.

Constanza, R., Norgaard, R., Daly, H., Goodland, R., & Cumberland, J. (2007). *An introduction to ecological economics.* Retrieved from www.eoearth.org/view/article/150041.

Dawkins, R. (1976). *The selfish gene.* Oxford: Oxford University Press.

Debref, R., Alijani, S., Thomas, L., Boudes, M., & Mangalagui, D. (2015). *Meta-analysis of social innovation across Europe.* Deliverable D3.1 of the project "Boosting the Impact of SI in Europe through Economic Underpinnings." (SIMPACT), European Commission – 7th Framework Programme, Brussels: European Commission, DG Research & Innovation.

Dey, P., & Teasdale, S. (2013). Social enterprise and dis/identification. *Administrative Theory & Praxis, 35*(2), 248–270. doi:10.2753/atp1084-1806350204.

During, R. (2014). *Understanding evolutionary pathways and societal embedding. Evolutionary theory of the social enterprise.* Working Document EFESEIIS. www.fp7-efeseiis.eu/evolutionary-theory/

During, R. (2017). *Evolutionary theory of social enterprise. On the use of evolutionary concepts in the field of social entrepreneurship.* Wageningen: WUR/EFESEIIS.

During, R., & van Dam, R. I. (2016). *Evolutionary pathways of social enterprising in the Netherlands: A contribution to grounded theory.* Working document EFESEIIS. www.fp7-efeseiis.eu/evolutionary-theory/

During, R., van Dam, R. I., Pleijte, M., & Salverda, I. E. (2016a). The Dutch participation society needs open data, but what is meant by open? In M. Adria & Y. Mao (Eds.), *Handbook of research on citizen engagement and public participation in the era of new media* (pp. 304–322). Hershey PA: IGI Global.

During, R., van Dam, R. I., & Salverda, I. E. (2016b). *Using evolutionary theory for pluralism in social policies.* Paper presented at the 2016 Social Policy Association Annual Conference: Radical, Resistant, Resolute, Symposium: Social Innovation and Social Policy: A Solution or Surrender to Welfare Austerity? Lost in Translation? Reconciling Social Innovation Discourse with Policy Implementation, Belfast.

Even Zohar, I. (1990). *Polysystem studies*. Durham, NC: Duke University Press.

Foster, J. (2003). Between economics and ecology: Some historical and philosophical considerations for modelers of natural capital. *Environmental Monitoring and Assessment, 86*(1–2), 63–74. doi:10.1023/a:1024002617932.

Fuchs, S. (2001). *Against essentialism. A theory of culture and society*. Cambridge, MA: Harvard University Press.

Granovetter, M. (2005). The impact of social structure on economic outcomes. *Journal of Economic Perspectives, 19*(1), 33–50.

Hazenberg, R., Bajwa-Patel, M., Mazzei, M., Roy, M. J., & Baglioni, S. (2016). The role of institutional and stakeholder networks in shaping social enterprise ecosystems in Europe. *Social Enterprise Journal, 12*(3), 205–222.

Hodgson, G. M. (2013). Understanding organizational evolution: Toward a research agenda using generalized Darwinism. *Organization Studies, 34*(7), 973–992. doi:10.1177/0170840613485855.

Hull, D. L. (1982). The naked meme. In H. C. Plotkin (Ed.), *Learning, development and culture: essays in evolutionary epistemology* (pp. 273–327). New York: Wiley.

Kamimura, A., Burani, G. F., & França, H. M. (2011). The economic system seen as a living system: A Lotka-Volterra framework. *Emergence: Complexity and Organization, 13*(3), 80–93.

Latour, B. (1987). *Science in action: How to follow scientists and engineers through society*. Cambridge, MA: Harvard University Press.

Luhmann, N. (1995). *Social systems*. Stanford, CA: Stanford University Press.

Mesoudi, A. (2011). *Cultural evolution: How Darwinin theory can explain human culture and synthesize the social sciences*. Chicago, IL: The University of Chicago Press.

Mesoudi, A., Chang, L., Dall, S. R. X., & Thornton, A. (2016). The evolution of individual and cultural variation in social learning. *Trends in Ecology and Evolution, 31*(3), 215–225.

Mohtsham Saeed, M., & Arshad, F. (2012). Corporate social responsibility as a source of competitive advantage: The mediating role of social capital and reputational capital. *Journal of Database Marketing and Customer Strategy Management, 19*(4), 219–232.

Nelson, R. R., & Winter, S. G. (2002). Evolutionary theorizing in economics. *Journal of Economic Perspectives, 16*(2), 23–46. doi:10.1257/0895330027247.

Pelikan, P. (2011). Evolutionary developmental economics: How to generalize Darwinism fruitfully to help comprehend economic change. *Journal of Evolutionary Economics, 21*(2), 341–366. doi:10.1007/s00191-010-0178-0.

Polanyi, K. (2001). *The great transformation. The Politica land economic origins of our time*. Boston, MA: Beacon Press.

Praszkier, R., Nowak, A., & Zablocka-Bursa, A. (2009). Social capital built by social entrepreneurs and the specific personality traits that facilitate the process. *Social Psychology (Psychologia Społeczna), 4*(1–2), 42–54.

Roy, M. J., McHugh, N., Huckfield, L., Kay, A., & Donaldson, C. (2015). "The most supportive environment in the world"? Tracing the development of an institutional 'ecosystem' for social enterprise. *Voluntas: International Journal of Voluntary and Nonprofit Organizations, 26*(3), 777–800. doi:10.1007/s11266-014-9459-9.

Scott, J. C. (1998). *Seeing like a state. How certain schemes to improve the human condition have failed*. New Haven, CA and London: Yale University Press.

SEFORIS. (2016). *Cross Country Report. A first cross-country analysis and profiling of social enterprises prepared by the SEFORIS research consortium.* Brussels: Oksigen Lab.

Svensson, C. F. (2015). *Contextualisation matters: Aligning social enterprises nation-state diversity.* Roskilde, Denmark: Roskilde University.

Tan, J. (2005). Venturing in turbulent water: A historical perspective of economic reform and entrepreneurial transformation. *Journal of Business Venturing, 20*(5), 689–704. doi:10.1016/j.jbusvent.2004.09.002.

Tata, J., & Prasad, S. (2010). Ethnic community involvement, entrepreneurial social capital, and business performance. *Global Business and Economics Review, 12*(1–2), 151–170.

Terstriep, J., Kleverbeck, M., Deserti, A., & Rizzo, F. (2015). *Comparative report on social innovation across Europe.* Deliverable D3.2 of the project Boosting the Impact of SI in Europe through Economic Underpinnings (SIMPACT). European Commission, 7th Framework Programme. Brussels: European Commission DG Research and Innovation.

van Dam, R. I., During, R., Glad, T., & N. De Sena. (2015). *Enabling social entrepreneurship for social innovation. Report of city Level Focus Groups with social entrepreneurs and stakeholders in Amsterdam, The Netherlands.* Working document EFESEIIS.

Verhoeven, K. F. J., & Preite, V. (2013). Epigenetic variation in asexually reproducing organisms. *Evolution, 68*(3), 644–655.

5 Emerging managerial aspects of social entrepreneurship in Europe

Marco Bellucci, Enrico Testi,
Serena Franchi, and Mario Biggeri

Introduction and research background

In the first sentence of *How to Change the World: Social Entrepreneurs and the Power of New Ideas*, David Bornstein states that his book "is about people who solve social problems on a large scale" (Bornstein, 2007, p. 1). The title itself reveals the author's perception of social entrepreneurs, who are identified as the best candidates to introduce innovative ideas that are capable of fostering significant global change. Is this just a rhetorical representation, or does it represent a clear depiction of what social entrepreneurship means in practice? This chapter contributes to the debate on social enterprises (SEs) and social entrepreneurship by focusing on the specific managerial characteristics that are often found in Europe.

While working on the EFESEIIS research project, we explored whether or not common perceptions of social entrepreneurs accurately describe the people who found or work in European SEs while also examining the various characteristics of individual organizations. We defined social entrepreneurs as individuals or groups who provide solutions to social problems through entrepreneurial activities. Consequently, we depicted social entrepreneurs as change agents who pursue new opportunities to create and sustain social value (Dees, 1998). SEs are operators in the social economy that emphasize the social impact of their activities rather than profit creation (European Commission, 2011).

These assumptions emerged from ideas on SEs, social entrepreneurship, and social entrepreneurs found in the scholarly literature (Dees, 1998; Borzaga & Defourny, 2004; Defourny & Nyssens, 2006, 2010, 2012; Kerlin, 2006; Nicholls, 2006; Galera & Borzaga, 2009). The research in this field allows us to summarize current perspectives and identify the strengths and weaknesses of the definitions at hand. Indeed, even though the concepts of SE and social entrepreneurs found expression simultaneously in the United States and Europe during the 1980s, diverse schools of thought emerged on both sides of the Atlantic (Kerlin, 2006). Significant conceptual convergences and divergences concerning the nature of the social mission, production activities, economic risks, governance structures, and the diffusion of social innovation have been identified (Defourny & Nyssens, 2010). As a result, SE and social entrepreneurship have different meanings in the United States and Europe.

It is important to note how these concepts were addressed on either side of the Atlantic. In Europe, for instance, emphasis has been placed on the collective, associative, and cooperative nature of SEs. The American approach, meanwhile, tends to focus on charismatic entrepreneurs, an approach that has gained momentum in recent years (Defourny & Nyssens, 2008). While European observers tend to point out that social entrepreneurship takes place within the third sector in a nonprofit context, North American tradition tends to stress blended value creation and the blurred boundaries between institutional and legal forms. Blended value stipulates that organizations create both financial and social value, and that these two kinds of value creation are not opposed to each other, but rather intrinsically connected (Emerson, 2003; Manetti, 2012).

While an SE tries to achieve social goals through entrepreneurial activities that usually originate as part of a community project or through collective action, social entrepreneurship is generally defined as the view of a single entrepreneur who strives to use entrepreneurial principles to organize and create something for disadvantaged people or the community as a whole (Travaglini, Bandini, & Mancinone, 2009). Collective and participatory dimensions are supposed to be key features of European SEs, which reduces the probability of opportunistic behavior by individuals. However, the collective dimension does not mean that charismatic leaders cannot play a key role in setting up the enterprise and furthering its development (Galera & Borzaga, 2009).

Although theoretical divergences might be solved by agreeing on a clear definition of SEs, no such consensus is forthcoming. Much of this variation depends on the nature and level of development of the national and regional ecosystems in which SEs are situated. Of course, SEs operate in different sectors, take on different legal forms, differ in their capacity to remain in the market, and depend on external finance (grants, donation, bequests, and benefactions) to varying degrees. They also differ in terms of their overall income, how they use their profits, and the number of employees and volunteers.

This chapter intends to move beyond the search for a common definition of SE or social entrepreneurship in Europe. Indeed, we hope to examine the most salient and interesting managerial traits of organizations that support SE in Europe. Through the use of surveys, interviews, case studies, and focus groups, the EFESEIIS project explored social entrepreneurs as both individuals and as representatives of their various enterprises.[1] Suffice it to say that its project data are of great use in terms of helping us explore the entrepreneurial, social, and innovative nature of European SEs.

"Primary objectives, legal forms, sectors, and motivations" provides an overview of the main objectives, sectors, and legal forms adopted by the

SEs in our sample as well as the motivations of the persons who founded or work in these organizations. "Multilevel governance and stakeholder engagement practice" investigates the participatory nature of European SEs, placing special emphasis on the wide array of stakeholders who have a vested interest in these organizations. "Drivers of innovation" and "Main challenges and obstacles" focus on the main drivers of innovation and the various obstacles and challenges faced by these organizations. "Conclusions and policy implications" summarizes our contribution and provides some final remarks.

Primary objectives, legal forms, sectors, and motivations

The term "social entrepreneur" has been emphasized by North American foundations and organizations—e.g. Ashoka—since the mid-1990s in order to identify and support individuals who launch new initiatives that are dedicated to a social mission while also stressing dynamism, personal involvement, and innovative practices (Defourny & Nyssens, 2008). In the EFESEIIS project, attaining a social or environmental impact was considered an important prerequisite for any organization that called itself an SE. Indeed, the economic activities of European SEs tend to be shaped by their social mission rather than the profit motive (Defourny & Nyssens, 2012). Consequently, our questionnaire asks whether solving a social or environmental issue was an objective of the social entrepreneur's organization. According to our data analysis, 79 percent of interviewees stated that pursuing a social or environmental issue is the primary objective of their organization. This is in line with Galera and Borzaga's work (2009) on the wide range of motivations that help bring about various forms of social entrepreneurship. They argue that the first objective of the organization is "to pursue a social goal in a stable and continuous way through the production of goods or services of general-interest" (Galera & Borzaga, 2009, p. 4).

The EFESEIIS data indicates that the majority of SEs in Europe are cooperatives and companies, followed by charities, NGOs, and associations. Most of the SEs operate in traditional service sectors, such as health care, social work, and education. Nonetheless, SEs devoted to the arts, entertainment and recreation, hotel and catering, media services, professional, scientific and technical activities, and administrative and support services are starting to play a greater role. The presence of SEs in non-traditional sectors suggests that the social economy is flourishing within varied and innovative environments.

The majority of SEs in our sample were either totally independent or only partially dependent on external financing (e.g. money from grants, bequests, and benefactions) and were involved in economically sustainable activities. SEs that are set up as foundations, associations, or NGOs appear to be more dependent on grants and benefactors. Nonetheless, around one-third of the SEs that were set up as companies depend on external financing, especially during the start-up phase. Our survey data clearly suggest that SEs tend to use both market and non-market revenues as sources of income. Market-oriented organizations employ a larger portion of paid staff than financially dependent SEs, many of which rely on volunteers (half of our total sample relied on volunteers). SEs that engage in market activities work with both private and public customers (including companies, citizens, and local authorities). The types of customers depend on both the sector and the market in which they operate, as well as how the welfare state is organized in their specific jurisdiction. For example, in countries such as Italy, where welfare services have been decentralized, many SEs work for public authorities in managing social services.

We asked social entrepreneurs to identify their main motivation for either founding or working in an SE. The data reveal that our respondents' motivations transcend the mere fulfillment of basic needs (e.g. to secure a source of income). Indeed, our survey results indicate that only 12 percent of respondents cited "self-employment" as their primary motive for participating in an SE; almost four times as many indicated that their primary goal was to address a social challenge. These findings are significant because our use of an anonymous online survey may have further mitigated the social desirability bias that often negatively impacts this type of data collection. Moreover, 20 percent of respondents mentioned either the importance of innovating existing practices or improving existing social services as being important factors.

We also crossed the question concerning the core aim of the enterprise with the question that addressed the personal motivations of social entrepreneurs. We discovered that addressing social challenges was often selected by social entrepreneurs who cited solving a social or environmental issue as a primary or secondary objective. Meanwhile, social entrepreneurs who do not place as much emphasis on addressing social challenges were more likely to found or work in an SE due to personal employment needs. When we distinguished between founders and employees, we found a general alignment between the motives for taking part in SEs. In fact, although a larger proportion of founders appear to be motivated by a social problem they have personally experienced (19 percent of founders and 8 percent of workers), the goal of addressing a social issue is shared by a majority of both workers and founders.

A range of other motives and aspirations drive participation in SEs. Approximately 20 percent of respondents mentioned either the importance of innovating existing practices or improving existing social services (many of which do not fulfill their basic aim). These intentions reflect the extent to which certain issues motivate social entrepreneurs and employees while also illustrating how both groups are motivated by a sense of community and sensitivity to individual social responsibilities. In our sample, just six percent of our respondents cite environmental aspirations as a primary

motivation for founding/working in an SE (especially founders and employees of NGOs). No significant differences in motivations can be detected
by gender or age. Nevertheless, younger people are slightly more likely to
view SEs as a self-employment opportunity. This is in line with the recent
evolution and growing popularity of this sector, which is increasingly seen
as a credible alternative to traditional business. Younger people are also
more likely to work with SEs in order to tackle inadequacies in existing
social services. This might be because the younger generation tends to see
traditional public services as unable to meet the basic needs of its users.
Lastly, motivations seem to be fairly similar across the countries surveyed.
Again, tackling a social issue is the main motivation to establish or work in
an SE, regardless of the respondent's nationality. Environmental concerns,
however, are cited by more than 10 percent of respondents in Albania and
Sweden, while more than 20 percent of respondents in Poland, Serbia, and
Italy cited economic factors.

Multilevel governance and stakeholder engagement practices

Another topic we want to explore in this chapter is the participatory nature of SEs and their relationship with stakeholders. The multi-stakeholder
nature of SEs has been studied often in recent years (Borzaga, Fiorentini, &
Matacena, 1996; Travaglini, 1997; Borzaga & Defourny, 2001; Antoldi,
2003; Campi, Defourny, & Gregoire, 2006; Spear, Cornforth, & Aiken, 2007;
Travaglini, Bandini, & Mancinone, 2009; Belloni, 2013; Borzaga &
Sacchetti, 2015). Indeed, SEs are generally described as organizations with
multi-stakeholder governance that guarantee direct participation in management and administration. Corporate governance in SEs is often characterized by a lack of ownership interests, a different set of motivations
driving the management of SE, and an expanded role for stakeholders
(Antoldi, 2003).

In order to analyze the extent to which specific categories of stakeholders
influence the decision-making processes of SEs in Europe, a section of our
questionnaire was dedicated to identifying methods of governance and primary stakeholders (including owners and board of directors, shareholders
and investors, employees, suppliers, customers and end users, state and public administrators, third-sector organizations and NGOs, and the broader
community). Traditionally, owners, members of the board of directors, and
shareholders are the most powerful stakeholders, oftentimes defining the
long-term objectives and various development strategies. It is important
to understand whether these power balances tend to shift towards other
categories of stakeholders in SEs while also determining whether or not
stakeholder engagement practices define the organization's entrepreneurial
strategy (Bellucci and Manetti, 2018).

We asked respondents to describe the degree to which various types
of stakeholders influence the decision-making process, using a scoring

system that ranged from 5 (high influence) to 1 (no influence). Our data shows that owners and members of the board of directors are considered "very influential" or "extremely influential" by 80 percent of SEs. Conversely, shareholders and investors are perceived as far less influential; in fact, 46 percent of respondents described them as "not at all influential," and more than half thought they had very little influence in the decision-making process.

The degree of influence and involvement of stakeholders in SEs is often different than it is in for-profit businesses. SEs are generally established through a process that involves a heterogeneous group of actors, each of whom have a "stake" in the achievement of one or more of the SE's objectives. Moreover, SEs usually opt for legal forms that call for broader governance structures that give voice, at least in theory, to all actors with whom the SE interacts. For example, the majority of SEs in our sample are cooperatives, implying that ownership is in the hands of stakeholders who are not only investors but also consumers or workers. Involving stakeholders in their day-to-day activities may be a pressing concern in nonprofit organizations, acting as a channel through which an organization's mission is pursued and realized. Primary stakeholders—most notably employees, customers, and users—have critical power within the organization, while suppliers seem to be less influential. This reinforces the intrinsic nature of SEs, which are, by definition, economic organizations with explicit social aims. Social objectives are usually achieved through the fruits of their production (e.g. provision of welfare services, health care, and education) or through the production process itself (e.g. fair trade principles, integration of disadvantaged workers, and environmental concerns). On the one hand, the economic goals of SEs create a situation in which customer and user satisfaction is essential to ensuring market competitiveness. On the other hand, SE activities can produce benefits that often surpass the market system. Thus, employees are not only extremely relevant for strategic reasons but also because enhancing their well-being may be one of the SE's objectives.

The fact that the social benefits of SEs often exceed the direct consumption of their goods or services proves that other stakeholders may also be influential. NGOs, third-sector organizations, and the communities they serve are recognized as "somewhat influential," "very influential," or "extremely influential" by the vast majority of respondents (just over four-fifths). Their importance may be attributed to either the SE's legitimacy-seeking activities (e.g. garnering public support to achieve specific social aims) or the SE's need for resources. Since SEs depend on a multitude of resources other than market revenues, potential resource providers—e.g. philanthropists (donors and volunteers) and the state (public funding and ad hoc regulation)—hold some influence over the decision-making processes of SEs. In fact, state and public administrations were perceived as "somewhat influential" or "very influential" by almost 40 percent of respondents.

Generally speaking, no significant differences can be detected when the sample is broken down by the size of a business. Third-sector organizations, NGOs, and the communities they serve seem to be slightly more influential among microenterprises (organizations with less than ten employees). This may be due to their greater dependency on external non-market resources. Our findings also show that state and public administration has more influence over medium enterprises (50–250 employees) and large enterprises (250+ employees).

SEs give voice to their stakeholders through various engagement practices. Stakeholder engagement—a process used by organizations to engage relevant stakeholders as a means of achieving agreed upon outcomes (AccountAbility, 2015)—is currently considered a fundamental accountability mechanism. Indeed, "it obliges an organization to involve stakeholders in identifying, understanding and responding to sustainability issues and concerns, and to report, explain and answer to stakeholders for decisions, actions and performance" (AccountAbility, 2015, p. 5). This topic is particularly interesting in a framework of high integration among organization and stakeholders, and within stakeholders themselves. SEs that are interested in measuring the views and perceptions of their stakeholders need to develop effective channels for interacting with relevant actors because a reliable process of stakeholder engagement can positively affect the accountability of SEs.

The respondents in our survey mostly rely on social media, questionnaires, satisfaction surveys, and public meetings to collect feedback from their constituents. Social media is increasingly used as a stakeholder engagement platform (Bellucci & Manetti, 2017), while telephone banks and more traditional tools are becoming less and less common. Social media can help organizations conduct stakeholder engagement because it allows one party (the organization) to interact with another (the stakeholder) in a two-way dialogue. Both parties are capable of learning from these interactions, which, in turn, allows them to revise their expectations and preconceptions (Manetti, 2011; Bellucci & Manetti, 2017). In fact, stakeholder engagement is acknowledged as a powerful tool of dialogic communication (Bebbington, Brown, & Frame, 2007; Brown, 2009; Brown & Dillard, 2013), offering interactive mutual learning processes that are capable of promoting transformative action and social change (Bebbington, Brown, & Frame, 2007). Interestingly enough, 34 percent of our respondents reported that stakeholders were members of executive boards. This type of co-optation strategy may reflect the SE's specific legal designation, which often involves the recognition of stakeholders other than shareholders, the right to take part in the governance structure, or the need to gain support from potential resource providers.

Involvement practices do not seem to be affected by the size of the organization. Indeed, it is interesting to note that large businesses tend to have a more heterogeneous involvement profile. Greater resources, capacity, and expertise—as well as the strategic importance of communicating transparency and accountability levels—may encourage SEs to engage in a more diversified set of stakeholder engagement practices.

Drivers of innovation

Various debates on SEs and social innovation have gained new momentum within the EU in recent years. Social innovation has often been defined in a broad manner; some definitions include every kind of innovation, while others are much more selective. Pol and Ville (2009) define social innovation as "any new idea with the potential to improve either the macroquality of life or the quantity of life." The authors also claim that social innovations consist of not only new products or services but also new processes and new ways of organizing production activities while also pointing out that social innovations should be replicable and capable of scaling up in order to achieve significant impact (Pol & Ville, 2009). Social innovation, in short, refers to innovative activities and services that try to address a social need and are offered through organizations whose primary purposes are social (Mulgan, 2006). Thus, SEs are well suited to create and spread social innovation.

According to Borzaga (2009), SE represents an innovation in and of itself. It is a private organization that also has objectives that are based on collective interests. Although it does not focus on material gain, it does have an entrepreneurial bent that is oriented towards the production of goods and services for specific beneficiaries while also generating benefits for a wide range of people. The SE could be described as an innovation of a specific institutional framework. According to Venturi and Zandonai (2009), innovation is a strategic instrument for SEs that allows them to respond to their main challenge: the need to find legitimization as a new community institution through the reinforcement of the internal management and with an open interaction with opportunities coming from the political and socioeconomic context. Three main steps are needed in order to achieve the most important outcomes of this "innovative" process. The first one is the individuation of new products and activities that are related to both the core business and completely new sectors. The second step involves the implementation of new processes—specifically the development of governance systems that enable different stakeholders to achieve goals associated with the "general interest." Finally, it is necessary to overcome the distinction between different types of policies by including this process in broader development policies and reinforcing the interconnected relationship between SEs and other institutions.

SE and social innovation have been adapted by public and private actors to suit specific social and economic goals. Indeed, nowadays debates over the relevance of social innovation are intensifying due to public finance crises and problems with managing services at the local level. SEs and social innovation are now seen as potential instruments for maintaining a sufficient level of well-being, despite cuts to public services. Nevertheless, the role of SEs has frequently been called into question, as commentators wonder whether SEs support the public sector or represent an innovative mediator between the market and the state. The experiences of Italian social cooperatives might provide an interesting perspective on this issue. For instance, Testi et al. (2017) claim that, historically speaking, social cooperatives have performed both functions. The innovative nature of social cooperatives emerged due to a push towards privatization in the 1990s, addressing unmet needs through personalized approaches that differed from the standardized policies provided by public authorities and offering a personalized supply of products or services. Thus, while the privatization process enabled nonprofit organizations to participate in the delivery of goods and services, it also influenced the new methods of addressing social needs (Testi et al., 2017).

What are the mechanisms through which innovative practices are embraced by SEs, and why do they pursue them in the first place? In an attempt to answer these questions, we asked respondents during the EFESEIIS project if their organization innovated in the last three years, be it in terms of product, process, finance, or marketing. Around 80 percent of the sample claimed to be engaged in innovative practices. This points towards improvements to product performance, product systems, services, and changes in core enabling processes; variations in business models and networking strategies; and reorganization of customer interactions, brand strategies, marketing channels, and public procurement practices. Moreover, our study shows that interest in innovation increases over time. Indeed, 12 percent of participants indicated that innovation was "not important" or only "slightly important" during the start-up phase. By contrast, the share of participants who regarded innovation as relatively unimportant decreased by four percentage points during the most recent phase. Similarly, around 80 percent of survey participants regarded innovation as "very important" or "extremely important" in the current phase.

Our findings also show that innovation in the initial stages of development is more important for relatively new SEs (organizations established since 1980). Organizations established between 1941 and 1980, meanwhile, exhibit different behavior during the start-up phase due to their relatively small numbers and different market and institutional conditions. In total, 80 percent of SEs set up in the last three years considered innovation to be either a "very important" or "extremely important" part of their start-up strategy. Highly competitive markets and the existence of oversaturated markets in many industries oblige younger enterprises to think in terms of innovation and product improvement from the very beginning.

Nowadays, SEs are increasingly compelled to innovate. According to our data, SEs set up between the 1980s and early 2000s were shown to produce the greatest amount of innovation. This is consistent with the need for well-established firms to reorganize in an effort to maintain their competitive advantage and successfully compete against newcomers. Furthermore, the main factors driving innovative change often come about in order to cater to new kinds of social needs or adapt to unmet social challenges. Indeed, half of our sample innovated in response to a change in the external environment. Innovation was also driven by financial distress, the desire to tap profitable market niches and increase competitiveness, and the need to respond to changes to legislative/policy frameworks. However, the share of SEs innovating in response to changes in media technology, the needs of vulnerable groups, changes in specific market sectors, and poor standards of quality is lower. Changes to the environment, public services, the trust of consumers, and business reputation have a marginal effect on innovation, as none of these reasons were endorsed by more than two percent of the survey sample. Although bureaucracy is seen as one of the main obstacles to developing an SE, only one percent of the sample innovated in response to bureaucratic issues, while demographic trends were mentioned by one percent of participants. However, demography may still be relevant for SEs dealing with health care, education, and job services. Innovation strategies vary according to the strategic objectives of the SE and the types of innovation these organizations pursue. In order to increase competitiveness, 71 percent of SEs ranked innovation in goods and services as "very important" or "extremely important." Meanwhile, 69 percent of participants believe that innovative marketing is important.

Many respondents claim that innovation in products and services is essential not only to beat competitors but also to achieve greater social impact. In this respect, marketing, financial, and process innovation are less relevant. Finally, the level of importance attributed to innovations that are meant to achieve environmental goals is lower, as less than 40 percent of respondents claimed that innovation to meet environmental changes was "very important" or "extremely important." Both market innovation and innovation in products and services represent the main strategies for tackling environmental issues. Product and service provision can become more environmentally friendly, while marketing strategies help explain the SE's environmental principles.

Main challenges and obstacles

Our data provides some insights into the main managerial challenges faced by European SEs. These challenges can be divided into two categories: exogenous (e.g. financing and supportive legislative/regulatory environments) and endogenous (e.g. upgrading skills and jobs and ensuring the quality of products and services). While the former cannot be fully controlled by SEs, the latter can be directly affected by taking proper action (Borzaga & Defourny, 2004). While discussing the main constraints faced by SEs in Europe, we asked respondents to rank the three most pressing challenges faced at each stage of their organization's development (start-up phase, current phase, future). The two main constraints reported by respondents were financing difficulties (which involve issues relating to the availability of finance and accessing funding) and market constraints (such as competition and an SE's economic activities). SEs frequently reported difficulties in getting funds to support their activities. Financing difficulties come from all kinds of sources, including private actors (14 percent), equity investment (5 percent), and government—either through direct funding (24 percent) or participation in a public tender (13 percent). Thus, both public and private funds seem insufficient to meet the needs of SEs. In our sample, SEs are mostly microenterprises that might not be granted credit because of their limited scale, limited collateral, and the risks associated with their activities. And although public authorities are more interested in the strategic importance of the social business in the long term than in short-term returns on investment, our respondents suggest that their support is still lacking. The heterogeneity of the sector and the absence of a systematic legal framework may similarly hinder the access SEs have to available funds.

Our research also indicates that SEs face several market constraints, such as small market share and strong competition from both third-sector organizations and for-profit businesses. Diminishing profit margins from business activities were cited by about 12 percent of our sample. This is largely a consequence of the current economic context, specifically the aftermath of the financial crisis of 2008. In addition, the relatively small scale of most of the SEs in our sample suggests that size might have a disproportionate effect on the results, which may further reduce profit margins among SEs.

The recruitment process is also negatively affected by various issues related to skills, motivations, compensating employees and volunteers, and creating positive networks. Recruiting employees and volunteers is an issue for 16 percent of the survey sample, while low pay was seen as a challenge for 13 percent of the sample. Fewer organizations saw low motivation (five percent) or low skills and experience (five percent) among employees to be pressing problems. Moreover, forging networks to build strategic partnerships and increase public awareness of SEs is a concern for about one-fifth of the organizations in our study. Networking issues appear to complicate an SE's integration into the socioeconomic arena, especially during the first six months of operation. The lack of support organizations makes integration networking even more complex. The lack of enabling organizations reflects a highly heterogeneous reality that includes several very different entities that are not completely institutionalized. Only five percent of the sample, however, ranked this as one of their three main challenges.

Breaking down the survey results by the year in which an SE was established helps us understand the main challenges facing these organizations with respect to both socioeconomic context and phase of development. Human resources management (i.e. recruiting and motivating workers, cultivating skills, and determining compensation) is seen as one of the three main challenges during the start-up phase, especially among SEs that were founded after 1980. The labor market currently emphasizes more complex skills and competencies, while job expectations among employees are expanding. Consequently, hiring and training may be harder for relatively new SEs. Competitive pressures and the relatively small scale of organizations have also served as prominent market constraints, regardless of the age of SEs. In addition, older SEs (established prior to 1980) report that problems relating to financial resources and juridical and fiscal obligations have been rising. By contrast, newer SEs do not exhibit significant differences with respect to constraining forces and initial challenges. Constraints relating to human resources weigh less on the SE's management strategy, which may be a result of its initial investment and efforts to recruit and train employees.

Broader access to funding remains a priority. SEs appear to be poorly integrated into the capital markets of most of the countries in which they operate. This might be due to legal constraints, the hybrid business models preferred by many SEs, and relatively scarce interest among private investors in supporting activities that are often seen as risky or unprofitable. Moreover, access to public resources is usually hindered by the slow and complex nature of bureaucracy. Meanwhile, networking activities that are meant to cultivate business reputation, build trust in the SE's activities, and raise public awareness of the organization seem to be less relevant (or at least fairly constant) among all the SEs in our study.

Conclusions and policy implications

This chapter contributes to the debates that have arisen on managerial issues among SEs in Europe. It updates the literature by addressing (a) the main objectives, sectors, and legal forms of SEs as well as the motivations of the people who founded or work in these organizations; (b) the participatory and multi-stakeholder nature of European SEs; (c) the main drivers of innovation; (d) and the main obstacles and challenges faced by these types of organizations.

We decided to integrate different data collection methods in order to examine the various perceptions of European social entrepreneurs. Several features of SE were especially noteworthy. For instance, we found similar opinions on the importance of expressing a clear social or environmental mission, guaranteeing the economic sustainability of the enterprise, and declaring the ultimate destination of profits, which supports Bornstein's claim that opened this chapter. The importance of having a clear social mission was also confirmed by taking note of why the social entrepreneurs in our study were motivated to either found or work in an SE as achieving a social or environmental impact was often cited as the main reason behind their professional choices. Acknowledging both the core aim of the enterprise and the internal motivations of the entrepreneur seems to have a positive impact on the innovative nature of SEs, which are oftentimes compelled to introduce innovations (and increase their competitiveness and social impact) in response to external change.

We also tried to determine the extent to which SEs take into account the views and perceptions of their stakeholders. A reliable process of stakeholder engagement can positively affect accountability, and SEs appear to be showing some commitment to developing effective processes for interacting with relevant stakeholders. The strategies SEs often use to engage with their stakeholders, including social media interaction, have been explored in this chapter.

At first glance, the multinational nature of our study stands out as an important aspect of our analysis. Since each national context needs to be properly taken into account, it might be useful to devise a standardized model of intervention for policy makers. If we look closely, common aspects and shared strengths and weaknesses can be found among various European SEs. For instance, the embeddedness of SEs in their specific territory, as well as their willingness to provide innovative services and offer inclusive practices that support local actors, should be seen as positive aspects of SE development in Europe. At the same time, unclear legal frameworks, a general lack of efficient funding mechanisms, significant market constraints, low public awareness, and excessive bureaucracy often hinder the development of SEs. These shared features provide significant insight into the complex nature of social entrepreneurship and SEs in Europe, thereby acting as an important starting point in shaping the policies that stakeholders and institutions require in order to promote the creation of a flourishing and inclusive ecosystem.

Note

1 The EFESEIIS project included an international survey, focus groups, interviews, and case studies. Albania, Austria, England, France, Germany, Italy, Poland, Scotland, Serbia, Sweden, and The Netherlands were part of the surveyed countries; 837 European social entrepreneurs filled out the questionnaire. More than a hundred interviews and focus groups were carried out with social entrepreneurs and their stakeholders. Finally, 55 case studies were carried out with "new generation social entrepreneurs" by applying a multidisciplinary methodology encompassing organizational life histories, in-depth interviews participatory exercises, desk analysis, and shadowing techniques. This chapter will focus on the results of the European survey. For more information on methodologies and data collection, see Chapter 2.

References

AccountAbility. (2015). *AA1000 stakeholder engagement standards*. Retrieved from www.accountability.org/wp-content/uploads/2016/10/AA1000SES_2015.pdf.

Antoldi, F. (2003). *Il governo strategico delle organizzazioni non profit. Strutture organizzative, strumenti di analisi e processi decisionali*. Milano: McGraw-Hill.

Bebbington, J., Brown, J., & Frame, B. (2007). Accounting technologies and sustainability assessment models. *Ecological Economics, 61*(2/3), 224–236.

Belloni, M. (2013). L'impresa sociale multistakeholder: sistemi e strutture di governo. Il caso studio delle MAG. *Impresa Sociale,* numero 1/6-2013.

Bellucci, M., & Manetti, G. (2017). Facebook as a tool for supporting dialogic accounting? Evidence from large philanthropic foundations in the United States. *Accounting, Auditing & Accountability Journal, 30*(4), 874–905.

Bellucci M. &, Manetti, G. (2018). *Stakeholder engagement and sustainability reporting.* London: Routledge, ISBN:978-0-8153-7315-5.

Bornstein, D. (2007). *How to change the world: Social entrepreneurs and the power of new ideas.* Oxford: Oxford University Press.

Borzaga, C. (2009). L'Impresa sociale. In L. Bruni & S. Zamagni (Eds.), *Dizionario di Economia Civile* (pp. 516–526). Roma: Città Nuova.

Borzaga, C., & Defourny, J. (2001). *L'impresa sociale in prospettiva europea.* Trento: Edizioni 31.

Borzaga, C., & Defourny, J. (2004). *The emergence of social enterprise.* London: Psychology Press.

Borzaga, C., & Sacchetti, S. (2015). *Why social enterprises are asking to be multistakeholder and deliberative: An explanation around the costs of exclusion* (Euricse Working Papers, 75|15). Trento: Euricse

Brown, J. (2009). Democracy, sustainability and dialogic accounting technologies: Taking pluralism seriously. *Critical Perspectives on Accounting, 20*(3), 313–342.

Brown, J., & Dillard, J. (2013) Critical accounting and communicative action: On the limits of consensual deliberation. *Critical Perspectives on Accounting, 24*(3), 176–190.

Campi, S., Defourny, J., & Grégoire, O. (2006). Work integration social enterprises: Are they multiple-goal and multi-stakeholder organizations? In M. Nyssens (Ed.), *Social enterprise* (pp. 29–49). London & New York: Routledge.

Dees, J. G. (1998). *The meaning of social entrepreneurship.* Working paper, Kansas city: Kauffman Center for Entrepreneurial Leadership.

Defourny, J., & Nyssens, M. (2006). Defining social enterprise. In M. Nyssens (Ed.), *Social enterprise, at the crossroads of market, public policies and the civil society* (pp. 3–26). London and New York: Routledge.

Defourny, J., & Nyssens, M. (2008). Social enterprise in Europe: recent trends and developments. *Social Enterprise Journal, 4*(3), 202–228.

Defourny, J., & Nyssens, M. (2010). Conceptions of social enterprise and social entrepreneurship in Europe and the United States: Convergences and divergences. *Journal of Social Entrepreneurship, 1*(1), 32–53.

Defourny, J., & Nyssens, M. (2012). Conceptions of social enterprise in Europe: A comparative perspective with the United States. In B. Gidron & Y. Hasenfeld (Eds.), *Social enterprises. An organizational perspective* (pp. 71–90). London: Palgrave Macmillan.

Emerson, J. (2003). The blended value proposition: Integrating social and financial returns. *California Management Review, 45*(4), 35–51.

European Commission. (2011). Communication from the Commission to the European Parliament, the Council, the European Economic and Social Committee and Committee of the Regions. *Social Business Initiative: Creating a favourable climate for social enterprises, key stakeholders in the social economy and innovation.* Brussels, 25.10. 2011.

Galera, G., & Borzaga, C. (2009). Social enterprise: An international overview of its conceptual evolution and legal implementation. *Social Enterprise Journal*, *5*(3), 210–228.

Kerlin, J. A. (2006). Social enterprise in the United States and Europe: Understanding and learning from the differences. *VOLUNTAS: International Journal of Voluntary and Nonprofit Organizations*, *17*(3), 246–262.

Manetti, G. (2011). The quality of stakeholder engagement in sustainability reporting: Empirical evidence and critical points. *Corporate Social Responsibility and Environmental Management*, *18*(2), 110–122.

Manetti, G. (2012). The role of blended value accounting in the evaluation of socio-economic impact of social enterprises. *VOLUNTAS: International Journal of Voluntary and Nonprofit Organizations*, *25*, 443–464.

Mulgan, G. (2006). The process of social innovation. *Innovations*, *1*(2), 145–162.

Nicholls, A. (2006). *Social entrepreneurship: New models of sustainable social change*. Oxford: Oxford University Press.

Pol, E., & Ville, S. (2009). Social innovation: Buzz word or enduring term? *The Journal of Socio-Economics*, *38*(6), 878–885.

Spear, R., Cornforth, C., & Aiken, M. (2007). *For love and money: Governance and social. enterprise*. London: National Council for Voluntary Organisations, London,UK.

Testi, E., Bellucci, M., Franchi, S., & Biggeri, M. (2017). Italian social enterprises at the crossroads: Their role in the evolution of the welfare state. *VOLUNTAS: International Journal of Voluntary and Nonprofit Organizations*, *28*(6), 2403–2422.

Travaglini, C. (1997). *Le cooperative sociali tra impresa e solidarietà. Caratteri economico-aziendali ed informativa economico-sociale*. Bologna: Clueb.

Travaglini, C., Bandini, F., & Mancinone, K. (2009). *Social enterprise in Europe: Governance models*. Paper presented at the Second EMES international conference on social enterprise. Retrieved from www.aiccon.it/file/convdoc/wp75.pdf.

Venturi, P., & Zandonai, F. (2009). Lo spazio dell'impresa sociale: dimensioni ed evoluzioni recenti. In C. Borzaga & F. Zandonai (Eds.), *Rapporto Iris Network. L'impresa sociale in Italia – Economia e istituzioni dei beni comuni* (pp. 9–18). Roma: Donzelli Editore.

6 Are decision makers in Social Enterprises more pro-social than their peers? An analysis of production and consumption choices

Enrico Testi, Mario Biggeri, Domenico Colucci, Nicola Doni, and Vincenzo Valori

Introduction

Social Enterprises (SEs) have been identified as valuable tools that can help solve societal problems. SEs are often driven by ideals and values rather than profit (Borzaga and Defourny, 2001; Defourny and Nyssen 2006), they contribute to community well-being, and they enhance the production of social capital and solve marginalization issues (Borzaga, Depedri, and Galera, 2012). SEs have, by definition, the primary objective of solving a social or environmental problem, whereas traditional companies might see this as a secondary objective behind profit maximization. Therefore, one could infer that SEs behave differently than traditional enterprises by making more pro-social choices.

In real-life situations, however, there is a continuum of organizational behaviours and objectives between for-profit firms and SEs (Borzaga, Depedri, and Tortia, 2010). In fact, decision makers in traditional enterprises can also make pro-social decisions that have a positive impact on society. Indeed, many authors have pointed out the continuous tension to balance social and economic objectives (Pearce, 2006; Peredo and Chrisman, 2006; Spear et al., 2009; Teasdale, 2010a, 2010b). This tension does not play out equally among SEs due to a host of factors, including the type of SE and how it produces social impact (Alegre, 2015). Therefore, identifying behaviours and choices as typical of SEs, for example being more cooperative or altruistic than traditional enterprises, risks to overgeneralize and be more driven by ideology rather than scientific evidence.

The "framework of social enterprises ecosystem" presented in Chapter 12 of the present book shows that the effects SEs have on society, and how they manage the tension between their social and economic objectives, depend on the choices made by decision makers in SE. Decision-makers are influenced by personal preferences, socio-institutional context, market factors, personal history, attitudes, and psychology, and the quality and quantity of information they have at their disposal. The decision-making process in SEs also depends on the legal and governance structure of the enterprise, the enterprises culture, its procedures, and internal group dynamics. For example, in cooperatives the decision-making process is by definition more democratic vis-à-vis SEs set up in a different legal form.

Decision-making processes in SEs—and any comparisons that can be drawn with decision-making processes in other enterprises—appear to be an under-researched topic.

The ecosystem perspective is based on the notion that it is important to understand the differences between both types of decision makers and how the system can incentivize pro-social behaviour. Although decisions are often made while considering a wide variety of issues, we will focus on two kinds of choices: the social quality of the goods and services provided (the higher the social quality, the greater the benefit for society), and the choice to buy goods and services, considering their social and environmental effects. We decided to focus on these factors because they reinforce each other and can lead to a virtuous cycle in which the ecosystem produces and consumes goods and services with high social quality.

This chapter contributes to the current literature on SEs by focussing on the following questions: do decision makers in SEs make more pro-social choices than other decision makers? What are the decision makers features that increase their pro-social choices? In order to answer these questions, we used both qualitative and quantitative methods.

This chapter is divided into six sections. The first section offers some definitions and a brief literature review concerning the features and attitudes of decision makers in SEs. The second section features the interpretative framework and our hypothesis. The third section, meanwhile, provides general information on the case study we used in our research, while the fourth section describes our methodology. The fifth section outlines the data we gathered through the survey and a series of semi-structured interviews. The final section of the chapter focuses on our conclusions and identifies preliminary policy suggestions.

Literature review: theoretical and empirical perspectives

Social entrepreneurship (SENT), SE, and Social Entrepreneur are sometimes used interchangeably, even though they have different definitions. As Mair and Martí (2006) state, definitions of social entrepreneurship typically refer to a process or behaviour; definitions of social entrepreneurs focus instead on the founder of the initiative; and definitions of SEs refer to the tangible outcome of social entrepreneurship (Mair and Martí, 2006, p. 37).

Even though there is no generally recognized definition of SE, there is widespread agreement on the basic features that an SE should have—most notably, a social objective and the ability to obtain resources from market or quasi-market exchanges. Following this shared understanding of SEs, we define SEs as those organizations that have five out of the nine indicators identified by the EMES group as describing the ideal type of SE (Borzaga and Defourny, 2001; Defourny and Nyssens, 2013). This includes the continuous production of goods and/or sale of services; a significant level of economic risk; a minimum amount of paid work; an explicit aim to benefit the community; and a limited profit distribution.

In our analysis we focus on organizations that have a social objective and are involved in a continuous activity of producing goods and/or selling services. Due to the different definitions and overlaps that exist between them, it is challenging to identify a single strand of literature that perfectly fits the definition of SE we use in this chapter while simultaneously addressing the issue of the features, preferences, and choices of its decision maker(s). Another challenge is that decision makers might be founders and/or managers or members of the enterprise as in the case of cooperatives. The distinction between founders and managers is similar to the distinction between entrepreneurs and managers. Indeed, a long-debated issue in the literature on entrepreneurship is who should be identified as an entrepreneur. In the economic literature, for instance, entrepreneurs have usually been characterized as having at least one of the following traits: they are a founder of an enterprise, they run a fairly new company, and they run or desire to run a high-growth company (Begley, 1995).

In much of the literature on social entrepreneurship, there is no distinction between founders and managers because social entrepreneurship and the connected idea of social entrepreneur are broader categories that often transcend the enterprise itself. As a matter of fact, social entrepreneurs can be found in both profit-seeking businesses that have a commitment to doing good and SEs that have a social purpose but are still businesses as well as in the voluntary sector (Parkinson and Howorth, 2008), and the public one (Hall et al., 2012; Hazenberg and Hall, 2016).

Due to these challenges, we decided to adopt a broad approach that encompasses literature on SE, social entrepreneurship (SENT), social entrepreneurs, and ethical decision-making. We will consider decision makers as a specific category of people who are involved in SENT through an SE. Since the broad approach that we adopt considerably enlarges the potential literature, we do not aim to provide a comprehensive literature review.

The literature on SENT usually features anecdotal (and at times idealistic) evidence about the traits, skills, and attitudes of social entrepreneurs. According to Prahbu (1999), perseverance, creativity, empathy, ability to instil confidence in others, and courage are the skills and attitudes most often associated with social entrepreneurial leaders. Similarly, ideas on creativity (Drayton, 2002), ability to recognize opportunities, collaborative leadership styles, teamwork capabilities, and community-oriented motivations (Morse and Dudley, 2002) are among the traits and skills identified most often when discussing social entrepreneurs. However, these traits and skills can also be found in other types of entrepreneurs.

The literature on behavioural economics has addressed the various determinants of entrepreneurship and what pushes people to become entrepreneurs (Baron, 2007; Åstebro et al., 2014). Similar issues have been raised when studying social entrepreneurs. For instance, Bird (1988) and Krueger Jr. (1993) have addressed the issue of entrepreneurial intentions and how the decision to set up a venture is made. Mair and Noboa (2006) combine insights from traditional entrepreneurship literature and anecdotal evidence in the field of SE in order to explain how behavioural intentions while starting a social venture are influenced by social venture desirability (which is affected by empathy and moral judgment) and social venture feasibility (which is often facilitated by social support and self-efficacy beliefs). Moreover, Renko (2013) finds that nascent social entrepreneurs who are guided by pro-social motivations are less likely to be successful in their start-up activities than their financially motivated peers.

Yitshaki and Kropp (2016) have analyzed the motivations and opportunity recognition of 30 Israeli social entrepreneurs. They found that 60% of them were motivated by pull factors, such as pro-social behaviours that were based on past life events. The other 40%, meanwhile, was motivated by push factors, such as career development. Miller et al. (2012) identify the mechanisms through which compassion, a pro-social motivation, can encourage social entrepreneurship.

The works of Harding and Cowling (2006) in the UK, using data from the Global Entrepreneurship Monitor (GEM), and Van Ryzin et al. (2009) in the US, using a voluntary online panel, identify common characteristics of social entrepreneurs. For instance, Harding (2006) claims that social entrepreneurs are more likely to be female, young, educated, and a minority. She also found that they are in general more positive than the average UK population but less positive than mainstream entrepreneurs, as they often become more disillusioned over time. Van Ryzin et al. (2009) argue that social entrepreneurs are more happy, extroverted, willing to give to others, and are more interested in politics. They are also more likely to be female, part of a minority group, educated, and reside in a big city. Bacq et al. (2016) use GEM in Belgium and the Netherlands to highlight the reluctant attitude among social entrepreneurs towards entrepreneurship and entrepreneurial commitment. It is important to point out, however, that all three of the studies cited earlier identified social entrepreneurs as people who performed (or intended to perform) a socially oriented activity through several different types of organizations.

Nga and Shamuganathan (2010) studied the relation between personality traits and social entrepreneurship dimensions, such as sustainability, vision, networking, and return orientation. Meanwhile, Cools and Vermeulen (2008) found that social and commercial entrepreneurs do not differ in terms of their cognitive style (Hayes and Allinson, 1998), and that they have the same information-processing preferences. Moreover, SEs do not differ from commercial enterprises with regards to their emphasis on proactive strategies. This is because SEs also have to compete with other SEs and commercial organizations for market opportunities and funding (Mort et al., 2003). Nonetheless, this same study did find that SEs are less likely to take risks than commercial enterprises.

In order to complement the ideas cited earlier, a brief discussion of the literature on ethical decision-making is needed. Much of this literature focuses on the different levels of influence that individual and organizational factors have on ethical decision-making (see, for example, O'Fallon and Butterfield, 2005). Most studies suggest that males and females do not tend to make different ethical decisions (Fleischman and Valentine, 2003; Lund, 2000). However, in studies where gender differences are reported, females have been shown to be more ethical than their male counterparts (Cohen et al., 2001; Sankaran and Bui, 2003).

Idealism and deontology are positively related to ethical decision-making (Singhapakdi et al., 1999), while relativism and teleology are negatively correlated (Cohen et al., 2001). Education, employment, and work experience are positively related to ethical decision-making, even though the type of education seems to have little or no effect (Green and Weber, 1997; Lund, 2000). The influence of age has produced mixed results (Kim and Chun, 2003; Ross and Robertson, 2003; Sankaran and Bui, 2003). Cognitive moral development, the capacity to understand ethical issues (Green and Weber, 1997; Bass et al. 1999), and religion appear to have a positive relationship as well (Singhapakdi et al., 2000). Interestingly enough, the size of an organization has been found to have a detrimental effect on ethical decision-making (Bartels et al. 1998).

Interpretative framework and hypothesis

The literature review highlights some of the features that might be more common to decision makers in SEs. Oftentimes, decision makers in social enterprises (DSE) are thought to be educated, interested in politics, guided by pro-social/community-oriented motivations, positive and open-minded, collaborative in the workplace, visionary, and creative. Other features, however, cast a shadow on the decision maker, as some observers believe that DSEs are more easily disillusioned by their experiences, less capable of reaching financial sustainability, and less likely to take risks than his or her peers in commercial enterprises. These individual features contribute, in different degrees and with other features of the ecosystem, to influence his or her choices and the results of the SE.

In order to disentangle the decision-making process in SEs and discuss the features that influence the choices faced by decision makers, we will use the framework elaborated in Chapter 12 of this book.

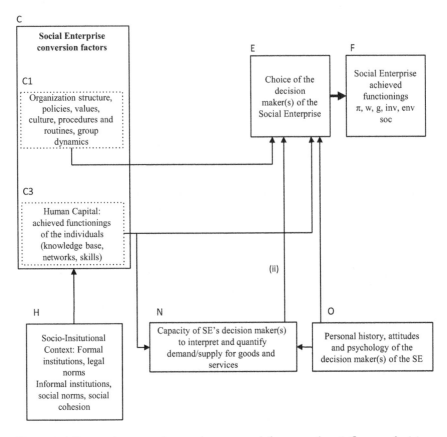

Figure 6.1 Personal, enterprise, and contextual features that influence decision-making.
Source: Adapted from Testi (2017).

Figure 6.1 shows the parts of the framework that describe the different features of the ecosystem that influence the choices (E) and the results achieved by the SE (F). According to the framework, choices (E) are influenced by:

- (O) Personal traits such as gender, age, personal history, attitudes and personality, social identity, religion, and education
- (C1) the organizational structure of the SE, its policies, identity, values, culture, procedures, and group interactions
- (C3) the human capital of the people making the decisions, such as their education level and knowledge base
- (H) socio-institutional context, which includes formal and informal institutions, social norms, culture, and social cohesion/conflict levels

- (ii) the information available to decision makers; this is influenced by the capacity of the decision maker/s to interpret the information (N), which is, in turn, influenced by both (C3) and (O).

Information (ii) plays an important role in how choices change. For example, an SE might be forced to take not pro-social choices in order to win the tender if it has the information that companies not concerned with social issues will take part to a tender and if the awarding criteria do not give a bonus to the production of social value.

Therefore, the features associated with (O), (C1), (I), and (ii) might influence the final decisions of an individual or an enterprise in a profoundly different manner.

Based on our research questions and the scholarly literature discussed earlier, we have formulated the following set of hypothesis, all of which will be tested empirically through the use of econometric estimates.

H1: *Decision-makers in SEs make more pro-social decisions in the production and consumption of various goods and services than decision makers in other types of enterprises (which will hereafter be known as Non-Social Enterprises or NSEs).*

This hypothesis is based on the work of Renko (2013) and Yitsaki and Kropp (2016). Since SEs are created in order to benefit the community, and since deciding to become a social entrepreneur is a life-choice, we can assume that decision makers in SEs are, on average, more pro-social than decision makers in NSEs.

H2: *Education level has a positive effect on the pro-social choices of decision makers.*

This hypothesis is based on the ethical decision-making literature review by O'Fallon and Butterfield (2005). They argue that one's education level positively contributes to a preference for ethical decision-making.

H3: *Decision-makers who perceive themselves as socially responsible make more pro-social choices.*

This hypothesis will allow us to determine whether or not decision makers who perceive themselves as being socially responsible make more pro-social choices, be they involved in either an SE or an NSE.

Case study

Our research focuses on the North-Eastern part of Tuscany, in particular the provinces of Florence, Prato, and Pistoia. The three provinces have a total of 1,558,434 inhabitants. According to the data from Infocamere (2016), the province of Florence had 109,435 registered enterprises in 2015, 48.9% of which are individual enterprises. The province of Prato had 28,975 registered enterprises in 2015, 56.5% of which were individual enterprises. Pistoia, meanwhile, had 32,832 registered enterprises in 2015, 54.7% of which were individual enterprises.

The entire metropolitan area, especially Tuscany, has a long tradition of civic participation. It has a thriving voluntary sector with approximately 1146 voluntary organizations and more than 30,000 volunteers. The region's strong civic spirit might have also positively contributed to the birth and growth of SEs in the 1970s. In fact this area boasts an impressive number of SEs. According to the data from the Chamber of Commerce, in 2017 there were 316 active SEs working in several different fields, most notably healthcare and education. Local foundations, public authorities, and various associations help SEs thrive in the area by providing grants, tenders, and support.

Research design, methodology, and data set

Research design and methodology

The present chapter uses qualitative and quantitative data. We decided to use a mixed method approach in order to better interpret the quantitative data and take into account information that is difficult to gather through a quantitative survey, such as the historical development of SEs in specific localities and the role that other organizations, institutions, and policies played in it.

Qualitative methods, sampling, and data collection

The interviewees and focus groups participants were selected on the basis of their knowledge of SEs and their different position in the ecosystem, thus enabling us to gather quality information from several different points of view. The content of the interviews and focus groups has been analyzed according to the ideas associated with grounded theory (Glaser and Strauss, 1967), an approach that enables researchers to code the most recurrent concepts. This allowed us to pinpoint the most relevant topics that emerged during the discussions and answer our research question. This integrated research methodology enabled us to identify the main historical, economic, political, cultural, and institutional factors that shaped SEs in the region we studied while also allowing us to understand the larger decision-making context.

The qualitative data was collected via semi-structured interviews that were performed as part of the Enabling the Flourishing and Evolution of Social Entrepreneurship for Innovative and Inclusive Societies (EFESEIIS) research project (for more information on the project please refer to Chapter 1). All the interviews were semi-structured with a few open-ended questions and were conducted in a face-to-face manner between April 2015 and May 2016. We carried out a total of 9 semi-structured interviews. The national and local experts who were interviewed consisted of two experts from think tanks on sustainable development and innovation, two from the finance sector, one from a social cooperative, one from a consulting agency, one from a national association of social cooperatives, one from a social cooperative consortium, and one university professor. The interviews focused on the professional experience of the respondents, especially country-specific SE issues and the role of key institutions, such as public entities, interest groups, and trade unions. In addition, two focus groups with a total of 20 subjects among social entrepreneurs and local stakeholders were held in Florence, Prato, and Pistoia between May and June 2015. Sixteen were social entrepreneurs (fourteen were members of social cooperatives), one stakeholder worked for the chamber of commerce, one worked for a financial institution, one worked for a support network, and one worked for a regional association of third-sector organizations.

Quantitative method: sampling design, questionnaire, and data collection

Quantitative data was gathered through a survey, which was designed according to the guidelines set by the EFESEIIS research project. Its goal was to obtain a random sample of decision makers from the north-eastern part of Tuscany, particularly the provinces of Florence, Prato, and Pistoia. The questionnaire, described in greater detail in Section 5.4, was administered between January 2016 and June 2016.

Participation in this study was restricted to founders and managers of SEs and for-profit enterprises. No enterprise size limit was set, which means that decision makers from individual enterprises were eligible as well. Following suggestions set out by Onwuegbuzie and Collins (2007, p. 288), we set the minimum sample size at 64 decision makers and the maximum sample size at 100 decision makers, dividing the sample equally between SEs and NSEs. The authors recommended this sample size on the basis of a statistical power analysis that was performed by Onwuegbuzie and Leech (2004). It was chosen in order to detect a medium, one-tailed, statistically significant relationship or difference with 0.80 power at 5% of significance for a correlational and causal-comparative research design.

Participants had to fill out a brief questionnaire featuring questions that allowed the researchers to determine whether or not the subject was eligible to take part in the experiment. The sample selection was separated between decision makers from SEs and decision makers from traditional enterprises. In the SE sample, all A and B type social cooperatives and SEs (according to law 155/2006) in the provinces of Florence, Prato, and Pistoia were contacted from a list provided by the Chambers of Commerce in all three provinces. Ultimately, 316 SEs were contacted by the researchers, 199 of which are based in the main cities in all three provinces (125 in Florence, 20 in Prato, and 44 in Pistoia). SEs were invited via e-mail to take part in our research.

The NSEs were invited (via email) by the local Chambers of Commerce to participate in this project. Once we secured the participation of 60 eligible decision makers for each type of enterprise, we identified the dates in which decision makers could come to the University of Florence and contribute to the project. Since the objective of the present study is to assess the differences between decision makers in SEs and NSEs, we assume that the time constraints cited by the entrepreneurs we contacted did not create a bias because they apply equally to both groups.

As a result, 74 out of 120 decision makers showed up to take part in the research activity, out of which 36 were SEs (11.4% of the entire population) and 38 NSEs.

The questionnaire

The decision makers were asked to fill out a questionnaire (see Appendix 1) that consists of 28 questions. The questions include background information (e.g. gender, level of education, marital status, number of family members, religious beliefs, presence of entrepreneurial background in the family, voluntary work, and previous experience in this field of study); satisfaction with one's personal financial situation and personal life (e.g. health, family relations, relationship with friends, professional life, and free time); and social awareness levels (e.g. the extent to which respondents consider themselves to be socially aware). Other questions addressed whether decision makers self-identify as social entrepreneurs, the year their organization was founded, the number of employees, the organization's religious affiliation, the sector of activity, the extent to which their organization cooperates with other organizations that are active in the same sector, and innovations introduced in the previous three years. The other variables are listed in Table 6.1.

The dependent variables used in our empirical research were related to the production and consumption choices made by the decision makers. These variables were inserted in the questionnaire. A dependent variable relating to the Social Value of Production was collected via a matrix in which a market interaction with another entrepreneur was simulated (see Appendix 1 for more on the matrix). Without knowing the choice of the hypothetical competitor, respondents had to choose which level of social quality/value to put into the goods sold by the enterprise. Social value could be 0, 10, 20, or 30, with 0 representing no benefit for society and 30 representing maximum benefit for society. Depending on the decision that was made by the other player, the respondent would achieve a certain financial return that was subsequently displayed in the matrix.

Another dependent variable relating to the Social Value of Consumption was created through a question that addressed the decision maker's ability to be a critical consumer, which was measured on a scale from 0 to 10 (0 representing the lowest level of critical thought and 10 representing the highest level of critical thought). We assumed that the response to this

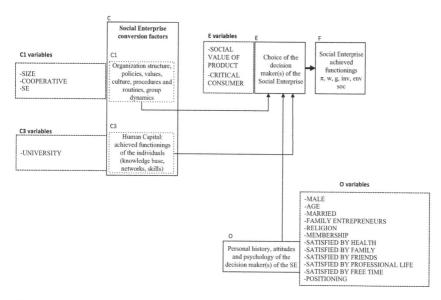

Figure 6.2 Interpretative framework and variables.
Source: Adapted from Testi (2017).

question was contingent on the decision makers consumption choices, be it at a personal or enterprise level.

All decision makers filled out the questionnaire. All of the decision makers involved in the study came from the same metropolitan areas of Florence, Prato, and Pistoia, all of which are socially and culturally similar (H). We did a pilot of the questionnaire with six decision makers of both types, and all decision makers understood the questions in the same way; therefore we took out (N) from our analysis. Moreover, since the matrix that was used to understand their production choices resulted in some fairly clear results, it is safe to say that the information (ii) upon which they based their decisions is the same for everyone. Therefore (H), (N), and (ii) have been taken out of the framework, even though the information pertaining to institutional context has been used to interpret the data. Figure 6.2 shows the reduced interpretative framework with the variables discussed in Table 6.1.

Data collection and management

Data was collected in three different sessions at the University of Florence between January 2016 and June 2016. After each session, researchers entered the data from the questionnaires into a database. Two entries were created for each session in order to avoid errors. The resulting database was then checked and cleaned. The complete database was finalized in August 2016. The resulting variables are indicated in Table 6.1.

Table 6.1 Variable definitions and descriptive statistics

Name	Definition	N	Min	Max	Mean	SD
Social value of consumption (Dependent variable)	0–10 scale of self-perception as a critical consumer; 0 = not critical, 10 = extremely critical consumer	74	0	10	6.53	1.97
Social value of production (Dependent variable)	0, 10, 20, 30 scale; 0 = no social value, 30 = Maximum social value	73	0	30	20.68	6.94
Male	Male = 1, Female = 0	74	0	1	0.69	0.46
Age	Age in years	74	23	62	40.97	10.00
University degree	1 = University and post university degree, 0 = other	74	0	1	0.46	0.50
Married	1 = married, 0 = other	74	0	1	0.45	0.50
Family entrepreneurs	1 = there are entrepreneurs in my family, 0 = there are no entrepreneurs in my family	74	0	1	0.55	0.50
Religion	1 = Attends religious functions more than once a year; 0 = never attends religious functions	74	0	1	0.54	0.50
Membership	1 = Part of a cultural or voluntary association, 0 = not member of cultural or voluntary associations	74	0	1	0.51	0.50
Satisfied by financial	1 = satisfied or very satisfied with financial situation, 0 = other	72	0	1	0.57	0.49
Satisfied by health	1 = satisfied or very satisfied with health, 0 = other	74	0	1	0.95	0.23
Satisfied by family	1 = satisfied or very satisfied with family relations, 0 = other	74	0	1	0.97	0.16
Satisfied by friends	1 = satisfied or very satisfied with friends, 0 = other	74	0	1	0.89	0.31
Satisfied with professional life	1 = satisfied or very satisfied with professional life, 0 = other	74	0	1	0.84	0.37
Satisfied with free time	1 = satisfied or very satisfied with free time, 0 = other	74	0	1	0.47	0.50
Positioning	Scale of 0–10; 0 = I do not self-define as a social entrepreneur, 10 = I totally define myself as a social entrepreneur	69	1.04	10	6.4	2.28
Size	No of employees in the company	67	1	2600	76.51	320.05
Size_log	No of employees in the company	67	0	7.86	2.57	1.62
SE	1 = the company is a social enterprise, 0 = other	74	0	1	0.49	0.503
Founder	1 = Yes, I am the founder of the company, 0 = No, I am not the founder of the company	67	0	1	0.55	0.501
ROLE	1 = Yes, I'm President or CEO of the company, 0 = No, I am not the president or CEO of the company	72	0	1	0.53	0.50
Cooperative	1 = Yes, the company is a cooperative, 0 = No, the company is not a cooperative	74	0	1	0.38	0.48

Estimation procedures and empirical results

We used the dummy variable SE (Table 6.1) in order to divide the decision makers into A- or B-type social cooperatives (as defined by Law 155/06, which distinguishes SEs in Italy from other types of enterprises). 36 out of 74 decision makers (48.64% of the total) were affiliated with SEs (DSEs), while the rest were affiliated with NSEs (DNSEs).

The average profile for each group was quite different. We ran a *t*-test to check the differences between the background variables. Most variables were similar; however, the following variables showed a Prob > *F* under 0.1: 61.1% of the DSEs have a university or post university degree compared to 31.6% of DNSEs. 65.8% of DNSE have an entrepreneur in the family, compared to 44.4% of DSEs. DSEs are on average less religious—41.7% compared to 65.8% of DNSEs—and tend to be more involved in cultural, political, and voluntary associations (63.9%) compared to DNSEs (39.5%). We therefore ran a regression analysis on both dependent variables in order to take into account and control for background variables.

To verify the first hypothesis we performed an OLS regression using "Social value of Consumption" as a dependent variable in order to explain the differences in pro-social consumption levels. The first regression performed on the "Social Value of Consumption" variable included independent variables, such as the sex, age, and education of the respondent; his/her religious affiliation and participation in cultural, political, and voluntary associations; whether or not the respondent was affiliated with an SE; satisfaction with their financial situation and life; the size of the enterprise; the respondent's role in the enterprise; and whether or not they had founded the enterprise. The formula of linear regression is:

$$y_i = \beta_0 + \sum_{j=1}^{k} \beta_j\, x_{ij} + \varepsilon_i$$

The regression shown in Table 6.2 suggests that having a University degree represents the only positive significant correlation with being a critical consumer.

We performed a second regression (Table 6.3) with "Social Value of Consumption" as a dependent variable. This time we substituted the independent variable "SE," which indicates whether or not the respondent is part of an SE, with the "Positioning" variable, which indicates the extent to which the respondent thinks of him or herself as a social entrepreneur (according to the definition indicated in Appendix 1). Including this variable reduces the number of observations from 72 to 67. As Table 6.3 illustrates, the variable "Positioning" is positively and strongly correlated to critical consumer variable, which means that decision makers who define themselves as critical consumers also tend to define themselves as social entrepreneurs. This regression also found that having higher levels of education is positively and significantly correlated to being a critical consumer.

Table 6.2 Regression between "Social Value of Consumption" (a dependent variable) and several independent variables

Source	SS	Df	MS		
				Number of obs = 72	
				F(11, 60) = 0.98	
	38.506531	11	3.50059373	Prob > F = 0.4706	
Residual	213.368469	60	3.55614115	R-squared = 0.1529	
				Adj R-squared =-0.0024	
Total	251.875	71	3.54753521	Root MSE = 1.8858	

Socvalconsum	Coef.	Std. Err.	t	P > |t|	[95% Conf. Interval]	
Male	0.1383411	0.5059035	0.27	0.785	−0.8736166	1.150299
Age	0.0209893	0.0260736	0.81	0.424	−0.0311657	0.0731443
University	1.113371	0.5460248	2.04	0.046	0.0211584	2.205583
Religious	−0.4988944	0.4878451	−1.02	0.311	−1.47473	0.4769411
Membership	−0.8324265	0.5068201	−1.64	0.106	−1.846218	0.1813646
SE	0.0434432	0.5441694	0.08	0.937	−1.045058	1.131944
S.Financial	−0.4119433	0.5047156	−0.82	0.418	−1.421525	0.5976382
S.Life	−0.8174549	0.5610388	−1.46	0.150	−1.9397	0.3047899
Size_log	−0.0418237	0.1489293	−0.28	0.780	−0.3397268	0.2560793
Founder	0.0779921	0.5095352	0.15	0.879	−0.9412299	1.097214
Role	0.1753639	0.4707036	0.37	0.711	−0.7661835	1.116911
_cons	6.160304	1.572125	3.92	0.000	3.015586	9.305023

Table 6.3 Regression between dependent variable Social Value of Consumption and independent variables including positioning

Source	SS	df	MS		
				Number of obs = 67	
				F(11,55) = 1.95	
Model	65.8085069	11	5.98259154	Prob > F = 0.0519	
Residual	168.490001	55	3.06345456	R-squared = 0.2809	
				Adj R-squared = 0.1370	
Total	234.298507	66	3.54997739	Root MSE = 1.7503	

SocValconsu	Coef.	Std. Err.	t	P > |t|	[95% Conf. Interval]	
Male	0.1340159	0.500836	0.27	0.790	−0.8696818	1.137714
Age	0.0063425	0.0258764	0.25	0.807	−0.045515	0.0582
University	0.8599945	0.5195338	1.67	0.100	−0.1811745	1.901163
Religious	−0.2152762	0.4807925	−0.45	0.656	−1.178806	0.7482534
Membership	−0.9273243	0.4794263	−1.93	0.058	−1.888116	0.0334674
Positioning	0.3531487	0.1046157	3.38	0.001	0.143494	0.5628033
S.Financial	−0.3331636	0.4957035	−0.67	0.504	−1.326576	0.6602484
S.Life	−0.4121586	0.5367508	−0.77	0.446	−1.487831	0.6635141
Size_log	−0.2200202	0.1566303	−1.40	0.166	−0.5339142	0.0938739
Founder	0.0910302	0.494594	0.18	0.855	−0.9001583	1.082219
Role	0.0138539	0.4629842	0.03	0.976	−0.9139871	0.9416948
_cons	4.479278	1.617071	2.77	0.008	1.238596	7.71996

Since the introduction of the variable "Positioning" reduced the number of observations, we performed another regression analysis (see Table 6.4) by imputing missing data using the ICE command that generates multiple data imputations. The results of this regression confirm the results of the previous analysis.

The data in Table 6.4 suggests that there is no relationship between being a decision maker in an SE and being a critical consumer, while those who choose to consume goods with a higher social value appear to be more educated—thus confirming hypothesis 2—and perceive themselves as being social entrepreneurs, regardless of whether or not they are affiliated with an SE.

In order to fully answer our research question we performed an ordered logit regression (Table 6.5) using "Social Value of Product" as a dependent variable and several independent variables, including the sex, age, and education of the respondent; his/her religious affiliation and participation in cultural, political and voluntary associations; whether or not the respondent is affiliated with an SE, satisfaction with one's financial situation and life; the size of the enterprise; the respondent's role in the enterprise; and whether or not they founded the enterprise. For the dependent variable "Social Value of Product," we decided to use an ordered logistic regression model because OLS common assumptions could be violated using a non-interval outcome variable (the outcome variable assumes four possible values: 0, 10, 20, and 30). The ordered logit function is as follows:

le 6.4 Regression between dependent variable Social Value of Consumption and independent variables including positioning, using multiple imputation for missing data

rce	SS	df	MS		
				Number of obs = 72	
				$F(11, 60)$ = 1.95	
del	66.3460669	11	6.03146063	Prob > F = 0.0502	
dual	185.528933	60	3.09214889	R-squared = 0.2634	
				Adj R-squared = 0.1284	
l	251.875	71	3.54753521	Root MSE = 1.7585	

Jalconsu	Coef.	Std. Err.	t	P > |t|	[95% Conf. Interval]	
e	−0.0625673	0.4713554	−0.13	0.895	−1.005418	0.8802839
	0.0107987	0.0245358	0.44	0.661	−0.0382801	0.0598776
ersity	0.8598722	0.496254	1.73	0.088	−0.1327836	1.852528
gious	−0.3309666	0.4553967	−0.73	0.470	−1.241896	0.5799623
bership	−0.8823912	0.4665884	−1.89	0.063	−1.815707	0.0509246
ioning	0.2949926	0.0982729	3.00	0.004	0.0984176	0.4915675
nancial	−0.404306	0.4649684	−0.87	0.388	−1.334381	0.5257692
fe	−0.6125959	0.5270516	−1.16	0.250	−1.666856	0.4416642
log	−0.0866095	0.1312246	−0.66	0.512	−0.3490978	0.1758788
der	0.3059451	0.4760007	0.64	0.523	−0.6461981	1.258088
	0.043115	0.4409734	0.10	0.922	−0.8389631	0.9251932
s	4.589788	1.555742	2.95	0.005	1.47784	7.701735

$$y_i^* = \beta_0 + \sum_{j=1}^{k} \beta_j \, x_{ij} + \varepsilon_i$$

y^* is the exact but unobserved dependent variable; x is the vector of independent variables, and is the vector of regression coefficients which we wish to estimate.

$$y = \begin{cases} 0 & \text{if} & y^* \leq \mu_{10} \\ 10 & \text{if} & \mu_{10} < y^* \leq \mu_{20} \\ 20 & \text{if} & \mu_{20} < y^* \leq \mu_{30} \\ 30 & \text{if} & \mu_{30} < y^* \end{cases}$$

Then the ordered logit technique will use the observations on y, which are a form of censored data on y^* to fit the parameter vector β.

The regression showed that the choice to produce goods with a higher social value is not related to these variables. This is in line with the literature on ethical decision-making highlighted previously in this chapter.

We also performed another regression that substituted the variable "SE" with the variable "Positioning." We found that there is a significant correlation between the self-perception of being a social entrepreneur and choosing to provide higher quality goods and services. Since the introduction of

Table 6.5 Ordered logit regression between "Social Value of product" (a dependent variable) and several independent variables with imputed values

Ordered logistic regression				Number of obs = 71		
Log likelihood = −69.790285				LR chi2(11)　= 5.97 Prob > chi2　= 0.8755 Pseudo R2　= 0.0410		

S. Value Pr	Coef.	Std. Err.	z	P > |z|	[95% Conf. Interval]	
Male	0.4972802	0.5325626	0.93	0.350	−0.5465234	1.541084
Age	−0.0022887	0.0272147	−0.08	0.933	−0.0556284	0.0510511
University	0.6839426	0.5789763	1.18	0.237	−0.4508301	1.818715
Religious	0.2550947	0.5133873	0.50	0.619	−0.751126	1.261315
Membership	0.2666293	0.526972	0.51	0.613	−0.7662168	1.299475
SE	0.1656675	0.5752274	0.29	0.773	−0.9617574	1.293092
S. Financial	−0.2118093	0.5196811	−0.41	0.684	−1.230366	0.806747
S. Satisfaction	0.2936297	0.5881348	0.50	0.618	−0.8590934	1.446353
Size	0.1440978	0.1536172	0.94	0.348	−0.1569864	0.4451819
Founder	0.1400252	0.5370847	0.26	0.794	−0.9126414	1.192692
Role	−0.2758805	0.5029528	−0.55	0.583	−1.26165	0.7098889
/cut1	−3.059809	1.890141			−6.764416	0.6447988
/cut2	−0.3387118	1.648313			−3.569347	2.891923
/cut3	2.462392	1.683387			−0.8369867	5.761771

Table 6.6 Ordered logit regression between dependent variable Social Value of product and independent variables including positioning

Ordered logistic regression			Number of obs = 66			
			LR chi2(11) = 11.69			
Log likelihood = −62.016696			Prob > chi2 = 0.3875			
			Pseudo R2 = 0.0861			

S. Value Pr	Coef.	Std.Err.	z	P > |z|	[95% Conf. Interval]	
Male	0.5834364	0.5684826	1.03	0.305	−0.530769	1.697642
Age	−0.0104525	0.0291953	−0.36	0.720	−0.0676743	0.0467693
University	0.5886885	0.5929295	0.99	0.321	−0.573432	1.750809
Religious	0.1554008	0.5562738	0.28	0.780	−0.9348757	1.245677
Membership	0.0549557	0.5459178	0.10	0.920	−1.015024	1.124935
Positioning	0.2545501	0.128479	1.98	**0.048**	0.0027358	0.5063643
S. Financial	−0.107597	0.5702467	−0.19	0.850	−1.22526	1.010066
. Satisfaction	0.5086819	0.6123102	0.83	0.406	−0.6914241	1.708788
Size	0.2006929	0.1783593	1.13	0.260	−0.1488849	0.5502706
Founder	0.5010916	0.5818716	0.86	0.389	−0.6393557	1.641539
Role	−0.4706782	0.5408418	−0.87	0.384	−1.530709	0.5893522
cut1	−1.434384	2.060269			−5.472438	2.60367
cut2	1.23892	1.849999			−2.387011	4.864852
cut3	4.252757	1.9451			0.4404313	8.065084

the variable "Positioning" reduced the number of observations, we performed another regression (Table 6.7) by imputing missing data using the ICE command that generates multiple data imputations. The results of this regression confirm the results of the previous analysis.

Concerning our first hypothesis (*H1*), we can state that there is no evidence that decision makers in SEs make more pro-social decisions in production and consumption. However, it is interesting to note that education level seems to play a role in determining whether or not our respondents consumed products with a higher social value, even though a similar causal relationship doesn't seem to exist with regards to making more socially-oriented production choices.

Pro-social choices (e.g. consuming and choosing to deliver goods and services with a higher social value) are strongly related to whether or not a decision maker identifies as a social entrepreneur. This suggests that the main difference between the decision makers who took part in our panel does not involve whether or not they are part of an SE or not but is rather dependent on their own pro-social attitudes or idealistic views of themselves. This confirms hypothesis *H3*.

However, we also need to discuss how these results were shaped by the various economic pressures that the respondents were facing when this project was first initiated. Most SEs, after all, work with the public sector through tenders. In the interviews and focus groups we conducted, a great deal of attention was paid to the topic of increased competition. SEs face greater competition from similar organizations to win public tenders. In some cases, they also have to

Table 6.7 Ordered logit regression between dependent variable Social Value of product and independent variables, including positioning with imputed values

Ordered logistic regression				Number of obs = 71		
				LR chi2(11) = 9.14		
Log likelihood = −68.203191				Prob > chi2 = 0.6088		
				Pseudo R2 = 0.0628		

S. Value Pr	Coef.	Std.Err.	z	P > |z|	[95% Conf. Interval]	
Male	0.333258	0.5304308	0.63	0.530	−0.7063672	1.372883
Age	−0.0098272	0.0279856	−0.35	0.725	−0.0646779	0.0450235
University	0.5182293	0.5664837	0.91	0.360	−0.5920584	1.628517
Religious	0.3484489	0.5224034	0.67	0.505	−0.675443	1.372341
Membership	0.2672245	0.5270464	0.51	0.612	−0.7657675	1.300217
Positioning	0.2130023	0.1189889	1.79	0.073	−0.0202117	0.4462163
S. Financial	−0.1513975	0.5236582	−0.29	0.772	−1.177749	0.8749536
S. Satisfaction	0.3752479	0.5985465	0.63	0.531	−0.7978817	1.548377
Size1	0.1367541	0.148297	0.92	0.356	−0.1539026	0.4274108
Founder	0.3301024	0.5451279	0.61	0.545	−0.7383287	1.398534
Role	−0.4380106	0.512374	−0.85	0.393	−1.442245	0.566224
/cut1	−2.047777	2.00548			−5.978446	1.882892
/cut2	0.674169	1.78093			−2.81639	4.164728
/cut3	3.569121	1.850157			−0.0571206	7.195363

compete with for-profit enterprises that are less concerned with the social quality of their goods and services, and can therefore reduce their costs more easily. According to some of the stakeholders interviewed, one of the problems faced by SEs is that they have to reduce—sometimes to zero—their operating margins in order to win tenders and pay their employees. However, SEs can only reduce costs to a certain point because, in many cases, they are very work intensive. Moreover, WISEs (Work Integration Social Enterprises) that include disadvantaged people in their workforce have a more difficult time cutting costs and/or increasing efficiency. The end result, according to the interviewed stakeholders, is that some SEs are unable to fully realize their social impact, which, in turn, forces some of them to start behaving like traditional enterprises, thereby placing less emphasis on the social aspects of their activities. This situation might have been reflected as well in the results of the questionnaire.

Conclusions

The results obtained in this study are consistent with much of the literature on SEs and SENTs while also providing us with some important information on ecosystems. On the one hand, decision makers in SEs do not seem to differ in terms of the pro-social choices they make. This could be because their differences, in the grand scheme of things, are not all that vast, or because, when faced with similar constraints and choices, they tend to mimic the behaviour of others (Parkinson and Howorth, 2008; Dey and Teasdale, 2015).

It is certain, however, that those who self-identify as social entrepreneurs often make pro-social choices, regardless of whether or not they work for an SE or a traditional for-profit enterprise.

These results can be interpreted in two different ways. For starters, we should recognize that if decision makers in SEs behave in the same way as decision makers in other enterprises, then it is safe to say that some of the idealistic arguments found in the literature on SEs and SENT might be somewhat overstated.

The second way to interpret the results is even more interesting because it might represent a first step in explaining the effects of the ecosystem and various contingencies on the behaviour of decision makers. Some decision makers, be they from SEs or other enterprises, are more socially aware and, as a result, tend to make more pro-social choices. However, other decision makers in SEs might start making less pro-social choices due to the intense pressures that arise due to competition and shrinking resources in the ecosystem, which, in turn, could cause them to start behaving like decision makers from traditional enterprises. Therefore, if we want SEs to provide as much social value as possible, we should create conditions that reduce price competition and foster competition based on quality, innovation, and social value (Biggeri et al., 2017). In fact, one of the solutions proposed by the stakeholders we interviewed involves the co-planning of services between SEs and public authorities (which will reduce price competition) and including in public tenders additional points if certain social requirements have been met in order to foster competition based on quality and innovation). These types of ideas have been promoted in recent studies (Federico et al. 2012) and by the new Public Procurement Directive (2014/24/EU) of the EU. And yet, despite what happens at the EU level, it is important to recognize that local authorities create many of the conditions that promote pro-social behaviours in the ecosystem. Many of the interviewees in our study claim that local authorities are often constrained by budgets and deadlines, and tend to misunderstand the consequences of their decisions on SEs and the ecosystem in which they operate. Positive efforts in this direction have been done in England with the Social Value Act (2012) and in Scotland with the Community Empowerment Bill and the Procurement Reform Act (2014).

The framework presented in Chapter 12 of this book shows that decisions made by SEs have an effect on the ecosystem and that different parts of the ecosystem can influence the decisions made by DSEs. The (positive) effects SEs have on the ecosystem are the result of both the choices made by SEs and the various features of the ecosystem itself, including institutional context, the market, and the goods and services available to SEs.

Based on the results of the present study, a policy maker interested in creating an enabling ecosystem should provide economic incentives, processes, and regulations that shift the focus away from competition based solely on price to competition that is based on quality, innovation, and social value. This will give SEs the means to fully pursue their social objectives and create positive effects on the ecosystem.

This work is just a first step in understanding the features of decision makers in SEs, and analysing the effects that institutional, social, and contextual factors have on their choices. In order to assess this phenomenon, we would need to engage in research that compares, through behavioural experiments, the behaviour of decision makers in SEs and decision makers in other enterprises that operate in different countries and ecosystems. This would allow us to assess whether or not different institutional, market, and cultural contexts influence decision-making and the results achieved by SEs. We acknowledge that this is a seminal chapter and we hope that this work will help raise awareness on this topic and encourage other researchers to build on our findings.

Appendix 1: Questionnaire

EFESEIIS

Enabling the Flourishing and Evolution of Social Entrepreneurship for Innovative and Inclusive Societies

Please send all inquiries to: info@arcolab.org

We are pleased to invite you and your organisation to participate in our survey. Participation in the survey is voluntary and you may decide to respond to the entire questionnaire or only to some questions. You may at any time withdraw your consent to participate. You do not have to give any reasons for withdrawing. If you withdraw your consent, all information about you and your organisation will be deleted.

The information collected in this survey will be treated in an anonymous and aggregated manner. It will be used for statistical and research purposes only, in accordance with national laws on privacy and data collecting.

Personal Code:
(Please, insert your personal code)

_____

1. **Sex:**
   ☐ Male
   ☐ Female
   ☐ Other
   ☐ Do not wish to answer
2. **Date of birth (year):** _____

3. **Place of birth:** _____

4. **What is your highest educational qualification?**
   ☐ No formal education (did not completing complete primary education)
   ☐ Primary education
   ☐ Secondary education
   ☐ Further education / College
   ☐ University – undergraduate
   ☐ University – postgraduate / Masters
   ☐ Ph.D. / Doctorate
   ☐ Do not wish to answer

5. **Family status**
   ☐ Single
   ☐ Married
   ☐ Co-habitating
   ☐ Widowed
   ☐ Separated
   ☐ Divorced
   ☐ Do not wish to answer

6. **How many relatives do you have?**
   (Please, fill the box below with the number of your relatives)

Parents	
Siblings	
Children	
Grandparents	
Grandchildren	
Cousins	

   ☐ Do not wish to answer

7. **How many people are in your family?**
   (Please, consider only the family members that are currently living with you)

   _____

8. **Is (or has) anyone in your family been an entrepreneur?**
   ☐ Yes
   ☐ No
   ☐ Do not know
   ☐ Do not wish to answer

9. **You are:**
   ☐ Catholic
   ☐ Atheist
   ☐ Agnostic
   ☐ Other religion: _____
   ☐ Do not wish to answer

10. **How often do you attend religious services?**
    ☐ More than once a week
    ☐ Once a week
    ☐ Once a month
    ☐ Once a year
    ☐ Practically never
    ☐ Do not wish to answer

11. **Are you currently a member of a voluntary organisation or association?**
    ☐ Yes
    ☐ No

12. **If yes, could you please specify the name of the organisation/association?**
    _____

13. **How would you define your current financial situation?**
    ☐ I live very comfortably
    ☐ I live comfortably
    ☐ I live in satisfactory condition
    ☐ I can barely afford to live
    ☐ It is bad
    ☐ Do not wish to answer

14. **All in all, at the date you can state to be:**
    ☐ Very satisfied
    ☐ Satisfied
    ☐ Not really satisfied
    ☐ Not at all satisfied
    ☐ Do not wish to answer

15. **How satisfied are you concerning the following aspects:**

	Not at all	A little	Sufficiently	Really	Do not wish to answer
Health					
Family relationships					
Friendships					
Professional life					
Free time					

16. **Are you familiar with game theory and the prisoner's dilemma?**
    ☐ Yes, I studied it during my time at university
    ☐ Yes, I've heard about it, but I have not studied it
    ☐ I do not know what they are
    ☐ I do not wish to answer

17. **Where would you like to work in 10 years?**
    ☐ In public administration (social, health, or welfare)
    ☐ In public administration (all other sectors)
    ☐ As a freelancer

☐ In a private enterprise
☐ In a non-profit organisation
☐ I do not wish to answer

18. **A critical consumer makes consumption choices based on predefined criteria, such as environmental and social sustainability, which have the same importance of price and quality of the products/services.**

    Given this definition, please use a scale from 0 to 10 to define your own level of critical thinking as a consumer (0 means you are not a critical consumer and 10 means you definitely are a critical consumer)

0	1	2	3	4	5	6	7	8	9	10

19. **Please look at the matrix below. It represents the pay-offs in an interaction between two entrepreneurs**

    You and another entrepreneur are involved in a market game. *You must choose the social value of the good you are producing: the numbers 0, 10, 20, and 30 correspond to the benefit you are choosing to create for society. The higher the number you choose, the higher the social responsibility of your firm.*

    In the following matrix, you can see the profits of each entrepreneur. In each cell of the matrix, corresponding to the choices you and the other entrepreneur do are indicated the profits for you, the other entrepreneur and the benefit for society.

    Your profit is the number in black; the other entrepreneur's profit is the number in blue; and the benefit for society is the number in red. For example, if You choose 0 (see the first row) and your rival chooses 30 (see the last column), you will achieve a profit of 45 (the black number in the last square) and the latter will achieve a profit of 20 (the blue number in the square). The total benefit for society will be 30 (the number in red). Similar calculations can be done for several different strategies.

		YOUR RIVAL							
		| 0		10		20		30	
0		10	10	40	35	50	30	45	20
		0		10		20		30	
10		35	40	10	10	40	25	25	15
		10		20		30		40	
20		30	50	25	40	10	10	20	10
		20		30		40		50	
30		20	45	15	25	10	20	10	10
		30		40		50		60	

Without knowing in advance the choice of your rival, which degree of goodness for your product will you choose? Please select a level between 0, 10, 20, and 30.

0	10	20	30

20. A social entrepreneur has as primary objective the achievement of a significant social impact through the introduction of innovative methodologies in both production and supply of services rather than the profit maximization. His or her main aim is to answer unmet social or environmental needs, thus guaranteeing the sustainability of the enterprise.

    Given this definition, what kind of entrepreneur do you think you are?
    □ A social entrepreneur
    □ Other kind of entrepreneur
    □ Do not wish to answer

21. To what extent would you define yourself as a social entrepreneur?
    Please, select a level between 0% and 100% in the line below
    0%   50%   100%
    !_____!_____!

22. When was your organization legally founded?
    _____

23. What is your current position in the enterprise?
    _____

24. How many people work in your organisation (including you)?
    _____

25. Is your organisation religiously affiliated?
    □ Yes, totally
    □ Yes, partially
    □ No
    □ Do not know
    □ Do not wish to answer

26. In which sector is the organization operating?
    _____

27. Do you cooperate with other organisations in the fields you work in (as indicated above)?
    □ Yes
    □ No
    □ Do not know
    □ Do not wish to answer

28. Has your organisation innovated in terms of products, process, finance, or marketing in the last 3 years?
    □ Yes
    □ No
    □ Do not know
    □ Do not wish to answer

The information collected in this survey will be treated in an anonymous and aggregated manner. It will be used for statistical and research purposes only, in accordance with national laws on privacy and data collecting.

Thank you for taking the time to complete this questionnaire!

References

Alegre, I. (2015). Social and economic tension in social enterprises: Does it exist? *Social Business, 5*(1), 17–32.

Åstebro, T., Herz, H., Nanda, R., & Weber, R. A. (2014). Seeking the roots of entrepreneurship: Insights from behavioral economics. *The Journal of Economic Perspectives, 28*(3), 49–69.

Bacq, S., Hartog, C., & Hoogendoorn, B. (2016). Beyond the moral portrayal of social entrepreneurs: An empirical approach to who they are and what drives them. *Journal of Business Ethics, 133*(4), 703–718.

Baron, R. A. (2007). Behavioral and cognitive factors in entrepreneurship: Entrepreneurs as the active element in new venture creation. *Strategic Entrepreneurship Journal, 1*(1–2), 167–182.

Bartels, K. K., Harrick, E., Martell, K., & Strickland, D. (1998). The relationship between ethical climate and ethical problems within human resource management. *Journal of Business Ethics, 17*(7), 799–804.

Bass, K., Barnett, T., & Brown, G. (1999). Individual difference variables, ethical judgments, and ethical behavioral intentions. *Business Ethics Quarterly, 9*(02), 183–205.

Begley, T. M. (1995). Using founder status, age of firm, and company growth rate as the basis for distinguishing entrepreneurs from managers of smaller businesses. *Journal of Business Venturing, 10*(3), 249–263.

Biggeri, M., Testi, E., & Bellucci, M., (2017), "Enabling ecosystems for social enterprises and social innovation: A capability approach perspective." *Journal of Human Development and Capabilities*, vol. 18(2), 299–306

Bird, B. (1988). Implementing entrepreneurial ideas: The case for intention. *Academy of Management Review, 13*(3), 442–453.

Borzaga, C., Depedri, S., & Tortia, E. (2010). *The growth of organizational variety in market economies: The case of social enterprises.* Euricse Working Papers, 003(10), Euricse, Trento

Borzaga, C., & Defourny, J. (2001). *The emergence of social enterprises.* London: Routledge.

Borzaga, C., Depedri, S., & Galera, G. (2012). Interpreting social enterprises. *Revista De Administracao, 47*(3), 398–409.

Cohen, J. R., Pant, L. W., & Sharp, D. J. (2001). An examination of differences in ethical decision-making between Canadian business students and accounting professionals. *Journal of Business Ethics, 30*(4), 319–336.

Cools, E., & Vermeulen, S. (2008). *What's in a name? An inquiry on the cognitive and entrepreneurial profile of the social entrepreneur.* Vlerick Leuven Ghent Management School Working Paper Series, 2008–02.

Defourny, J., & Nyssens, M. (2006). Defining social enterprise. In M. Nyssens (Eds.), *Social enterprise. At the crossroads of market, public policies and civil society* (pp. 3–26). London: Routledge.

Defourny, J., & Nyssens, M. (2013). *The EMES approach of social enterprises in a comparative perspective.* EMES Working Papers, 12(03).

Dey, P., & Teasdale, S. (2015). The tactical mimicry of social enterprise strategies: Acting 'as if' in the everyday life of third sector organizations. *Organization,* 23(4), 485–504.

Drayton, W. (2002). The citizen sector: Becoming as entrepreneurial and competitive as business. *California Management Review,* 44(3), 120–132.

Federico, V., Russo, D., & Testi, E. (2012). *Impresa sociale, concorrenza e valore aggiunto. Un approccio europeo.* CEDAM.

Fleischman, G., & Valentine, S. (2003). Professionals' tax liability assessments and ethical evaluations in an equitable relief innocent spouse case. *Journal of Business Ethics,* 42(1), 27–44.

Glaser, B. G., & Strauss, A. L. (1967). *The discovery of grounded theory.* Chicago, IL: Aldine.

Green, S., & Weber, J. (1997). Influencing ethical development: Exposing students to the AICPA code of conduct. *Journal of Business Ethics,* 16(8), 777–790.

Hall, J., Matos, S., Sheehan, L., & Silvestre, B. (2012). Entrepreneurship and innovation at the base of the pyramid: A recipe for inclusive growth or social exclusion? *Journal of Management Studies,* 49(4), 785–812.

Harding, R., & Cowling, M. (2006). *Social entrepreneurship monitor.* London: Global Entrepreneurship Monitor.

Hazenberg, R., Bajwa-Patel, M., Mazzei, M., Roy, M. J., & Baglioni, S. (2016). The role of institutional and stakeholder networks in shaping social enterprise ecosystems in Europe. *Social Enterprise Journal,* 12(3), 302–321.

Hazenberg, R., & Hall, K. (2016). Public service mutuals: towards a theoretical understanding of the spin-out process. *Policy & Politics,* 44(3), 441–463.

Infocamere. (2016). Retrieved from www.infocamere.it/web/infocamere/movimprese/-/asset_publisher/ueRnd4KL4Z0I/content/dati-totali-imprese-1995-2015.

Kim, S. Y., & Chun, S. Y. (2003). A study of marketing ethics in Korea: What do Koreans care about? *International Journal of Management,* 20(3), 377.

Krueger, N. (1993). The impact of prior entrepreneurial exposure on perceptions of new venture feasibility and desirability. *Entrepreneurship: Theory and Practice,* 18(1), 5–22.

Lund, D. B. (2000). An empirical examination of marketing professionals' ethical behavior in differing situations. *Journal of Business Ethics,* 24(4), 331–342.

Mair, J., & Marti, I. (2006). Social entrepreneurship research: A source of explanation, prediction, and delight. *Journal of world business,* 41(1), 36–44.

Mair, J., & Noboa, E. (2006). Social entrepreneurship: How intentions to create a social venture are formed. In J. Mair, J. Robinson, & K. Hockerts (Eds.), *Social entrepreneurship* (pp. 121–135). New York: Palgrave Macmillan.

Miller, T. L., Grimes, M. G., McMullen, J. S., & Vogus, T. J. (2012). Venturing for others with heart and head: How compassion encourages social entrepreneurship. *Academy of Management Review,* 37(4), 616–640.

Morse, R., & Dudley, L. (2002). Civic entrepreneurs and collaborative leadership. *PA Times,* 25(8), 2.

Mort, G. S., Weerawardena, J., & Carnegie, K. (2002). Social entrepreneurship: Towards conceptualisation. *International Journal of Nonprofit and Voluntary Sector Marketing*, 8, 76–88.

Nga, J. K. H., & Shamuganathan, G. (2010). The influence of personality traits and demographic factors on social entrepreneurship start up intentions. *Journal of Business Ethics*, 95(2), 259–282.

O'Fallon, M. J., & Butterfield, K. D. (2005). A review of the empirical ethical decision-making literature: 1996–2003. *Journal of Business Ethics*, 59(4), 375–413.

Onwuegbuzie, A. J., & Collins, K. M. (2007). A typology of mixed methods sampling designs in social science research. *The Qualitative Report*, 12(2), 281–316.

Onwuegbuzie, A. J., & Leech, N. L. (2004). Enhancing the interpretation of significant findings: The role of mixed methods research. *The Qualitative Report*, 9(4), 770–792.

Parkinson, C., & Howorth, C. (2008). The language of social entrepreneurs. *Entrepreneurship & Regional Development*, 20(3), 285–309.

Pearce, J. (2006). *Learning from failure: Lessons in how to strengthen and build the social enterprise sector*. Plymouth: Co-active Ltd.

Peredo, A., & M., McLean, M. (2006). Social entrepreneurship: A critical review of the concept. *Journal of World Business*, 41(1), 56–65.

Prabhu, G. N. (1999). Social entrepreneurial leadership. *Career Development International*, 4(3), 140–145.

Renko, M. (2013). Early challenges of nascent social entrepreneurs. *Entrepreneurship Theory and Practice*, 37(5), 1045–1069.

Ross Jr, W. T., & Robertson, D. C. (2003). A typology of situational factors: Impact on salesperson decision-making about ethical issues. *Journal of Business Ethics*, 46(3), 213–234.

Sankaran, S., & Bui, T. (2003). Ethical attitudes among accounting majors: An empirical study. *Journal of American Academy of Business, Cambridge*, 3(1/2), 71–77.

Singhapakdi, A. (1999). Perceived importance of ethics and ethical decisions in marketing. *Journal of Business Research*, 45(1), 89–99.

Singhapakdi, A., Marta, J. K., Rallapalli, K. C., & Rao, C. P. (2000). Toward an understanding of religiousness and marketing ethics: An empirical study. *Journal of Business Ethics*, 27(4), 305–319.

Spear, R., Cornforth, C., & Aiken, M. (2009). The governance challenges of social enterprises: Evidence from a UK empirical study. *Annals of Public and Cooperative Economics*, 80(2), 247–273.

Teasdale, S. (2010a). How can social enterprise address disadvantage? Evidence from an inner city community. *Journal of Nonprofit & Public Sector Marketing*, 22(2), 89–107. doi: 10.1080/10495141003601278.

Teasdale, S. (2010b). Models of social enterprise in the homelessness field. *Social Enterprise Journal*, 6(1), 23–34. doi: 10.1108/17508611011043039.

Testi, E. (2017). Analysing social enterprises and their ecosystem, PhD Thesis PhD in Economics, Curriculum Economia e Gestione dello Sviluppo Locale, University of Florence, Italy.

Van Ryzin, G. G., Grossman, S., DiPadova-Stocks, L., & Bergrud, E. (2009). Portrait of the social entrepreneur: Statistical evidence from a US panel. *Voluntas: International Journal of Voluntary and Nonprofit Organizations*, 20(2), 129–140.

Yitshaki, R., & Kropp, F. (2016). Motivations and opportunity recognition of social entrepreneurs. *Journal of Small Business Management*, 54(2), 546–565.

7 Social capital in social enterprises

Agata Zabłocka, Ryszard Praszkier, Marta Kacprzyk-Murawska, and Ewa Petrushak

Introduction

Social capital has become both important (Trigilia, 2001) and popular in recent years (Portes, 2000). It is seen as essential in business circles (Bosma et al., 2004; DiMauro, 2015; Lock Lee & Guthrie, 2008; Tsai & Ghoshal, 1988) and in the social sector (Praszkier & Nowak, 2012; Putnam, 2000). However, few scholars have actually documented the role of social capital in the social economy (e.g. Borzaga and Sforzi, 2014; Spear and Hulgård, 2006; Kay, 2006). "With respect to social enterprises," Weber and his peers (2013) argue, "little is known about the importance of social capital" (p. 1). We will elaborate on this issue, as social capital is critical for the development of social enterprises.

Scholars have also ignored the conditions for social capital creation. Some studies discuss how social entrepreneurs build social capital (Praszkier et al., 2009; Praszkier & Nowak, 2012; Zabłocka-Bursa & Praszkier, 2012), while others are based on case studies (Flores & Rello, 2003). However, little work has been done on the individual properties that support building social capital. This seems to be an essential issue because understanding some of the personality characteristics required to build social capital could help train social activists. Thus, the key question raised in this chapter involves how to characterize and measure an individual's propensity for building social capital.

The significance of social capital in human, social, and economic development

The positive impact of social capital

Despite the somewhat vague definition of social capital (Lin et al., 2001; Portes, 1998; Yang, 2007), there is consensus that it is important to both individuals (Adler & Kwon, 2002; Brehm & Rahn, 1997; Burt, 1997; 2001; Coleman, 1988; Ellison et al., 2007), groups and organizations, and society at large (Fine, 2001; Woolcock & Narayan, 2000). Moreover, many scholars highlight the significance of social capital as a catalyst for economic growth (Claridge, 2004; Fukuyama 2001; Maskell, 2000; Neace, 1999; Putnam, 1993). In the 1990s, Putnam (1993, 1996) defined social capital as the various features of social organizations, such as trust, norms, and networks, that can improve the efficiency of society by facilitating coordinated actions, thus enabling participants to act together more effectively. Once the century turned, however, he added to this definition (2000) by claiming that social capital refers to connections among individuals and the social networks and norms of reciprocity and trustworthiness that arise from them. In other words, we all have access to social capital through our networks, but the networks are not always equally robust.

Bourdieu (1997) defines social capital as "the aggregate of the actual or potential resources which are linked to possession of a durable network of more or less institutionalized relationships of mutual acquaintance and recognition." Similarly, Coleman's definition of social capital refers to "aspects of social structure to actors, as resources that can be used by the actors to realize their interests" (1990, p. 305). In simpler terms, social capital appears when a person's family, friends, and associates become important assets that can be called upon in a crisis or enjoyed for their own sake (Woolcock & Narayan, 2000). Social capital also makes it easier to achieve certain ends (Coleman, 2000; Putnam & Gross, 2002). For example, it has been shown to reduce turnover rates (Krackhardt & Hanson, 1993) and facilitate entrepreneurship (Chong & Gibbons, 1997) and the formation of start-up companies (Walker et al., 1997). Social capital is an especially critical factor in sustaining bottom-up mechanisms (Woolcock, 1998), while the power of bottom-up change mechanisms is seen as critical for the introduction of social change (McAdam, 1999; Piven, 2008).

There is some consensus that social capital represents not only the institutionalized relationships between people but also the shared values and understandings that enable individuals and teams to trust each other and thus work together. Mutual trust reinforces societal development (Bourdieu, 2003; Coleman, 2000; Fukuyama, 1996). Higher trust yields better societal outcomes, thereby raising mutual trust levels, which in turn positively influences future outcomes (Putnam, 1993). Social capital also produces positive results at the individual level. For example, it empowers people to take risks and explore new opportunities (Brehm & Rahn, 1997; Coleman, 1988) while also influencing career success (Burt, 1992; Gabbay & Zuckerman, 1998; Podolny & Baron, 1997).

One important caveat: we are focusing on social capital among groups and the community at large, rather than the social capital of individuals, which often depends on individual support networks. Nonetheless, support networks will serve as one of the indicators for an individual's penchant for building social capital among groups and communities.

Given the positive impact of social capital, several questions arise. For instance, what factors support its development? What personality characteristics help an individual build his or her own social capital?

Social capital and social enterprises

The European Commission has found that a significant proportion of Europe's economy—otherwise known as the "social economy"—includes a wide variety of structurally divergent organizations, including cooperatives, mutual societies, nonprofit associations, foundations, and social enterprises (Social Economy in the EU). They engage in several different types of commercial activities, provide a wide range of products and services across the European single market, and generate millions of workplaces. Social enterprises, in particular, represent an important and ever-growing part of the social economy. Their main objective is to have a social, societal, or environmental impact on the communities they serve. Social enterprises are also drivers of social innovation.

Unlike for-profit enterprises, the primary objective of social enterprises is to serve their members rather than obtain a return on investment (Social Economy in the EU; Nicholls, 2008). The potential benefits of social enterprises—for example, to regenerate disadvantaged urban areas (Bertotti et al., 2011)—have generated intense interest from scholars and practitioners in the past 10–20 years. Some observers highlight the importance of social economy within different contextualization in order to find synergy with the local production and use of social capital (Bertotti et al., 2011; Evans & Syrett, 2007). This is why social capital is increasingly used in the field of community development and the social economy as a whole (Kay, 2006).

Our analysis of Enabling the Flourishing and Evolution of Social Entrepreneurship for Innovative and Inclusive Societies (EFESEIIS) interviews and case studies found that most social enterprises are based on bonding social capital (which involves creating common goals, culture, and practices within select groups) and bridging social capital (which involves networking with local stakeholders and creating ties with the local community and addressing its critical challenges).

Bridging and bonding social capital: the power of weak ties

Our previous research (Zabłocka-Bursa et al., 2016) shows that the propensity to build social capital is not inherent among individuals—that it depends, above all else, on the perceived strength of their ties with other individuals. For example, some people may establish trusting and cooperative relationships in situations where we perceive the bonds as strong (e.g. with family members or long-term close friends, professional colleagues, and well-known neighbors). However, we're typically slower to trust and cooperate with strangers.

Strong ties are relationships among people who work, live, or spend some quality time together; they engender a tendency for group members to think alike and reduce the diversity of ideas (Porter, 2007). Establishing weak ties requires cognitive flexibility and an ability to function in complex organizations (Granovetter, 1973, 1995; Lin, 2001). Even though strong ties clearly play a crucial role in our lives—particularly in terms of establishing and maintaining the norms and mutual understandings of society—in certain situations weak ties can be quite powerful. In his research on finding employment, Granovetter (1973) claimed that the most effective connections were not close friends, but rather distant acquaintances. This led to the hypothesis that there is strength of weak ties (Barabási, 2003; Granovetter, 1973). Granovetter's work confirmed not only that weak ties resulted in greater job opportunities but also that those who found jobs through strong ties were far more likely to have had a period of unemployment between jobs (Granovetter, 1983, 1995). Weak ties are powerful because they bridge the gap between groups, resulting in the emergence of productive opportunities that may have been unavailable in tightly knit groups (Granovetter, 1973, 1983). They not only provide access to heterogeneous resources but also enhance a person's opportunity for social mobility (Granovetter, 1973, 1995; Lin, 2001).

A dearth of team members with weak ties deprives close-knit groups of information from distant parts of the social system. Consequently, its members are restricted to the provincial views of their friends and family, which may isolated them from new ideas and trends. They may also be poorly integrated into political or other goal-oriented movements (Granovetter, 1973, 1983, 1995). Societies that lack weak ties will tend to ignore avenues of mutual support and become fragmented (Granovetter, 1983). Moreover, effective social leaders do not limit themselves to their immediate social environment; instead, they create and maintain relationships based on weak ties (Praszkier, 2012; Praszkier & Nowak, 2012).

That being said, there has been considerable ambiguity over the definition and operationalization of the weak-ties concept. On the one hand, Granovetter (1973) assessed the strength of any given tie by discussing four indicators: its longevity, its emotional intensity, the intimacy quotient, and the reciprocal services that emerge as a result of this relationship. He conceded that these parameters are mostly intuitive. Indeed, this concept has been based on subjective judgments and, consequently, researchers have created divergent definitions that tend to suit their particular research context (Petróczi et al., 2007).

What helps individuals foster social capital?

Social capital can be an individual asset (Portes, 1998) that consists of social groups or networks that individuals can access and use to obtain further benefits (Yang, 2007). Drawing from this notion, we assumed that three variables determine an individual's ability to foster social capital: trust, cooperation, and sense of support.

Trust

Trust is seen as an essential dimension of social capital. When it exists among neighbors, peers, and group members, trust leads to a high level of solidarity. It is the key driver for undertaking cooperative action (Bourdieu, 2003; Coleman, 2000; Cook et al., 2005; Fukuyama, 1996; Putnam, 1993, Tyler, 2003). Some authors even equate trust with social capital (La Porta et al., 1996). We posit that trusting others plays an essential role in allowing individuals to develop social capital (Praszkier & Nowak, 2012; Zabłocka-Bursa & Praszkier, 2012).

Cooperation

The second pivotal dimension of social capital development is cooperation (Bouma et al., 2008; Knack & Keefer, 1997; Putnam, 1993; da Silva, 2006). It takes mutual commitment and cooperation from all parties to build social capital (Adler & Kwon, 2002). Individuals are more likely to develop a habit of cooperation and act collectively when they are in regular contact with each other (Wasko & Faraj, 2005). Thus, cooperation is often seen as a value in and of itself (Kenworthy, 1997; Maxwell, 2002; Praszkier & Nowak, 2012; Zabłocka-Bursa & Praszkier, 2012). We therefore argue that one's willingness to cooperate is an essential personality trait among individuals who are seeking to develop social capital.

Sense of support

The third component in the development of social capital is Sense of Support. This aspect is strongly related to a feeling of security in one's social relations. Several different kinds of support are significant—be they emotional, informative, instrumental, or spiritual—as is the extent to which these types of support are accessible to an individual (Tardy, 1985). Some scholars have demonstrated that social networks and social contacts deliver positive experiences, strengthen one's feeling of security, and reinforce the perception that one's life is predictable and stable (Knoll & Schwarzer, 2004; Sęk, 2001; Sheridan & Radmacher, 1998). In other words, someone with a strong sense of support is more likely to benefit from previously inaccessible resources. These assets empower the individual to take risks and explore new opportunities (Brehm & Rahn, 1997; Coleman, 1988). The opposite personality type—someone who suffers from "Lone Ranger" syndrome—disregards the need for support from others. This individual is doomed to fail in the long run (Praszkier & Nowak, 2012; Zabłocka-Bursa & Praszkier, 2012) and is less able to develop social capital for others.

Strength of ties as an intuitive concept

In 2012–2013 we used Granovetter's four indicators—longevity, emotional intensity, intimacy quotient, and reciprocal services—to test several questions in five separate pilot studies. However, the reliability of the questions, as measured by their correlation with one another, was insufficient, and the factor analyses produced results that were unclear and difficult to interpret. This strengthened arguments posed by other scholars suggesting that there were some problems with Granovetter's original theoretical framework while also confirming that the best means of estimation is the subject's intuitive perception of the strength of his or her ties.

As a result, we decided to base our assessments on the subjects' individual perceptions. Indeed, our questionnaire asks that the subject answer all of the questions by referring to three different people—a close relation, a fairly close relation, and a distant relation.

EFESEIIS research results

The main focus of our study was to understand how three variables that often determine an individual's ability to foster social capital—Trust, Sense of Support, and Cooperation—are represented in different types of organizations. This knowledge could help us better understand the specific character of social enterprises (in comparison to traditional businesses) and provide information on how social capital evolves or diminishes in organizations over time.

The EFESEIIS project focused on both traditional entrepreneurs and social entrepreneurs in ten European countries. Thirteen participants (7.7%) came from Scotland, 29 (17.2%) from Italy, 10 (5.9%) from Sweden, 22 (13%) from Poland, 11 (6.5%) from England, 10 (5.9%) from Serbia, 26 (15.4%) from Germany, 23 (13.6%) from Austria, 4 (2.4%) from France, and 12 (7.1%) from the Netherlands. Out of 169 participants, 43.2% of the 169 participants were female, and the average age was 43.36 (SD = 11.89).

Four types of organizations were identified: nonprofit (N = 46; 27.2%), socioeconomic (N = 50; 29.6%), for-profit (N = 58; 34.3%), and other (N = 13; 7.7%). Three subcategories were also created based on when the organization was established: old enterprises (established before 2006; N = 69; 40.8%), new generation enterprises (established between 2006 and 2012; N = 62; 36.7%), and newborn enterprises (established after 2012; N = 25; 14.8%).

Trust, sense of support, and cooperation among different types of organizations were analyzed. The average number of contacts was used to measure all three factors.

Trust levels in various types of organizations

The results confirmed the presupposition that the level of trust increases with the closeness of the relationship (Figure 7.1). Indeed, differences in trust levels were significant: [Huynh-Feldt test: $F(1.78, 240.11) = 94.54$, $p < 0.001$, $\eta^2 = 0.41$].

Moreover, it turned out that socioeconomic organizations differed significantly from for-profit organizations because trust levels in the former were significantly higher than in the latter (Figure 7.2): [$F(2, 135) = 5.73$, $p = 0.004$, $\eta^2 = 0.077$].

Remarkably enough, trust levels were higher among older organizations: [$F(2, 135) = 3.14$, $p = 0.046$, $\eta^2 = 0.044$]. However, old enterprises differed

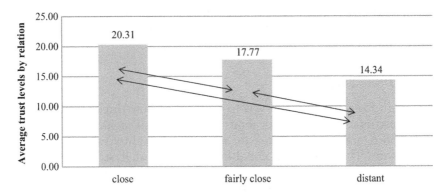

Figure 7.1 Trust levels by relation (average number of contacts).

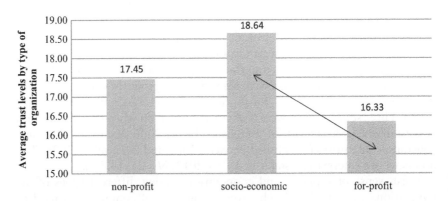

Figure 7.2 Trust levels by type of organization (average number of contacts).

significantly from newborn enterprises (Figure 7.3): (p = 0.042). This confirms that trust among employees is built systematically and evolves over time.

Sense of support levels from social networks in various types of organizations

Sense of support levels tend to increase as the closeness of a relationship increases. The differences that emerged between the three types of relations were significant (Figure 7.4): [Huynh-Feldt test: $F(1.47, 211.93)$ = 72.5, $p < 0.001$, η^2 = 0.349].

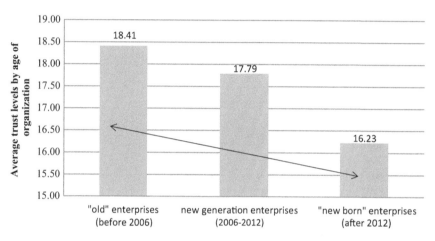

Figure 7.3 Trust levels by age of organization (average number of contacts).

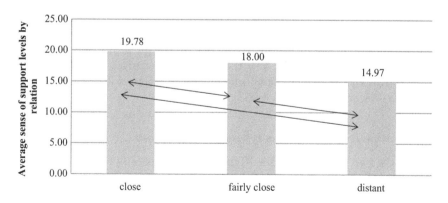

Figure 7.4 Sense of support levels from social networks by relation (average number of contacts).

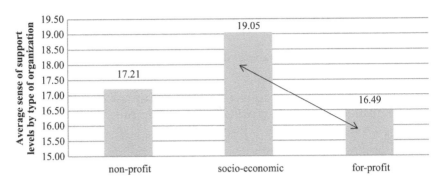

Figure 7.5 Sense of support levels from social networks by type of organization (average number of contacts).

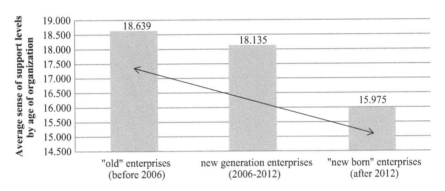

Figure 7.6 Sense of support levels from social networks by age of the organization (average number of contacts).

Additionally, these results suggest that sense of support levels differed according to the type of organization. Indeed, support levels are higher in socioeconomic organizations than they are in for-profit organizations: [$F(2, 135) = 6.05$, $p = 0.003$, $\eta^2 = 0.082$]. Old enterprises also have higher sense of support levels than newborn enterprises (Figures 7.5 and 7.6): [$F(2, 135) = 3.788$, $p = 0.025$, $\eta^2 = 0.053$].

Cooperation levels in various types of organizations

Unlike the two previous factors—Trust and Sense of Support—cooperation levels actually decreased as the closeness of a relation increased (Figure 7.7). In fact, higher levels of cooperation were more often observed among distant relations than they were among both fairly close relations ($p = 0.015$) and close relations ($p = 0.031$): [Huynh-Feldt test: $F(1.59, 214.93) = 6.16$, $p = 0.005$, $\eta^2 = 0.044$].

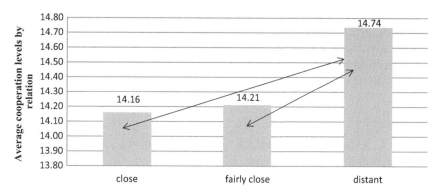

Figure 7.7 Cooperation levels by perceived closeness of relations (average number of contacts).

Due to the small sample size, these results are only an approximation and illustrate potential trends and dependencies; they also reveal the potentials of the questionnaire (see: Zabłocka-Bursa et al., 2016).

Questions for future research

Social capital can be studied in a wide variety of contexts. Future research should attempt to broaden our understanding of how social capital is being built within networks and what effects the personal traits of leaders have on this process. For instance, it might be interesting to determine whether empathy levels can influence the creation of trustworthy and cooperative relationships among less closely connected people while also assessing whether or not leaders with lower empathy levels are more likely to trust people in close-knit circles. Future research should also try to determine whether innovators tend to develop social capital regardless of the strength of their connections while also paying attention to the outsized role closely connected individuals play when social activists try to build social capital.

Moreover, it is also worth exploring the dynamics of organizations that decide to shift away from top-down management strategies in order to emphasize bottom-up initiatives and grassroots participation. It might be interesting, in particular, to determine whether or not team members are prone to distribute social capital to less connected team members. In other words, future work in this area should ask whether these types of structural changes force organizations to adopt new social capital distribution strategies.

European history is full of examples in which economic hardship resulted in greater social solidarity, which, in turn, suggests that the development of social capital among individuals might be dependent not only on personal characteristics but also on larger social forces. For instance, it could be argued that social capital development is stronger during transitional eras of history—during periods of profound social, cultural, economic, and political change. Thus, it might be worth considering whether or not members of disadvantaged communities tend to limit the distribution of social capital to their own close-knit circles and whether, when experiencing a constructive transition, they tend to open up to the outside world and trust groups or individuals to whom they are less closely connected.

References

Adler, P. S., & Kwon, S.-W. (2002). Social capital: Prospects for a new concept. *The Academy of Management Review, 27*(1), 17–40.

Barabási, A. L. (2003). *Linked.* Cambridge, MA: A Plume Book.

Bertotti, M., Harden, A., Renton, A., & Sheridan, K. (2012). The contribution of a social enterprise to the building of social capital in a disadvantaged urban area of London. *Community Development Journal, 47*(2), 168–183.

Brehm, J., & Rahn, W. (1997). Individual-level evidence for the causes and consequences of social capital. *American Journal of Political Science, 41*(3), 999–1023.

Borzaga, C. and Sforzi, J. (2014). Social capital, cooperatives and social enterprises. In: A. Christoforou and J. B. Davis (Eds.), *Social capital and economics; social values, power, and social identity* (pp. 193–214). London: Routledge.

Bosma, N., van Praag, M., Thurik, R., & de Wit, G. (2004), The value of human and social capital investments for the business performance of startups. *Small Business Economics, 23*(3), 227–236.

Bouma, J., Bulte. E., & van Soest, D. (2008). Trust and cooperation: Social capital and community resource management. *Journal of Environmental Economics and Management, 56*(2), 155–166.

Bourdieu, P. (1997). The forms of capital. In A. H. Halsey, H. Lauder, P. Brown, & A. S. Wells (Eds.), *Education: Culture, economy, society* (pp. 46–58). Oxford: Oxford University Press.

Bourdieu, P. (2003). The forms of capital. In A. H. Halsey, H. Lauder, P. Brown, & A. S. Wells (Eds.), *Education: Culture, economy, society* (pp. 46–58). Oxford: Oxford University Press.

Burt, R. S. (1992). *Structural holes: The social structure of competition.* Cambridge, MA: Harvard University Press.

Burt, R. S. (1997). The contingent value of social capital. *Administrative Science Quarterly, 42*(2), 339–365.

Burt, R. S. (2001). Structural holes versus network closure as social capital. In N. Lin, K. S. Cook, & R. S. Burt (Eds.), *Social capital; Theory and research* (pp. 31–56). New York, NY: Aldine de Gruyter.

Chong, L., & Gibbons, P. (1997). Corporate entrepreneurship: The roles of ideology and social capital. *Group and Organization Management, 22*(1), 10–30.

Claridge, T. (2004). *Benefits and importance of social capital.* Retrieved 29 January 2017, from www.socialcapitalresearch.com/literature/theory/benefits.html.

Coleman, J. S. (1988). Social capital in the creation of human capital. *The American Journal of Sociology, 94*, 95–12.

Coleman, J. S. (1990). *The foundations of social theory.* Cambridge, MA: The Belknap Press of Harvard University Press.

Coleman, J. S. (2000). *Foundations of social theory.* Cambridge, MA: Belknap Press.

Cook, K. S., Hardin, R., & Levi, M. (2005). *Cooperation without trust?* New York, NY: Russell Sage Foundation Publication.

da Silva, M. F. (2006). Cooperation, social capital and economic performance. *Revista de Economia Política, 26*(3), 345–363.

DiMauro, V. (2015). *Why building social capital matters in business.* Retrieved 29 January 2017, from www.leadernetworks.com/2015/05/building-social-capital-matters-business.html.

Ellison, N. B., Steinfield, C., & Lampe, C. (2007). The benefits of Facebook "Friends:" Social capital and college students' use of online social network sites. *Journal of Computer-Mediated Communication, 12*(4), 1143–1168.

European Commission's Growth. (2018). *Social economy in the EU.* Retrieved from http://ec.europa.eu/growth/sectors/social-economy_en.

Evans, M., & Syrett, S. (2007). Generating social capital?: The social economy and local economic development. *European Urban and Regional Studies, 14*(1), 55–74.

Fine, B. (2001). *Social capital versus social theory: Political economy and social science at the turn of the millennium.* London: Routledge.

Flores, M., & Rello, F. (2003). Social capital and poverty: Lessons from case studies in Mexico and Central America. *Culture and Agriculture, 25*(1), 1–10.

Fukuyama, F. (1996). *Trust. The social virtues and the creation of prosperity.* New York, NY: A Free Press Paperbacks.

Fukuyama, F. (2001). Social capital, civil society and development. *Third World Quarterly, 22*(1), 7–20.

Gabbay, S. M., & Zuckerman, E. W. (1998). Social capital and opportunity in corporate R and D: The contingent effect of contact density on mobility expectations. *Social Science Research, 27*(2), 189–217.

Granovetter, M. S. (1973). The strength of weak ties. *The American Journal of Sociology, 78*(6), 1360–1380.

Granovetter, M. S. (1983). The strength of weak ties: A network theory revisited. *Sociological Theory, 1*(1), 201–233.

Granovetter, M. S. (1995). *Getting a job: A study of contacts and careers.* Chicago, IL: University of Chicago Press.

Kay, A. (2006). Social capital, the social economy and community development. *Community Development Journal, 41*(2), 160–173.

Kenworthy, L. (1997). Civic engagement, social capital, and economic cooperation. *American Behavioral Scientist, 40*(5), 645–656.

Knack, S., & Keefer, P. (1997). Does social capital have an economic payoff? A cross-country investigation. *The Quarterly Journal of Economics, 112*(4), 1251–1288.

Knoll, N., & Schwarzer R. (2004). Prawdziwych przyjaciół... Wsparcie społeczne, stres, choroba i śmierć. In H. Sęk & R. Cieślak (Eds.), *Wsparcie społeczne, stres i zdrowie* (pp. 29–48). Warszawa: PWN.

Krackhardt, D., & Hanson, J. R. (1993). Informal networks: The company behind the chart. *Harvard Business Review, 71*(4), 104–111.

La Porta, R., Lopez-de-Silanes, F., Shleifer, A., & Vishny, R. W. (1996). *Trust in Large Organizations.* Working paper 5864, National Bureau of Economic Research Cambridge.

Lin, N. (2001). *Social capital: A theory of social structure and action.* Cambridge: Cambridge University Press.

Lin, N, Cook, K., & Burt, R. S. (2001). Preface. In N. Lin, K. Cook, & R. S. Burt (Eds.), *Social capital: Theory and research* (pp. vii–xii). New York, NY: Aldine de Gruyter.

Lock Lee, L., & Guthrie, J. (2008). *The role of corporate social capital in business innovation networks*. Presented to the International Forum on Knowledge Asset Dynamics, 26–27 June 2008, Matera, Italy. Retrieved 29 January 2017, from https://papers.ssrn.com/sol3/papers.cfm?abstract_id=1358752.

Maskell, P. (2000). Social capital, innovation, and competitiveness. In S. Baron, J. Field, & T. Schuller (Eds.), *Social capital; Critical perspective* (pp. 111–123). New York, NY: Oxford University Press.

Maxwell, J. C. (2002). *Teamwork makes the dreamwork*. Nashville, TN: Thomas Nelson.

McAdam, D. (1999). *Political process and the development of black insurgency, 1930–1970*. Chicago, IL: The University Of Chicago Press.

Neace, M. B. (1999). Entrepreneurs in emerging economies: Creating trust, social capital, and civil society. *The ANNALS of the American Academy of Political and Social Science, 565*(1), 148–161.

Nicholls, A. (2008). *Social entrepreneurship: New models of sustainable social change*. New York, NY: Oxford University Press.

Petróczi, A., Nepusz, T., & Bazsó, F. (2007). Measuring tie-strength in virtual social networks. *Connections, 27*(2), 39–52.

Piven, F. F. (2008). Can power from below change the world? *American Sociological Review, 73*(1), 1–14.

Podolny, J. M., & Baron, J. N. (1997). Resources and relationships: Social networks and mobility in the workplace. *American Sociological Review, 62*(5), 673–693.

Porter, J. (2007). *Weak ties and diversity in social networks*. Retrieved 29 January 2017, from http://bokardo.com/archives/weak-ties-and-diversity-in-social-networks.

Portes, A. (1998). Social capital: Its origins and applications in modern sociology. *Annual Review of Sociology, 24*, 1–24.

Portes, A. (2000). Social capital: Its origins and applications in modern sociology. In E. L. Lesser (Ed.), *Knowledge and social capital: Foundations and applications* (pp. 43–67). Boston, MA: Butterworth-Heinemann.

Praszkier, R. (2012). Social entrepreneurs open closed worlds: The transformative influence of weak ties. In A. Nowak, K. Winkowska-Nowak, & D. Bree (Eds.), *Complex human dynamics, from mind to societies* (pp. 111–129). New York, NY: Springer.

Praszkier, R., & Nowak, A. (2012). *Social entrepreneurship: Theory and practice*. New York, NY: Cambridge University Press.

Praszkier, R., Nowak, A., & Zabłocka-Bursa, A. (2009). Social capital built by social entrepreneurs and the specific personality traits that facilitate the process. *Psychologia Społeczna, 4*(1–2), 42–54.

Putnam, R. D. (1993). The prosperous community: Social capital and public life. *The American Prospect, 13*, 35–42.

Putnam, R. D. (1996). Who killed civic America? *Prospect, 6*, 66–72.

Putnam, R. D. (2000). *Bowling alone. The collapse and revival of American community*. New York, NY: Simon and Shuster.

Putnam, R. D., & Gross, K. A. (2002). Introduction. In R. D. Putnam (Ed.), *Democracies in flux* (pp. 3–19). New York, NY: Oxford University Press.

Sęk, H. (2001).*Wprowadzenie do psychologii klinicznej.* Warszawa: Wydawnictwo Naukowe Scholar.

Sheridan, C. L., & Radmacher, S. A. (1998). *Psychologia zdrowia. Wyzwanie dla biomedycznego modelu zdrowia.* Warsaw: Instytut Psychologii Zdrowia PTP.

Spear, R, & Hulgård, L. (2006). Social entrepreneurship and the mobilisation of social capital in European social enterprises. *Research Gate,* doi: 10.4324/9780203946909.

Tardy, C. H. (1985). Social support measurement. *American Journal of Community Psychology, 13*(2), 187–202.

Trigilia, C. (2001). Social capital and local development. *European Journal of Social Theory, 4*(4), 427–442.

Tsai, W., & Ghoshal, S. (1988). Social capital and value creation: The role of intrafirm networks. *The Academy of Management Journal, 41*(4), 464–476.

Tyler, T. R. (2003). Why do people rely on others? Social identity and social aspects of trust. In K. S. Cook (Ed.), *Trust in society* (pp. 285–306). New York, NY: Russell Sage Foundation Publication.

Walker, G., Kogut, B., & Shan, W. (1997). Social capital, structural holes and the formation of an industry network. *Organization Science, 8*(2), 109–125.

Wasko, M. M., & Faraj, S. (2005). Why should I share? Examining social capital and knowledge contribution in electronic networks of practice. *Management Information Systems Quarterly, 29*(1), 35–57.

Weber, C., Wallace, J., & Tuschke, A. (2013). Social capital, social innovation and social impact. *Frontiers of Entrepreneurship Research, 33*(18), 1–15.

Woolcock, M. (1998). Social capital and economic development: Toward a theoretical synthesis and policy framework. *Theory and Society, 27*(2), 151–208.

Woolcock, M., & Narayan, D. (2000). Social capital: Implications for development; theory, research, and policy. *The World Bank Research Observer, 15*(2), 225–249.

Yang, K. (2007). Individual social capital and its measurement in social surveys. *Survey Research Methods, 1*(1), 19–27.

Zabłocka-Bursa, A., & Praszkier, R. (2012). Social change initiated by social entrepreneurs. In A. Nowak, K. Winkowska-Nowak, & D. Bree (Eds.), *Complex human dynamics: From mind to societies* (pp. 153–169). New York, NY: Springer.

Zabłocka-Bursa, A., Praszkier, R, Józwik, E., & Kacprzyk-Murawska, M. (2016). Measuring the propensity for building social capital depending on ties-strength. *Journal of Positive Management, 7*(4), 19–39.

8 The role of stakeholder networks in shaping the development of social enterprise ecosystems

Richard Hazenberg, Meanu Bajwa-Patel, and Toa Giroletti

Introduction

The field of social entrepreneurship and the study of social enterprises have grown rapidly over the last decade, with scholarly interest in the field emerging around the world. Indeed, explorations of social entrepreneurship have identified several different types of social enterprises (see, for example, Defourny & Nyssens, 2008, 2010; Doherty et al., 2009; Galera & Borzaga, 2009; Kerlin, 2006, 2010, 2013), while prior research by Mendell (2010) found that their emergence is often rooted in the various institutional contexts of the countries and/or regions in which they operate. This focus on geographic differences and institutional factors has also been complemented by growing scholarly interest in the various processes and social structures that underpin the emergence of these geographic and institutional differences—especially political, socioeconomic, and cultural factors (Doherty et al., 2009; Hazenberg et al., 2016a, 2016b; Mazzei 2017; Salamon et al., 2003). Most recently, a focus on social structures and the network ties that link different stakeholders in the social enterprise sector has led to the creation of an ecosystem typology based on biological evolutionary theory, which argues that there is a need for greater pluralism in social enterprise ecosystems (Hazenberg et al., 2016b).

This chapter adds to this scholarship by examining the power structures that exist within social enterprise ecosystems, many of which inhibit or support the emergence of pluralism in relation to power and resources. Our decision to adopt a Weberian view of power allows us to explore how actors within ecosystems act "purposefully" and "rationally" to create value for themselves and others while also emphasizing how these actions occur within social structures (i.e. networks) that facilitate the flow of resources to different segments of the ecosystem (i.e. social action) (Weber, 1978). By adopting this focus on power, we argue that social entrepreneurship, like social innovation, is a loaded term that is politically and socially constructed (Nicholls & Murdock, 2012), and that dominant stakeholders use their power to develop narratives that compel actors within social enterprise ecosystems to behave in certain ways

(Dey & Steyaert, 2014). As Montgomery (2016) argues in relation to social innovation, dominant discourse can limit or liberate the social and political capacities of citizens. Therefore, understanding how power structures shape discourse within social enterprise ecosystems and stakeholder networks is crucial in ensuring that sustainable social enterprise ecosystems can emerge.

Theoretical framework

Evolutionary theory and social networks in social enterprise ecosystems

A growing body of literature has emerged recently emphasizing the conceptualization of social enterprise sectors as ecosystems and the importance of "place" in the development of social economies (see, for example, Arthur et al., 2006; During, 2014; Grassl, 2012; Hazenberg et al., 2016a, 2016b; Mazzei, 2017; Roy et al., 2015). The biological evolutionary approach often utilizes the concept of "autopoiesis," which argues that every organism (used as a metaphor here for stakeholders) within an ecosystem is a product of evolution within that system (Maturana & Varela, 1987). Stakeholders are referred to here in the context of stakeholder theory, in which organizations are viewed as being responsible to a wider group of stakeholders—including suppliers, customers, partners, financiers, and wider society—upon which the organization relies to exist (Freeman & Reed, 1983; Freeman, 2010). Stakeholder theory also has resonance when discussing issues of power and social identity, as the power held by actors and institutions is central to how groups coalesce, mobilize, and act in response to hierarchy and political responsibility (Crane & Ruebottom, 2011; Jensen & Sandström, 2011).

Since social enterprise ecosystems are made up of several institutional actors, the identification of stakeholders as key organisms within the ecosystem is pertinent to the evolution of the ecosystem itself. Furthermore, this evolution is a two-way process in which environmental factors and the organism's "internal logics" shape its development (i.e. they behave individually depending upon their interpretation of environmental stimuli) (Van Assche, Beunen, & Duineveld, 2014). These internal logics are shaped by three main factors:

- *genetic*—the historical antecedents passed down through the generations to shape current organizational types within the ecosystem (for instance, shared/similar economic, political, and legal systems);
- *phenotype*—variations that emerge within species due to environmental factors (such as the diversity of existing social enterprise organizational forms);

- *epigenetics*—when the nature of the organism's genetic coding is shaped by environmental factors and/or experiences (the role of political and socioeconomic factors and policy) (During, 2014; During, Van Dam, & Salverda, 2016; Hazenberg et al., 2016b).

These three factors can lead to both divergent and convergent evolution in an ecosystem, a phenomenon that was identified by Hazenberg et al. (2016a) when exploring the evolution of the Scottish and English social enterprise ecosystems (see Figure 8.1).

While the use of biological evolutionary theory provides a useful metaphor for understanding the emergence and development of social enterprise ecosystems, it does not account for the social interactions that are crucial to any understanding of human socioeconomic systems (although it can be argued that the "social" experience of stakeholders is an epigenetic factor). Communication in human ecosystems often shapes how people interpret and react to their environment (Luhmann, 1989). Therefore, the socially embedded nature of economic systems (Granovetter, 1985) also needs to be accounted for when seeking to understand the development of social enterprise ecosystems, a new sub-species of enterprises that is based upon economic *and* social environmental factors (During, Van Dam, & Salverda, 2016). Indeed, the importance of "embeddedness" and stakeholder network analysis in social enterprise and social innovation research has already been identified as requiring further study (Shaw & Bruin, 2013).

Granovetter's (1985) work on "embeddedness" is crucial in understanding how social networks, the relations between stakeholders, and hence power can mediate behavior within an ecosystem and create dominant narratives. Social network theory posits that the position of stakeholders (individual actors and organizations) within ecosystems both enables and inhibits the pursuit of their goals (Brass, 1984; Mehra, Kilduff, & Brass, 2001; Qureshi, Kistruck, & Bhatt, 2016), as it influences the flow of resources (economic as well as other forms of capital) between them (Jack, 2005; Uzzi, 1996). The growth of businesses and social enterprise does not occur in a vacuum, but is of course subject to socioeconomic and political factors (Zafeiropoulou & Koufopoulos, 2013). The extent to which these socioeconomic and political factors affect social networks—and hence relations between stakeholders in ecosystems—often determines the type of ecosystem that emerges, the phenotypes that exist within them, and the power structures that actively shape the environment. Indeed, the role of power within an ecosystem is fundamental to its development. In the same way that a dominant species can shape its environment both positively and negatively—we need look no further than ourselves here—or that a dominant individual within a group can coerce/persuade others to their own goals, so can powerful individuals/organizations/groups have a significant impact on a social enterprise ecosystem.

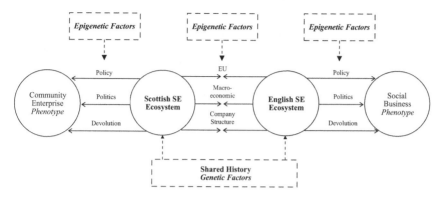

Figure 8.1. Comparative development of the Scottish and English ecosystems. Taken from Hazenberg et al. (2016a).

Power in social enterprise ecosystems

Power and the ability to shape networks and resource flows are a fundamental element of this process, as stakeholders with power can shape narratives and defend or challenge dominant discourses (Weber, 1978). Furthermore, it could be argued that power is one of the most important factors in the evolution of social enterprise ecosystems as it can act as a genetic factor and an epigenetic factor, and actively shape the emergence of phenotypes through the control of resource flows (i.e. policy and funding).[1] If we accept that this is the case (see Dey & Steyaert, 2014; Dey & Teasdale, 2016; Nicholls, 2010), or at least that power is one of the more dominant factors in shaping discourse, then an exploration of pluralism in social enterprise ecosystems by analyzing concentrations of power is fundamental to understanding how sustainable and resilient ecosystems can be produced.

A Weberian view of the role of power in social networks argues that dominant stakeholders can control the flow of resources in order to shape social action to their own ends (Weber, 1978). Weber also examines the role of power and class, identifying that class distinctions are, to a degree, aligned with access to power and resources. Indeed, Weberian ideas of power and class are particularly pertinent to the current study due to the emergence of social enterprises in disadvantaged communities, many of whom traditionally lack access to power and resources, as many of these organizations (particularly at the smaller more localized end of the sector) lack the social networks and power required to leverage in resources. In ecosystems where relatively high levels of power and resources are concentrated among a small number of stakeholders, large sections of the ecosystem can be left exposed to the decisions made by a select group of actors, a process that Puumalainen et al. (2015) refer to as "high power distance." These actors can therefore wield disproportionate influence on the development of an ecosystem and drive paradigmatic shifts within it (Hazenberg et al., 2016b; Nicholls, 2010). This is a process that Montgomery (2016) identifies in relation to neoliberal manipulation of the concept of social innovation, and the way that neoliberal actors have used the language of social innovation (and social entrepreneurship) to shape discourse around public policy (see, for example, Have & Rubalcaba, 2016).

This ability to compel and/or influence others to think and act in certain ways (Dey & Steyaert, 2014) reinforces Weber's (1978) focus on the use of power and social structures to shape social action. While this can have positive ramifications for an ecosystem, it can also lead to reduced resistance to dominant discourses (Jones et al., 2015) and inhibit innovation, as stakeholders are less likely to challenge the social equilibrium (Dey & Steyaert, 2014; Zahra et al., 2009). Thus the role of power in controlling discourse, resource-flow, and potentially reducing pluralism in social enterprise ecosystems acts as the theoretical focus of this chapter and the research that underpins it. We argue that sustainable and resilient social enterprise ecosystems can only be achieved by creating low power distance (Puumalainen et al., 2015) and increasing pluralism.

Methodology

The findings reported in this chapter are the product of a mixed-methods research methodology, utilizing focus groups, semi-structured interviews, and stakeholder network mapping. We sought to identify the conditions under which social entrepreneurship and social innovation emerged across Europe, map the stakeholder networks that existed within social enterprise ecosystems, and understand the relative power dynamics at play in each ecosystem. The data-gathering process was cut into three phases. The first phase involved two city-level focus groups with local stakeholders—one that was targeted at social entrepreneurs and another that targeted other stakeholders (e.g. representatives from local government, policy-makers, and members of social enterprise support organizations) in each EFESEIIS participant country.[2] A total of 20 focus groups were held involving 141 participants.

The second stage involved semi-structured interviews of national stakeholders that were identified through the local focus groups (the interview questions were based upon the data that emerged in the focus groups). A total of 117 interviews were conducted, which meant that a total of 258 social enterprise stakeholders took part in our research. The data from the first two phases was then used to produce a stakeholder map for each country's ecosystem, which was then compared and contrasted with other countries in the study by the research leads (the EFESEIIS English team) in order to explore differences and commonalities. This analysis led to the creation of the social enterprise ecosystem typology discussed later in this chapter.

Our data analysis strategies featured a Straussian approach to grounded theory (Hekkala, 2007). The researchers have a general idea of where to begin, force the theory through structured questions, and rigorously code the data in order to reveal theory through structured analysis (Halewah, Fidler, & McRobb, 2008). The Constant Comparative Method (CCM) was used to analyze the data (Glaser & Strauss, 1967; Lincoln & Guba, 1985). This approach has been successfully applied in previous studies of social venture creation and social enterprises (see Haugh, 2007; Hazenberg, 2017).

Seven main themes emerged from our research: procurement policies/regulation for social innovation; financial activities for ecosystem growth; inclusive labor market practices; collaborative stakeholder systems; training and education in support of ecosystem growth; impact and dissemination; and system drivers. All of these themes will be discussed in relation to two main areas of interest: the development of a stakeholder typology and pluralism in social enterprise ecosystems. Our data analysis methods and the development of the stakeholder typology discussed later were originally enunciated in Hazenberg et al. (2016b, 2016c).

Developing a stakeholder typology

Our data analysis led to the creation of a typology for social enterprise ecosystems that included four specific types: Statist-macro, Statist-micro, Private-macro, and Private-micro (see Figure 8.2 for an overview of each typology). These types of ecosystems emerge based upon the dominant stakeholder types present in an ecosystem. For example, a Statist-macro ecosystem will feature a concentration of power among national and transnational public sector organizations. Conversely, a Private-micro ecosystem will have its discourse shaped by local, private-sector stakeholders. This is not to say that other stakeholder types do not exist within an ecosystem; rather, we propose a generalized ecosystem typology that can be applied to different countries and/or regions depending upon the stakeholders that exist within them, the relational and structural links between these actors, and the power held by individual stakeholder groups. For each ecosystem type outlined later, the relevant countries engaged in the EFESEIIS project are listed next to the type that best aligns with their current situation. Our research also identified a "pluralistic zone," in which it is argued the ecosystem is balanced with low power distance and diffused concentrations of power.

Statist-macro ecosystems (Albania, Austria, France, Poland, and Serbia)

Statist-macro ecosystems are typified by the predominance of state institutions in delivering support to social enterprise ecosystems (through funding, policy and legal/regulatory mechanisms) that emerge at the national and supra-national levels (European Union). Supra-national support is often received from international NGOs such as Ashoka, and there is a distinct lack of localism in relation to developing micro- and meso-level support for the social economy. Indeed, stakeholders in Poland bemoaned the lack of collaboration between local government and social enterprises, despite the obvious benefits to both stakeholder groups and a general alignment in values. This lack of localism and bottom-up social innovation does result in more homogenous support mechanisms across the ecosystem, but it also creates high power distance between stakeholders (Puumalainen et al., 2015). As one participant noted,

> The money is inefficiently spent on social problems. While money is invested in the right projects, the way this is done is old-fashioned. The beneficiary group is seen as an object of support and not as subject/ actors of change.
>
> (SE Practitioner, Austria)

In addition, the homogeneity of the support mechanism creates a lack of diversity in the "gene pool" of ecosystem actors (During, Van Dam, & Salverda,2016) that can damage the sustainability and ability of the ecosystem to resist external exogenous shocks. This leads to the emergence of specific organizational forms—phenotypes—that are the result of public policy support and are therefore acutely vulnerable to changes in public policy (Hazenberg et al., 2016a). This lack of diversity leaves stakeholders subject to the whims of those wielding power within the ecosystem, and further encourages dominant stakeholders to use their power to shape social action in line with their own goals (Weber, 1978), ultimately reducing bottom-up social innovation (Have & Rubalcaba, 2016). This demonstrates the ability of stakeholder (social) networks within ecosystems to enable and/or inhibit the actions of others and guide how they interpret their environment (Luhmann, 1989; Mehra, Kilduff, & Brass, 2001; Qureshi, Kistruck, & Bhatt, 2016). This allows certain stakeholders to be bypassed in Statist-macro ecosystems, as was recognized in Albania:

> Local government would be most appropriate to engage; of course it hasn't been engaged so far. A form would be providing public facilities with economic prices for social enterprises.
>
> (International NGO, Albania)

Statist-micro ecosystems (Scotland and Sweden)

Statist-micro ecosystems, while still utilizing public sector bodies to deliver support to social enterprise ecosystems, are typified by a greater focus on localism through local state institutions, even though supra-national financial support is often present (e.g. the European Social Fund and European Regional Development Fund). National policy and funding programs are limited, which leads to the emergence of heterogeneous local social enterprise ecosystems. This creates a more fragmentary landscape at the national level, as some local authorities/municipalities are more supportive of the social economy than others. This was identified by a Swedish stakeholder:

> A significant feature of the Swedish SE sector is that it is built around the work of local authorities, not national institutions. This has to do with the fact that many social entrepreneurs address local problems. Inevitably, the municipalities become their ally. The dependency is obviously mutual, but the fact remains that social enterprises always evolve on local basis. Thus, to enhance the development of the SE sector we need a better collaboration between the government and the municipalities.
>
> (Association of Local Authorities
> and Regions, Sweden)

The issue of power is central here, as it creates an ecosystem with both high and low power distances (Puumalainen et al., 2015), depending on levels of support from local authorities. This type of ecosystem leads to a greater diversification of the gene pool of social enterprises (During, Van Dam, & Salverda, 2016), albeit one that is skewed towards "community businesses" (Hazenberg et al., 2016a, 2016b). Among local authorities in Statist-micro ecosystems—at least those local authorities that are supportive of the social economy—greater emphasis is placed on the empowerment of communities and creating low power distance while still acknowledging that convincing stakeholders to relinquish power is difficult. This is difficult because stakeholders are effectively being asked to surrender (or at least reduce) their ability to shape social actions (Weber, 1978), even if the surrender of power can lead to increases in bottom-up social innovation (Have & Rubalcaba, 2016), greater independence (Dey & Steyaert, 2014), and increased resistance to the emergence of dominant discourses (Jones et al., 2015), such as neo-liberal narratives on social innovation/entrepreneurship (Montgomery, 2016). Policy-makers in Scotland recognized this when talking about their own experiences:

> We've got ALEOs in the Council - Arm's Length External Organizations - so the likes of Jobs & Business Glasgow and Community Safety Glasgow, as well as Glasgow Life. They've all got a role to play in this. Part of this is about relinquishing power and that's a very difficult thing to persuade people to do. In fact, it's the hardest thing.
>
> (Local Authority, Scotland)

Private-macro ecosystems (England and Germany)

Private-macro ecosystems are epitomized by a dichotomy between limited state funding at the national level for social enterprise ecosystems, but significant levels of policy support and/or the creation of legal/regulatory frameworks. National governments tend to emphasize the marketization of the third sector in this type of ecosystem, an area that has received considerable focus in England (see, for instance, McKay et al., 2015). Marketization is a process in which the state develops policy mechanisms that are designed to encourage the growth of the social economy through the support of the private sector (i.e. social investors) and the public sector (competitive procurement processes). This often means that larger social enterprises are given preference over smaller, more localized organizations:

> I think they [local authorities] prioritize getting the bigger companies up and running and I think a conversation about policy and supporting smaller SEs might be helpful.
>
> (Social Entrepreneur, England)

While grant funding for the social economy comes mainly from national NGOS and supranational bodies such as the European Union, focus is often placed on homogenizing the third sector around the theme of marketization/sustainability. In Germany, for instance, research has shown that personal networks amongst stakeholders can inhibit or enable the winning of procurement contracts, again demonstrating the role of social interactions and stakeholder networks in shaping power (Luhmann, 1989; Mehra, Kilduff, & Brass, 2001; Qureshi, Kistruck, & Bhatt, 2016) and consolidating power (Weber, 1978).

> In a nutshell, in a relatively well functioning and structured country like Germany, we have an unbelievable dependency on persons [in procurement processes.]
>
> (Social Entrepreneur, Germany)

This ecosystem type embodies the role of centralized state power—albeit one that seeks to homogenize the ecosystem through market mechanisms—and, like its Statist-macro counterpart, is characterized by high power distance (Puumalainen et al., 2015). The development of the social investment market in England provides a good example of this Weberian use of power by stakeholders (in this case policy-makers) to drive social action (see, for example, Hazenberg, 2017; Hazenberg & Denny, In Press). While market forces can lead to some diversification in the "gene pool" of social enterprises (During, Van Dam, & Salverda, 2016), the homogenizing role of national policies and supra-national funding mechanisms often undermines this process. Furthermore, these factors also reduce bottom-up innovation and prevent social enterprises from acting in an innovative manner (Dey & Steyaert, 2014; Have & Rubalcaba, 2016). This, in turn, leaves social enterprises powerless to challenge the status quo or pushes them towards challenging dominant narratives by engaging in "tactical mimicry" (Dey & Teasdale, 2016; Zahra et al., 2009). Private-macro ecosystems represent what Montgomery (2016) refers to as the "technocratic paradigm of social innovation," which is an important feature of neoliberalism. Therefore, this ecosystem type demonstrates the ability of powerful actors across all sectors to drive social action and shape discourse based on their own dominant narratives (Weber, 1978).

> I think we suffer generally from a confused message from national government on these issues...Now government talks about localism and big society, there is nothing put on the table in terms of initial feasibility funding for people to take advantage of...It is about how things are addressed at local level.
>
> (SE stakeholder, England)

Private-micro ecosystems (Italy and the Netherlands)

The Private-micro type, like its macro counterpart, is exemplified by a lack of state funding and a focus on marketization. However, this focus on market forces in shaping social enterprise ecosystems is not driven by centralized state policy, but rather by disparate third- and private-sector organizations operating at the local level. These organizations include associations, cooperatives, regional funding bodies, and NGOs. Depending upon the political approaches of local authorities and local procurement strategies, formal links are sometimes present between local social enterprises and government, oftentimes through service delivery contracts. This ecosystem type has emerged as a localized response to perceptions that the traditional welfare state is dysfunctional, and that the private sector is incapable of filling gaps in provision. This, in turn, leads to the creation of networks between third-sector organizations and ecosystems that contain low power distance (Puumalainen et al., 2015) and diffuse actors who use the social networks to shape action (Mehra, Kilduff, & Brass, 2001; Qureshi, Kistruck, & Bhatt, 2016).

> The welfare state model is definitely dead. The redistributive model and thus the public services cannot answer to the social needs. Hence, new enterprises emerge to cope with the rising demand. Nevertheless, the new contribution from the social sector cannot be reduced only as an answer to the shortage of public funding. I consider the value of social enterprise as a model that differs from the State intervention...The SEs'

contribution rises from two premises: i) there are unmet needs; ii) [there] exists a different answer in providing supply: the demand should be personalized rather than standardized.

(SE Support Organisation, Italy)

Indeed, a large number of respondents from the Netherlands identified the importance of personal networks (informal and formal) in shaping social entrepreneurial success, over and above state bodies or public policy. This leads to a more diversified and heterogeneous ecosystem in which power is not centralized, although pockets of power invariably exist through stakeholders, such as regional associations and funders. As a result, bottom-up social innovation that challenges existing paradigms is more prevalent in these types of ecosystems (Dey & Steyaert, 2014; Have & Rubalcaba, 2016; Zahra et al., 2009). The ability of smaller social enterprise actors/ stakeholders to shape local ecosystem conditions is, from a Weberian perspective, easier to achieve, as power is more dispersed and individual horizons for social action are broader. This also leads to the emergence of more democratic organizations within the ecosystem and an ecosystem that is more aligned to what Montgomery (2016) terms the "Democratic Paradigm of Social Innovation."

> Europe is far away from here in practice...I do connect to the national government, but in a minimum way. My 'reality' is mostly here. When talking about an enabling environment, I experience other governmental organizations mostly abstractly, in a way that I do have to reckon with them, but I do not have a relationship with them...But I do have a lot of relations with people and companies here in the area. That is my enabling environment.
>
> (Academic, Netherlands)

Overall social enterprise ecosystem typology

The four ecosystem types outlined earlier form an overall typology of social enterprise ecosystems that is delineated by two axes: localism versus national/supranational forces, and the involvement of private, public, and third sectors in the ecosystem. These four ecosystem types have emerged as a result of each region's historical/cultural context (genetic), environmental factors in the socioeconomic and political spheres (epigenetic), and the social and stakeholder networks that exist within each ecosystem (During, Van Dam, & Salverda, 2016; Hazenberg et al., 2016a, 2016b; Luhmann, 1989). This emphasizes the importance of "place" in the emergence of social enterprise ecosystems (Mazzei, 2017), as well as social and stakeholder networks (Mehra, Kilduff, & Brass, 2001; Qureshi, Kistruck, & Bhatt, 2016). However, it is important to stress that the identification of these four ecosystem types in each of the 11 countries is intended to provide a broad template for identifying social enterprise ecosystems, and that the use of

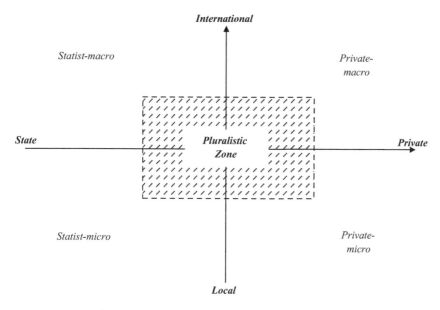

Figure 8.2. Social enterprise ecosystem typologies. Taken from Hazenberg et al. (2016b).

biological evolutionary theory is largely metaphorical in nature (Hazenberg et al., 2016a, 2016b). Indeed, the boundaries between different ecosystem types are fluid, as ecosystems constantly shift in terms of their make-up and distinctive features. Nevertheless, this typology acts as a model for policy-makers and other stakeholders who support the social economy, allowing them to identify the types of support that might work best in a specific regional context. It also allows us to conceptualize a "pluralistic zone" for ecosystems that embody multiple characteristics, and where diverse stakeholder networks/relationships exist alongside low power distance and multiple narratives to enable flourishing, sustainable, and robust social enterprise ecosystems (Hazenberg et al., 2016b). This conceptual typology is illustrated in Figure 8.2. The pluralism concept and its relation to Weberian power dynamics will be explored in greater depth in the next section.

Pluralism in social enterprise ecosystems

The typology presented earlier seeks to provide a template for understanding the types of social enterprise ecosystems that can emerge in geographic regions across Europe, and how their "embedded" nature shapes their emergence and ongoing development (Granovetter, 1985). Their "embeddedness" is characterized by the stakeholder and social networks that exist within the ecosystem, particularly the various actors that use these networks to access resources and interpret/shape their environment (Jack, 2005; Luhmann, 1989; Uzzi, 1996). This process also relates to stakeholder theory, as the manner in which ecosystem stakeholders respond to environmental factors and integrate into social networks is often shaped by power, hierarchy, and identity (Crane & Ruebottom, 2011; Jensen & Sandström, 2011). Indeed, stakeholders can use these networks—and their positions within them—to access or wield power while also using this power to influence discourse in the environment, control resource flows, and enable/inhibit the social actions of others while pursuing their own goals (Weber, 1978). Using a Weberian view of power as a theoretical lens to understand social networks within the social economy enables academics (and other stakeholders) to better understand how to support the development of robust and sustainable social enterprise ecosystems. As noted earlier, ecosystems that are characterized by high power distance (Puumalainen et al., 2015)—where high levels of power are concentrated in the hands of relatively few stakeholders—tend to produce lower levels of social innovation (Have & Rubalcaba, 2016) and encourage the emergence of dominant narratives that distort reality and conceal truth (Dey & Steyaert, 2014).

Greater network pluralism in social enterprise ecosystems should therefore be the goal of all social enterprise stakeholders who wish to see the development of robust and flourishing social economies around the world. Greater pluralism through diversified income streams, cultural relativism, informed policy, heterogeneous stakeholder groupings, and cross-sector trade (involving the private, public, and third sectors) makes social enterprise ecosystems more resistant to exogenous shocks and improves the ability of social enterprises to compete for survival (During, Van Dam, & Salverda, 2016; Hazenberg et al., 2016b). This is because pluralism increases the heterogeneity of organizational types (the genetic biodiversity of the ecosystem) and facilitates increased communication between stakeholders, thereby encouraging them to continually reassess their environment, challenge dominant narratives, enhance trust and collaboration, and increase innovation (Dey & Steyaert, 2014; During, Van Dam, & Salverda, 2016; Have & Rubalcaba, 2016; Jones et al., 2015; Luhmann, 1989; Qureshi, Kistruck & Bhatt, 2016; Zafeiropoulou & Koufopoulos, 2013). This creates low power distance within social enterprise ecosystems (Puumalainen et al., 2015) and limits the ability of certain actors to drive paradigmatic shifts (Hazenberg et al., 2016b; Nicholls, 2010). Increasing network pluralism is therefore fundamental to the development of sustainable ecosystems and empowering socially disadvantaged people.

Summary and implications

This chapter has sought to demonstrate how biological evolutionary theory, social network theory, and Weberian conceptions of power can inform our understanding of social enterprise ecosystems in relation to stakeholder networks and relationships, and how power can shape these networks and ecosystem development. Indeed, power within networks is crucial to the emergence of dominant narratives and discourses that shape how actors within the ecosystem perceive their environment and engage in social action. This, in turn, has powerful effects on the types of organizations that emerge, the policy frameworks that are developed, and the overall sustainability of the ecosystem itself.

We argue that the negative effects of power can best be countered through greater network pluralism within social enterprise ecosystems, which will reduce power distance and increase social innovation. By developing a fluid typology of social enterprise ecosystems across Europe, our research encourages stakeholders to increase pluralism in their own ecosystems and improve the sustainability of the social economy more generally. The findings outlined in this chapter (and more broadly in relation to stakeholder networks in the EFESEIIS project as a whole) also allow stakeholders to identify the most suitable support mechanisms in their locality. Further research that explores this typology outside of Europe would be beneficial, as would ongoing analysis of the 11 countries involved in this research, with special emphasis on their trajectories—their success in increasing pluralism.

Notes

1 This chapter avoids developing a hierarchy of factors for the development of social enterprises, as this over-simplifies other factors at play, including individual agency and responsibility.
2 EFESEIIS supports individuals, institutions, and governments seeking to develop the social economy by improving knowledge on social entrepreneurship. The 11 countries include Albania, Austria, England, France, Germany, Italy, Netherlands, Poland, Scotland, Serbia, and Sweden. For more information about the project, see Chapter 2.

References

Brass, D. J. (1984). Being in the right place: A structural analysis of individual influence in an organization. *Administrative Science Quarterly*, 29, 518–539.

Crane, A., & Ruebottom, T. (2011). Stakeholder theory and social identity: Rethinking stakeholder identification. *Journal of Business Ethics*, 101(1), 77–87.

Defourny, J., & Nyssens, M. (2008). Social enterprise in Europe: Recent trends and developments. *Social Enterprise Journal*, 4(3), 202–228.

Defourny, J., & Nyssens, M. (2010). Conceptions of social enterprise and social entrepreneurship in Europe and the United States: Convergences and divergences. *Journal of Social Entrepreneurship*, 1(1), 32–53.

Dey, P., & Steyaert, C. (2014). Rethinking the space of ethics in social entrepreneurship: Power, subjectivity and practices of freedom. *Journal of Business Ethics*, 133, 627–641.

Dey, P., & Teasdale, S. (2016). The tactical mimicry of social enterprise strategies: Acting 'as if' in the everyday life of third sector organisations. *Organization*, 23(4), 485–504.

Doherty, B., Foster, G., Mason, C., Meehan, J., Meehan, K., Rotheroe, N., & Royce, M. (2009). *Management for social enterprise.* London: Sage Publications.

During, R. (2014). *The evolutionary perspective on social enterprise.* EFESEIIS FP7 Draft Paper, July 2014.

During, R., Van Dam, R., & Salverda, I. (2016). *Using evolutionary theory for pluralism in social policies.* Paper presented at the Social Policy Association Conference – July 4th–6th 2016, Belfast, Northern Ireland.

Freeman, R. E. (2010). *Strategic management: A stakeholder approach.* Cambridge: Cambridge University Press.

Freeman, R. E., & Reed, D. L. (1983). Stockholders and stakeholders: A new perspective on corporate governance. *California Management Review, 25*(3), 88–106.

Galera, G., & Borzaga, C. (2009). Social enterprise: An international overview of its conceptual evolution and legal implementation. *Social Enterprise Journal, 5*(3), 210–228.

Glaser, B. G., & Strauss, A. L. (1967). *The discovery of grounded theory.* Chicago, IL: Aldine.

Granovetter, M. (1985). Economic action and social structure: The problem of embeddedness. *American Journal of Sociology, 91,* 481–510.

Grassl, W. (2012). Business models of social enterprise: A design approach to hybridity. *ACRN Journal of Social Entrepreneurship Perspectives, 1*(1), 37–60.

Halewah, M., Fidler, C., & McRobb, S. (2008). *Integrating the grounded theory method and case-study research methodology within IS research: A possible 'road map'.* Paper presented at the International Conference on Information Systems, ICIS Conference Proceedings Paper 165.

Haugh, H. (2007). Community-led social venture creation. *Entrepreneurship, Theory & Practice, 31*(2), 161–182.

Have, R. P., & Rubalcaba, L. (2016). Social innovation research: An emerging area of innovation studies. *Research Policy, 45,* 1923–1935.

Hazenberg, R. (2017). *Investment readiness and sustainability: Social investment as a third sector policy panacea?* Paper presented at the 21st IRSPM Conference – April 19th–21st 2017, Budapest, Hungary.

Hazenberg, R., Bajwa-Patel, M., Roy, M. J., Mazzei, M., & Baglioni, S. (2016a). A comparative overview of social enterprise 'Ecosystems' in Scotland and England: An evolutionary perspective. *International Review of Sociology, 26*(2), 205–222.

Hazenberg, R., Bajwa-Patel, M., Roy, M. J., Mazzei, M., & Baglioni, S. (2016b). The role of institutional and stakeholder networks in shaping social enterprise ecosystems in Europe. *Social Enterprise Journal, 12*(3), 302–321.

Hazenberg, R., Bajwa-Patel, M., Qureshi, S., & Field, M. (2016c). *Stakeholder networks within social enterprise ecosystems across Europe.* EFESEIIS Work Package 4 Report, August 2016.

Hazenberg, R., & Denny, S. (In Press). Critiquing the social investment market in England: Marketisation before sustainability. In P. Palmer & M. Salway (Eds.), *Social investment around the world.* Gower Book Series.

Hekkala, R. (2007). *Grounded theory – The two faces of the methodology and their manifestation in IS research.* Proceedings of the 30th Information Systems Research Seminar in Scandinavia IRIS, Scandinavia.

Jack, S. L. (2005). The role, use and activation of strong and weak network ties: A qualitative analysis. *Journal of Management Studies, 42,* 1233–1259.

Jensen T., & Sandström, J. (2011), Stakeholder theory and globalization: The challenges of power and responsibility, *Organization Studies*, *32*(4), 473–488.

Jones, R., Betta, M., Latham, J., & Gross, D. (2009). Female social entrepreneurship as a discursive struggle. *AGSE*, 871–885.

Kerlin, J. A. (2006). Social enterprise in the United States and Europe: Understanding and learning from the differences. *Voluntas*, *17*(3), 246–262.

Kerlin, J. A. (2010). A comparative analysis of the global emergence of social enterprise. *Voluntas*, *21*, 162–179.

Kerlin, J. A. (2013). Defining social enterprise across different contexts: A conceptual framework based on institutional factors. *Nonprofit and Voluntary Sector Quarterly*, *42*(1), 84–108.

Lincoln, Y., & Guba, E. (1985). *Naturalistic inquiry*. Beverly Hills, CA: Sage.

Luhmann, N. (1989). *Ecological communication*. Chicago, IL: University of Chicago Press.

Maturana, H., & Varela, F. (1987). *The tree of knowledge: The biological roots of human understanding*. Boston, MA: Shambhala Publications.

Mazzei, M. (2017). Understanding difference: The importance of 'place' in the shaping of local social economies. *Voluntas*, *28*(6), 2763–2784.

McKay, S., Moro, D., Teasdale, S., & Clifford, D. (2015). The marketisation of charities in England and Wales. *Voluntas*, *26*(1), 336–354.

Mehra, A., Kilduff, M., & Brass, D. J. (2001). The social networks of high and low self-monitors: Implications for workplace performance. *Administrative Science Quarterly*, *46*, 121–146.

Mendell, M. (2010). Reflections on the evolving landscape of social enterprise in North America. *Policy and Society*, *29*(3), 243–256.

Montgomery, T. (2016). Are social innovation paradigms incommensurable? *Voluntas*, *27*, 1979–2000.

Nicholls, A. (2010). The legitimacy of social entrepreneurship: Reflexive isomorphism in a pre-paradigmatic field. *Entrepreneurship, Theory and Practice*, *34*(4), 611–633.

Nicholls, A., & Murdock, A. (2012). The nature of social innovation. In A. Nicholls & A. Murdock (Eds.), *Social innovation: Blurring boundaries to reconfigure markets* (pp. 1–30). Basingstoke and New York: Palgrave Macmillan.

Phillips, W., Lee, H., Ghobadian, A., O'Regan, N., & James, P. (2015). Social innovation and social entrepreneurship: A systematic review. *Group and Organisation Management*, *40*(3), 428–461.

Puumalainen, K., Sjögrén, H., Syrjä, P., & Barraket, J. (2015). Comparing social entrepreneurship across nations: An explanatory study of institutional effects. *Canadian Journal of Administrative Sciences*, *32*, 276–287.

Qureshi, I., Kistruck, G. M., & Bhatt, B. (2016). The enabling and constraining effects of social ties in the process of institutional entrepreneurship. *Organization Studies*, *37*(3), 425–447.

Roy, M. J., McHugh, N., Huckfield, L., Kay, A., & Donaldson, C. (2015). The most supportive environment in the world'? Tracing the development of an institutional 'Ecosystem' for social enterprise. *Voluntas*, *26*(3), 777–800.

Salamon, L. M., Sokolowski, S. W., & List, R. (2003). *Global civil society: An overview*. The John Hopkins Comparative Nonprofit Sector Project. Retrieved from http://ccss.jhu.edu/wp-content/uploads/downloads/2011/09/Book_GCSOverview_2003.pdf.

Shaw, E., & Bruin, A. (2013). Reconsidering capitalism: The promise of social innovation and social entrepreneurship. *International Small Business Journal, 31*(7), 737–746.

Uzzi, B. (1996). The sources and consequences of embeddedness for the economic performance of organizations: The network effect. *American Sociological Review, 61,* 674–698.

Van Assche, K., Beunen, R., & Duineveld, M. (2014). *Evolutionary governance theory: An introduction.* Wageningen: Springer.

Weber, M. (1978). *Economy and society: An outline of interpretative sociology.* Berkeley, CA: California University Press.

Zafeiropoulou, F. A., & Koufopoulos, D. N. (2013). The influence of relational embeddedness on the formation and performance of social franchising. *Journal of Marketing Channels, 20*(1–2), 73–98.

Zahra, S. A., Gedajlovicb, E., Neubaumc, D. O. & Shulmand, J. M. (2009). A typology of social entrepreneurs: Motives, search processes and ethical challenges. *Journal of Business Venturing, 24*(5), 519–532.

9 Understanding the innovative behavior of social enterprises

Ana Aleksić Mirić, Marina Petrović, and Zorica Aničić

Introduction

Social enterprises are currently developing in an environment in which balancing an organization's social impact and generating sustainable sources of economic survival is imperative. This simultaneous search for more effective solutions that meet emerging social needs, together with the exploration of new ways to operate more efficiently, is becoming a dominant feature of social enterprises, which, in turn, differentiates them from other types of entrepreneurial initiatives.

Social entrepreneurs can be defined as individuals who are able to bring about social innovation in various fields. Like traditional entrepreneurs, social entrepreneurs are motivated by passion and new ideas about how unfulfilled social needs can be met. An intense drive often leads social entrepreneurs into economic ventures and, at the same time, keeps their energies high, allowing them to overcome obstacles and remain engaged with their project. Still, the pressure to innovate does not diminish as the business grows, but seems to increase over time, as well-established enterprises are motivated to adapt in order to meet competitive market requirements. However, the existing literature on this topic does not address the issue of innovation in social enterprises in anything but a cursory manner. Therefore, this chapter examines the factors that drive social enterprises to behave in an innovative manner. It is cut into two main components— theoretical and empirical. The theoretical part of the chapter provides an overview of various terms and concepts, as well as how they relate to each other in the scholarly literature. This includes discussions of innovation and entrepreneurship, social entrepreneurship, and the role of innovation in addressing larger social issues in the community. The theoretical part of the chapter outlines the key factors motivating social enterprises to act in innovative way. The second part of the paper, which is based on the field data derived from the EFESEIIS research project, explores several traits associated with innovation, including individual response to envisioned social needs, organizational factors, and the influence of external environmental factors.

Theoretical background

Entrepreneurship cannot be separated from innovation. According to Schumpeter (1961), innovation often encompasses the creation of new products or production methods, new ways to organize labor, and new supply sources or markets. The relationship between entrepreneurship and innovation is also discussed by Drucker (1985), who defines entrepreneurship as an act of innovation that often emphasizes the various resources available for generating wealth. Therefore, understanding innovation as merely the development of new products and processes is incomplete and superficial. This is acknowledged by Schumpeter's (1961) claim that innovation is a "new combination" of already existing resources. Therefore, innovative activities should not be *a priori* related to discovering and exploring completely new opportunities, but also seen as a means of improving already implemented ideas (Schumpeter, 1961). Indeed, Schumpeter saw innovation as a driving force for technological progress and economic development.

Social entrepreneurship is a process that catalyzes social change and addresses important social needs in a way that is not necessarily dependent on direct financial benefits for the entrepreneurs (Mair and Marti, 2004). Unfortunately, the concept of social innovation, and the relationship between social entrepreneurship and innovation in general, is not explored in the scholarly literature to any great extent. Though social entrepreneurship and social innovation was often discussed in the works of Piter Drucker during the 1960s, it is important to note these concepts have been around for centuries. For example, Mumford (2002) suggests that Benjamin Franklin used to talk about "small modifications within socially oriented communities." According to Baumeister et al. (2004), a "social entrepreneur is an individual who uses profitable strategies in order to achieve goals, simultaneously seeking financial as well as social return on investment." Social entrepreneurs focus on transforming systems and practices that are the root causes of poverty, marginalization, environmental deterioration, and the accompanying loss of human dignity. In so doing, they may set up for-profit or not-for-profit organizations and create sustainable systematic change. On the other hand, social innovation often refers to new ideas that work towards meeting social goals. Mouglan (2006) also defines social innovation as a special type of innovation that refers to activities and services that are motivated by the goal of meeting a social need while also pointing out that they are predominantly diffused through organizations whose primary purposes are social in nature.

It is crucial to understand that social entrepreneurship transforms social issues into management issues, as these social issues are approached by organizations or entrepreneurs in an innovative and/or entrepreneurial manner. The development and expansion of social entrepreneurship makes it possible to address the needs of socially sensitive groups and problems in local communities. Social entrepreneurship can also have a stabilizing effect on labor markets as well. Oftentimes, social enterprises stress labor integration and the inclusion of marginalized groups by combining traditional business approaches with activities that focus on the greater good. Social enterprises can provide social services that were not adequately regulated by the government while also providing certain products on the market that both achieve social goals and create profit.

Founding new companies with social goals (or revising existing companies) may be driven by the government, religious organizations, health-care providers, volunteer organizations, or the activities of individuals (e.g. social entrepreneurs). Although not much has been said in the scholarly literature about the motivations of social entrepreneurs, our research has found that social entrepreneurs are not only driven by profits, but also by a desire to affect social change, by their ability to recognize opportunities for new entrepreneurial ventures, and by a need to organize and motivate others to join them in meeting their stated goals (Spreckley, 2010). As Anita Roddick from The Body Shop is often quoted as saying, "to succeed you have to believe in something with such a passion that it becomes a reality" (Vermeire & Collewaert, 2013). Sharma (2010) suggests that people who bring about social innovation need two types of skills—the capacity to bridge diverse stakeholder communities and long-term adaptive skills in response to changing circumstances.

The various motivations that encourage individuals and organizations to engage in innovative activities are inadequately addressed in the existing literature on entrepreneurship. Social entrepreneurs have received even less attention. The starting point for innovation is an awareness of a need that is not being met, and some idea of how it could be met. Researchers have shown that the willingness of people to pursue entrepreneurial opportunities depends on their social ties to investors (Aldrich & Zimmer, 1986); stocks of financial capital (Evans & Leighton, 1989); career experience (Carroll & Mosakowski, 1987; Cooper, Woo, & Dunkleberg, 1989); opportunity costs (Amit, Meuller, & Cockburn, 1995); an organization's strategic framework (Ozsomer et al., 1997); support from management, organizational climate, and means of rewarding entrepreneurial activities (Hornsby et al., 1999); education and diversity of the company's top management (Carmen et al., 2005; Andersson et al., 2009); entrepreneurial empathy (Mulgan, 2007); and access to finance (OECD, 2011). Four other factors—all of which will be discussed later in greater detail—also play significant roles in fostering innovation among traditional and social enterprises alike: access to capital, organizational framework, size of the organization, and access to skilled labor.

Since innovation is often associated with risks and costly investments in knowledge and technology, both internal financial resources and access to external capital can often determine a firm's innovative activities. Research has shown that companies that have greater access to funds, especially in the early stages of their development, are more innovative. In addition, social innovation can be driven by competition, open cultures, and accessible capital, and it will be blocked where capital is monopolized by urban elites or government (Mulgan, 2006).

Another factor that shapes the innovative behavior of an organization and the individuals within it is its strategic framework. As Ozsomer et al. (1997) point out, developing a proactive strategic framework often leads to a more flexible organizational structure and encourages innovative behavior. Support from management, organizational climate, and methods for rewarding innovation are also seen (Hornsby et al., 1999). Companies that receive higher levels of support from management, and have more advanced rewards systems, less rigid organizational structures, and more developed communication networks have proven to be more innovative.

It has often been noted that the size of the company plays an important role in shaping innovative behavior—and that innovation is most often associated with smaller companies. However, several studies have shown that the size of the company does not necessarily determine its ability to innovate (Zahra, 1991). Klette and Kortum (2004) have similarly confirmed that research and development levels are not always related to the size of a company.

Lastly, there is a strong correlation between employing skilled labor—defined here as any employee that has at least three years of university education—and innovation (Andersson et al., 2009). It has been shown that more innovative companies are usually managed by highly educated teams and managers with prior experience in creating and implementing new goods and services, and that innovation levels are often dependent on the functional diversity of the company's top management (Carmen et al., 2005). Some authors point out that innovation is similarly connected to entrepreneurial empathy levels (Mulgan, 2007). Although social entrepreneurs are often motivated by the desire to address their own problems, some individuals may be motivated by the suffering of their friends, family, or local community. Nevertheless, the scholarly literature also points out that despite having limited access to financial resources—and other types of resources for that matter—a true entrepreneur will always find a way to implement his or her idea, if only because he or she has been driven by passion and a belief in his or her idea (Cardon et al., 2009).

Having said all that, it is important to note that social innovation is driven by several different forces. On an individual level, social innovation may come out of a need to solve one's own problems or from empathy towards other groups and individuals in their social circle. However, on a macro-organizational level, innovation is usually driven by a desire to address social issues within the broader community, or perhaps as a consequence of maintaining an organization's competitive position in that area. Regardless, in the absence of any scholarly consensus on this matter, the remainder of this chapter will examine the various drivers of social innovation that emerged from our own research.

Methodology

The data for this study was drawn from EFESEIIS' field research,[1] which is based on an online survey. The link to the questionnaire was sent by e-mail to various social enterprises, with a brief explanation of the purpose of the survey and the benefits of participating in it. Respondents were owners or managers of social enterprises, all of whom were 18 years of age or older. Non-founders were allowed to respond to the questionnaire whenever they were granted decision-making rights and the authority to manage the organization by the owner.

The questionnaire consisted of several modules. The first three modules were designed to collect data on the personal characteristics of the respondents (e.g. gender, age, education, previous experience in founding/managing social enterprises, and motivation) and the general characteristics of the enterprise (e.g. type, number of employees, ownership structure, year of establishment, sector, and sales turnover). The other modules addressed the following dimensions of social enterprises: access to capital, challenges and constraints, the role of innovation, the influence of different stakeholders on decision-making processes, and the social capital of entrepreneurs.

We hoped to determine which factors encourage social enterprises to behave in an innovative way. We therefore focused on identifying factors from both within the organization (micro and macro organizational factors) and the external environment. We define innovative social enterprises (ISEs) as organizations that have created innovative products in the last three years—placing special emphasis on managers or owners who responded positively when answering the question "*Has your organization innovated in terms of products, processes, finances, or marketing in the last 3 years?*" By contrast, managers or owners who responded "no" when answering the same question were categorized as social enterprises that have not innovated in the last three years (NISEs).

Statistical analysis was performed using t-test for testing equality of means, z-test for testing equality of proportion, and both hi-square tests and non-parametric tests to confirm the results obtained using parametric tests. For numerical variables we used t-test for testing equality of means between ISEs and NISEs. Since the answers offered in the questionnaire follow Likert item logics—e.g. 1—Completely disagree, 2—Disagree, 3—Neither agree or disagree, 4—Agree, and 5—Completely agree—the results of the test have been checked via non-parametric tests. Our analysis has produced similar results. We used a p-value of 0.05 when making statistical inferences in this chapter. Our data came from the countries mentioned in the EFESEIIS research project and our conclusions refer to the entire sample.

Research Findings

Macro-organizational factors and innovation

Social awareness

After conducting a statistical analysis of the data, we found that ISEs are more likely than NISEs to recognize that solving a social problem is a primary or secondary goal of their organization. This difference is statistically significant (Table 9.1).

Organizational life cycle

One of the main macro-organizational factors that can affect innovation is organizational life cycle. Our statistical analysis suggests that innovation was more important among ISEs during early stages of development than it was among NISEs. Previous can be seen from Table 9.2.

Since growth is as important as innovation among social enterprises, we examined whether growth is equally important to innovative and non-innovative organizations. Table 9.3 shows that a majority of the respondents believe that it is important for social enterprises to grow—to increase the number or range of activities, recruit more employees, etc. Nonetheless, ISEs tend to see growth as being much more important—in a statistically significant manner—than NISEs do.

Table 9.1 Problem solving and innovativeness

Question/Factor		Innovative social organization (ISE)	
		Yes	No
A1—Is contributing to solve a social or environmental issue an objective of your organization?	Yes	98.8%	93.0%
	No	1.2%	7.0%
No. of respondents		521	100

Table 9.2 Importance of innovation during different stages of the life cycle—testing equality of means

Questions/Factors*	Test results	p-value	Innovative social organizations (mean)	
			Yes	No
F1—How important was innovation in the start-up phase of your organization (e.g. in terms of products, processes, finances, or marketing)?	≠	0.00	4.02	3.19
F2—How important is such innovation now?	≠	0.00	4.14	3.35

*Possible responses: 1—Not at all satisfied/important, 2—Slightly satisfied/important, 3—Moderately satisfied/Neutral, 4—Very satisfied/important, and 5—Extremely satisfied/important. No ISE = 522; No NISE = 101.

Table 9.3 Importance of growth and innovativeness

Questions/Factors	Test results		Innovative social organizations	
			Yes	No
E2—Is it important for your organization to grow (e.g. increase the number or range of activities, recruit more employees, etc.)?	≠	Yes	91.0%	83.7%
		No	9.0%	16.3%
No. of respondents			502	92

Table 9.4 Size of enterprises and innovativeness

Company category		Innovative social organizations	
		Yes	No
Large	Count	13_a	0_a
	% within innovative org.	2.5%	0.0%
Medium	Count	49_a	3_b
	% within innovative org.	9.4%	3.0%
Small	Count	140_a	23_a
	% within innovative org.	26.8%	22.8%
Micro	Count	321_a	75_b
	% within innovative org.	61.4%	74.3%
Total	Count	523	100.0%
	100.0% % within innovative org.	100.0%	100.0%

Each subscript letter denotes a subset of innovative organizations categories whose column proportions do not differ significantly from each other at the .05 level.

Organizational size and innovation

We examined whether or not organizational size shapes innovation. After determining the average number of employees in both ISEs and NISEs, it was concluded that the size of the organization does not affect innovation, and that ISEs and NISEs do not differ when assessing the average number of employees. Nonetheless, in order to gain better insight on the impact of an organization's size on innovation, a deeper analysis was conducted. Namely, the companies were divided into four categories based on the number of employees: Micro (up to 10 employees), Small (10–49 employees), Medium (50–249), and Large (more than 249 employees). Our statistical analysis concluded that ISEs and NISEs have the same percentage of large and small enterprises. However, differences emerge in medium and micro enterprises. The percentage of medium-sized enterprises is higher among ISEs than it is among NISEs, while the percentage of micro enterprises is higher among NISEs (Table 9.4).

Table 9.5 Turnover and innovativeness

Turnover in 2014		Innovative organizations	
		Yes	No
€0–6,250	Count	56ₐ	23_b
	% within innovative org.	11.0%	23.5%
€6,251–12,500	Count	27ₐ	4ₐ
	% within innovative org.	5.3%	4.1%
€12,501–25,000	Count	35ₐ	12ₐ
	% within innovative org.	6.9%	12.2%
€25,001–50,000	Count	51ₐ	8ₐ
	% within innovative org.	10.0%	8.2%
€50,001–100,000	Count	54ₐ	12ₐ
	% within innovative org.	10.6%	12.2%
€100,001–200,000	Count	53ₐ	13ₐ
	% within innovative org.	10.4%	13.3%
€200,001–350,000	Count	48ₐ	7ₐ
	% within innovative org.	9.4%	7.1%
€350,000–500,000	Count	28ₐ	6ₐ
	% within innovative org.	5.5%	6.1%
€500.001–1 M	Count	54ₐ	7ₐ
	% within innovative org.	10.6%	7.1%
1 M–2 M	Count	38ₐ	2_b
	% within innovative org.	7.5%	2.0%
2 M–4 M	Count	24ₐ	2ₐ
	% within innovative org.	4.7%	2.0%
4 M–8 M	Count	42ₐ	2_b
	% within innovative org.	8.2%	2.0%
Total	Count	510	98
	% within innovative org.	100.0%	100.0%

Each subscript letter denotes a subset of innovative organizations categories whose column proportions do not differ significantly from each other at the 0.05 level.

As Table 9.5 illustrates, the share of ISEs with a turnover of 1 M–2 M and 4 M–8 M is higher, while NISEs have a higher share of social enterprises with a turnover of up to 6,250 Euros.

Micro-organizational factors and innovation

Education

Innovation can also be influenced by some micro-organizational factors, such as the age of the founder/manager, his or her education, previous experience, motivations, professional satisfaction, staff issues, and team characteristics.

The education of the founder/manager of a social enterprise influences innovation in a positive manner. Indeed, the ISEs within our sample have a higher percentage of university-educated founders/managers than the NISEs (Table 9.6).

Table 9.6 Education and innovativeness

13—What is your highest educational qualification?		Innovative organizations	
		Yes	No
Secondary education	Count	27_a	5_a
	% within innovative org.	6.7%	7.2%
College	Count	66_a	16_a
	% within innovative org.	16.3%	23.2%
University–undergraduate	Count	115_a	11_b
	% within innovative org.	28.4%	15.9%
University–postgraduate (master's)	Count	177_a	37_a
	% within innovative org.	43.7%	53.6%
University–postgraduate (Doctorate)	Count	20_a	0_a
	% within innovative org.	4.9%	0.0%
Total	Count	405	99
	% within innovative org.	100.0%	100.0%

Each subscript letter denotes a subset of innovative organizations categories whose column proportions do not differ significantly from each other at the 0.05 level.

Table 9.7 Age and innovativeness

Age groups		Innovative social organizations	
		Yes	No
18–30	Count	25_a	9_a
	% within innovative org.	4.8%	8.9%
31–40	Count	98_a	7_b
	% within innovative org.	18.7%	6.9%
41–50	Count	93_a	18_a
	% within innovative org.	17.8%	17.8%
51–60	Count	106_a	17_a
	% within innovative org.	20.3%	16.8%
60+	Count	201_a	50_b
	% within innovative org.	38.4%	49.5%
Total	Count	523	101
	% within innovative org.	100.0%	100.0%

Each subscript letter denotes a subset of innovative organizations categories whose column proportions do not differ significantly from each other at the 0.05 level.

An organization's ability to innovate can also be influenced by the founder's age. After determining the average age of founders/managers in the ISEs and NISEs involved in our research, we concluded that there is no statistically significant difference in age. However, further analysis found that differences emerge when individual age groups are taken into consideration (see Table 9.7). In fact, ISEs report a higher percentage of

Table 9.8 Previous founding and/or managing experience

Questions/Factors		Innovative organization	
		Yes	No
B4—Have you been involved in founding a social enterprise before this one?	Yes	30.8%	17.8%
	No	69.2%	82.2%
B5—Have you managed a social enterprise before this one?	Yes	27.1%	15.8%
	No	72.9%	84.2%
	No. of respondents	516	101

founders/managers in the 31–40 age group, and a smaller percentage of founders/managers over 60 years of age, than NISEs do.

Previous experience

Most of the owners/managers who took part in our research did not have previous experience establishing and/or running an enterprise (Table 9.8). However, further statistical analysis reveals that this factor positively influences innovation levels in their current social ventures.[2] In other words, the percentage of employees with experience in founding social enterprises is higher among ISEs than among NSEs. We reached the same conclusion when we examined the role experience plays in managing social businesses. The percentage of owners or employees with experience in managing social business is higher among ISEs than it is among NSES. This difference, moreover, is statistically significant.

Motivations and innovation

In terms of what motivates people to work with/found social enterprises, our results show statistically significant differences between ISEs and NISEs, especially when it comes to the creation of personal employment opportunities. Indeed, the founders of ISEs are less likely than their peers in NISEs to start a social enterprise in order to create a personal employment opportunity (Table 9.9).

Professional satisfaction and innovation

While trying to determine whether satisfaction with one's professional life is the same in ISEs and NISEs, our research found that there is a statistically significant difference in the satisfaction levels between both groups.[3] Basically, respondents from ISEs are more satisfied with their professional lives than their counterparts in NISEs. Moreover, this difference is statistically significant (Table 9.10).

Table 9.9 Motivations and innovativeness

What is your main motivation for working with/founding a Social Enterprise?		Innovative organizations	
		Yes	No
Address a social problem I personally experienced	Count	73_a	16_a
	% within innovative org.	14.1%	16.8%
Address social challenges	Count	211_a	36_a
	% within innovative org.	40.8%	37.9%
Address environmental challenges	Count	29_a	8_a
	% within innovative org.	5.6%	8.4%
Create a personal employment opportunity	Count	59_a	19_b
	% within innovative org.	11.4%	20.0%
Inadequacy of existing social service	Count	43_a	5_a
	% within innovative org.	8.3%	5.3%
Needed to innovate specific practices	Count	61_a	7_a
	% within innovative org.	11.8%	7.4%
Other (please specify)	Count	41_a	4_a
	% within innovative org.	7.9%	4.2%
Count		517	95
% within innovative org.		100.0%	100.0%

Each subscript letter denotes a subset of innovative organizations categories whose column proportions do not differ significantly from each other at the 0.05 level.

Table 9.10 Satisfaction with professional life and innovativeness testing equality of means

Questions/Factors*	Test results	p-value	Innovative organizations (mean)	
			Yes	No
B8—How satisfied are you with your professional life, in general?	$\neq$	0.00	3.88	3.41
No. of respondents			522	100

Staff and team characteristics

All of the organizations involved in our study use both paid staff and volunteers. However, ISEs hire paid employees to a much greater extent than NISEs do, and the difference is statistically significant (Tables 9.11 and 9.12).

Our statistical analysis shows that team members cooperate well in both ISEs and NISE, and that there is no statistically significant difference in the attitudes about team collaboration in both groups. However, trust levels are significantly higher among team members who work in ISEs than among those who work in NISEs. Interestingly enough, ISEs also appear to be more likely to develop diverse networks of business relations.

Table 9.11 Paid staff involvement

Questions/Factors		Innovative organization	
		Yes	No
A5—Does your organization employ paid staff?	Yes	92.1%	83.2%
	No	7.9%	16.8%
No. of respondents		521	101

Table 9.12 Team characteristics and innovativeness—testing equality of means

Statements*	Test results	p-value	Innovative social organizations (mean)***	
			Yes	No
H2_1—People in my team generally trust each other	≠	0.005	4.22	3.95
H2_2—People in my team generally co-operate effectively	=	0.562	4.15	4.10
H2_3—I generally trust people in my team**	≠	0.042	4.30	4.12
H2_4—I generally co-operate with my team members	=	0.356	4.40	4.32
H2_5—The enterprise has a large network of business relations	≠	0.000	3.67	3.04

* Offered answers to respondents: 1—Not at all, 2—A little, 3—Medium, 4—Quite a lot, and 5—Completely.
** Realized $p = 0.1$ when performed nonparametric test to verify results of t-test.
*** No ISE = 470; no NISE = 82.

Table 9.13 Impact of the external environment on organizational innovativeness

Questions/Factors	Test results		Innovative social organizations	
			Yes	No
F5—Did you innovate in response to a change in your external environment?	≠	Yes	65.8%	30.3%
		No	34.2%	69.7%
No. of respondents			445	76

External environmental forces

In addition to macro-organizational and micro-organizational factors, innovation can also be influenced by the external environment. However, ISEs are more likely to have had their innovation activities shaped by the external environment than NISEs do (Table 9.13).

Social enterprises that have innovated in the past three years report using personal savings as a source of financing more so than those that have not innovated. ISEs are also more likely than NISEs to obtain start-up funds from bank loans (see Table 9.14). Furthermore, ISEs report that they are more likely to rely on project grants than NISEs do. This difference is statistically significant (see Table 9.15).

Key actors

Major stakeholders in ISEs—including owners/boards of directors, employees, suppliers, customers and users, third-sector organizations and NGOs,

Table 9.14 Starter funds and innovativeness

Where did your organization get the funds to start its activities?	Test results		Innovative social organizations	
			Yes	No
Bank loans	≠	Yes	12.3%	4.2%
		No	87.7%	95.8%
Grants from projects	=			
Personal savings	=			
Donations/fundraising	=			
Crowdfunding	=			
Microcredit	=			
Regulated market (e.g. insurance)	=			
Social investment	=			
Private investment	=			
No. of respondents			473	96

Table 9.15 Actual funds and innovativeness

Which funds do you actually use for your activity?	Test results		Innovative social organizations	
			Yes	No
Bank loans	=			
Grants from projects	≠	Yes	57.5%	45.8%
		No	42.5%	54.2%
Personal savings	=			
Donations/fundraising	=			
Crowdfunding	=			
Microcredit	=			
Regulated market (e.g. insurance)	=			
Social investment	=			
Private investment	=			
No. of respondents			473	96

and the local community—have a greater impact on decision-making processes than their counterparts in NISEs (see Table 9.16). However, the difference is minimal between ISEs and NISEs in terms of the impact investors and state/public administrators have on decision-making processes. ISEs are also more likely than NISEs to evaluate user satisfaction and use surveys and social media in order to engage with their stakeholders. This difference is statistically significant (Table 9.17).

Table 9.16 Stakeholder influence and innovativeness—testing equality of means

G.1) Degree to which stakeholders influence decision-making of organization (5 = high influence; 1 = no influence)	Test results	Innovative social organization	N	Mean
Owner/boards of directors	≠	Yes	497	4.2354
		No	94	3.9574
Shareholders/investors	=	Yes	497	2.3682
		No	94	2.2553
Employees	≠	Yes	497	3.5835
		No	94	3.1809
Suppliers	≠	Yes	497	2.2757
		No	94	1.8723
Costumers and users	≠	Yes	497	3.8773
		No	94	3.3511
State and public administration	=	Yes	497	2.9095
		No	94	2.7021
Third-sector organizations and NGOs	≠	Yes	497	2.6197
		No	94	2.1915
Community	≠	Yes	497	3.2294
		No	94	2.8404

Table 9.17 Stakeholder engagement practices and innovativeness

G.2) What stakeholder engagement practices do you use?	Test results	Innovative social organization	
		Yes	No
Dedicated telephone lines	=		
Public meetings	=		
Surveys and evaluating user satisfaction	≠	Yes	64.2% 37.2%
		No	35.8% 62.8%
Advisory groups	=		
Stakeholder involvement in the reporting of activities (e.g. sustainability reporting)	≠	Yes	36.6% 25.5%
		No	63.4% 74.5%
Membership of executive board	=		
Social media	≠	Yes	66.0% 40.4%
		No	34.0% 59.6%
No. of respondents		497	94

Discussion and conclusions

Our findings suggest that innovation in social enterprises is connected to both organizational and external factors. Some macro-organizational factors include being conscious of their social mission, believing that innovation is an important element of their activities at an early stage of organizational development, and seeing a growth-oriented approach as an important contributor to organizational innovation.

We also found that micro-organizational factors influence innovation, including the education levels of founders and managers, and previous personal experience in founding or managing a social enterprise. Innovation seems to be connected to professional satisfaction levels as well, as respondents from ISEs are more likely to report being satisfied with their professional lives than their peers in NISEs.

Employment policies are also worth noting. After all, ISEs are more likely than NISEs to hire paid employees. Our findings also suggest that trust between team members can influence innovation levels, as this trait is often significantly higher among ISEs than it is among NISEs.

The extent to which the external environment shapes innovation should not be underestimated either. Indeed, ISEs are more likely than NISEs

Table 9.18 Summary table

Question group	Question	Factor influences innovativeness
A. General questions	A1—Is contributing to solve a social or environmental issue an objective of your organization?	Yes
	A2—Is your organization involved in any economic activity, such as selling goods and services?	No
	A3—Is your organization's core income dependent on grants, donation, bequests, or benefactors?	No
	A4—Does your organization use any of its profits to fund core activities?	No
	A5—Does your organization employ paid staff?	Yes
B. Personal experience	B1—Are you the founder of the enterprise?	No
	B3—Does your current position give you the authority to decide/manage major issues in the enterprise (e.g. strategy, enterprise objectives, activities, organization of teamwork, etc.)?	No
	B4—Have you been involved in founding a social enterprise before this one?	Yes
	B5—Have you managed a social enterprise before this one?	Yes
	B6—Is anyone in your family an entrepreneur? Has anyone in your family been an entrepreneur?	No
	B7—What is your main motivation for working with/founding a social enterprise?	Yes
	B8—How satisfied are you with your professional life in general?	Yes

(*Continued*)

Question group	Question	Factor influences innovativeness
D. Financing	D1—Which of the following sources of funding are available for social enterprises in your country?	Yes
	D2—Where did your organization get the funds to start its activities?	Yes
	D3—Which funds do you actually use for your activities?	Yes
E. Challenges	E2—Is it important for your organization to grow (e.g. increase the number or range of activities, recruit more employees, etc.)?	Yes
F. Innovation	F1—How important was innovation in the start-up phase of your organization (e.g. in terms of products, processes, finances, or marketing)?	Yes
	F2—How important is such innovation now?	Yes
	F5—Did you innovate in response to a change in your external environment?	Yes
G. Governance & stakeholders	G1—Please describe the degree to which the following categories of stakeholder influence decision-making processes in your organization (5 = high influence; 1 = no influence)	Yes
	G2—What stakeholder engagement practices do you use?	Yes
H. Social Capital	H2—Please rate the following statements:	Yes
I. Personal data	I1—Sex	No
	I3—What is your highest educational qualification?	Yes
	I4—Did you undertake any additional vocational training or education for your current position?	No
	I6—Do you identify yourself as a person with severe disabilities?	Yes

to report engaging in activities associated with innovation as a result of changes in the external environment. Innovative social organizations are also more likely to develop diverse networks of business relations and involve stakeholders—most notably owners/boards of directors, employees, suppliers, customers and users, third-sector organizations and NGOs, and the local community—in their decision-making processes. On a related note, ISEs are more likely than NISEs to engage in stakeholder engagement practices via surveys, social media, and other means of collecting feedback.

Lastly, access to personal savings, bank loans, and project grants seem to be connected to higher innovation levels among social enterprises. For a list of all of the factors influencing innovation among social enterprises, see Table 9.18.

Notes

1 For more details concerning the methodological issue see Chapter 2.
2 Previous experience includes not only being a founder of a social enterprise, but also being involved in this process in a lesser role.
3 We should emphasize that the results of the non-parametric tests are in accordance with the results of the *t*-test.

References

Amabile, T. M. (1997). Entrepreneurial creativity through motivational synergy. *Journal of Creative Behaviour, 31,* 18–26.

Andersson, M., & Loof, H. (2009). *Key characteristics of the small innovative firm.* Centre of Excellence for Science and Innovation Studies (CESIS), Working Paper 175. Jönköping University.

Baron, J. N., & Hannan, M. T. (2002). Organizational blueprints for success in high-tech start-ups: Lessons from the Stanford project on emerging companies. *California Management Review, 44*(3), 8–36.

Baum, J. R., & Locke, E. A. (2004). The relationship of entrepreneurial traits, skill, and motivation to subsequent venture growth. *Journal of Applied Psychology, 89,* 587–598.

Baum, J. R., Locke, E. A., & Smith, K. G. (2001). A multidimensional model of venture growth. *Academy of Management Journal, 44,* 292–303.

Baumeister, R. F., Vohs, K. D., DeWall, C. N., & Zhang, L. (2007). How emotion shapes behaviour: Feedback, anticipation, and reflection, rather than direct causation. *Personality and Social Psychology Review, 11,* 167–203.

Camelo-Ordaz, C., Hernández-Lara, A. B., & Valle-Cabrera, R. (2005). The relationship between top management teams and innovative capacity in companies. *Journal of Management Development, 24*(8), 683–705.

Cardon, M. S. (2008). Is passion contagious? The transference of entrepreneurial emotion to employees. *Human Resource Management Review, 18,* 77–86.

Cardon, M. S., Wincent, J., Singh, J., & Drnovsek, M. (2009). The nature and experience of entrepreneurial passion. *Academy of Management Review, 34*(3), 511–532.

Cova, B., & Svanfeldt, C. (1993). Societal innovations and the postmodern aestheticization of everyday life. *International Journal of Research in Marketing, 10,* 297–311.

Dees, J. G., Anderson, B. B., & Wei-Skillern, J. (2002). *Pathways to social impact: Strategies for scaling out successful social innovations.* CASE Working Paper Series 3. Durham: Duke University.

D'Intino, R. S., Goldsby, M. G., Houghton, J. D., & Neck, C. P. (2007). Self-leadership: A process for entrepreneurial success. *Journal of Leadership & Organizational Studies, 13,* 105–120.

Filion, L. J. (1991). Vision and relations: Elements for an entrepreneurial metamodel. *International Small Business Journal, 9,* 26–40.

Fraczak, P., & Wygnanski, J. (2008). *The Polish model of the social economy: Recommendations for growth.* Warsaw: Foundation for Social and Economic Initiatives.

Gartner, W. B. (1985). A conceptual framework for describing the phenomenon of new venture creation. *Academy of Management Review, 10,* 696–706.

Gimeno, J., Folta, T. B., Cooper, A. C., & Woo, C. Y. (1997). Survival of the fittest? Entrepreneurial human capital and the persistence of underperforming firms. *Administrative Science Quarterly, 42,* 750–783.

Hornsby, J. S., Kuratko, D. F., & Montagno, R. V. (1999). Perception of internal factors for corporate entrepreneurship: A comparison of Canadian and U.S. managers. *Entrepreneurship Theory and Practice, 24*(2), 9–24.

Klette, T. J., & Kortum, S. (2004). Innovating firms and aggregate innovation. *Journal of Political Economy, 112,* 896–1018.

Mair, J., & Marti, L. I. (2004). *Social entrepreneurship: A source of explanation, prediction and delight.* IESE Business School Working Paper 546. Retrieved from SSRN: https://ssrn.com/abstract=673446 or http://dx.doi.org/10.2139/ssrn.673446.

Mulgan, G. (2006). The process of social innovation. *Innovations, 1*(2), 145–162.

Mulgan, G. (2007). *Social innovation what it is, why it matters and how it can be accelerated.* Skoll centre for social entrepreneurship Working Paper, University of Oxford. London: The Basingstoke Press.

Mumford, M. D. (2002). Social innovation: Ten cases from Benjamin Franklin. *Creativity Research Journal, 14*(2), 253–266.

Ozsomer, A., Calantone, R. J., & Bonetto, A. D. (1997). What makes firms more innovative? A look at organizational and environmental factors. *Journal of Business & Industrial Marketing, 12*(6), 400–416.

Schumpeter, J. (1961). *The theory of economic development: An inquiry into profits, capital, credit, interest, and the business cycle.* Cambridge, MA: Harvard University Press.

Serna, C. (2009). *The reflexive assembly: Embryon of a virtous circle in evaluating the cooperative social economy.* Working paper CIRIEC, 2009/05. Liege.

Shane, S., Locke, E. A., & Collins, C. J. (2003). Entrepreneurial motivation. *Human Resource Management Review, 13,* 257–279.

Sharma, A. (2010). Sustainable social development through innovations: understanding Indian cases. *Business and Globalisation, 5*(1), 17–30.

Spreckley, F. (2010). *Social enterprise business planning.* British Council, unpublished.

Vermeire, J., & Collewaert, V. (2013). *Passion in new entrepreneurs.* Flanders, DC: Knowledge Centre at Vlerick Business School, pp. 1–4.

Woodman, R. W., Sawyer, J. E., & Griffin, R. W. 1993. Towards a theory of organizational creativity. *Academy of Management Review, 18,* 293–321.

Zahra, S. A. (1991). Predictors and financial outcomes of corporate entrepreneurship: An exploratory study. *Journal of Business Venturing, 6,* 259–285.

10 Social innovation in niches

Christina Grabbe, Katharina Obuch, and Annette Zimmer

Introduction

The global economic crisis has led to greater attention to social enterprises (SEs) (Defourny & Nyssens, 2015; Kerlin, 2010; Meng, 2016), many of which are seen as innovative and universal "all-rounders" that are capable of tackling present and future challenges (e.g. demographic change, social cohesion, and migration). The idea of combining entrepreneurial spirit with social goals has received a warm welcome of late, particularly among politicians who see social innovation as a means of addressing the problems of overburdened welfare states—including, most notably, increased demands for social services and shrinking funding opportunities. Our comparative study of two SEs in Germany highlights the divergent spaces these new actors occupy, the different functions they fulfill, and the various challenges they face. After all, different socioeconomic and political contexts require different types of social innovation.

This chapter explains how SEs serve as drivers of social innovation in conservative welfare states with well-established organizational fields. At first glance, these jurisdictions seem to leave little space for new actors and ideas. According to Esping-Andersen (1990), conservative welfare structures are characterized by moderate decommodification levels, a comparatively high degree of welfare entitlements that are dependent on both contributions and status, and an overall aim of preserving the status quo. Moreover, conservative welfare regimes are often marked by cooperation between the state and nonprofit welfare providers whose activities are based on the principle of subsidiarity.

Using Germany as a prime example of a conservative welfare regime (Esping-Andersen, 1990), we argue that new SEs are able to successfully emerge and position themselves in highly regulated and established organizational fields by following a niche approach. Their strategy focuses on innovation, relies on new and private resources during the start-up phase, and addresses recent changes to social service production in Germany. New social risks and demands related to rising rates of inequality, unemployment, and child poverty are opening up new opportunities for SEs to occupy specific "niches," where they can focus on emerging or neglected social problems and target groups.

"Methodology" and "Terminology: social innovation and social enterprise" offer a brief discussion of our methodology and how we define both social innovation and SE. "The German context" provides an overview of Germany's welfare system, with a focus on youth welfare as a field that has drawn special attention from SEs. "Social enterprises as social innovators" presents two case studies of new generation SEs that were analyzed in the EFESEIIS project. "Discussion: social innovation in established organizational fields" explains how new SEs make inroads and establish themselves as social innovators in a highly regulated organizational field that is already served by several well-established organizations.

Methodology

Our research builds on the EFESEIIS project, which analyzed the new generation of social entrepreneurs and their ecosystems in Germany and ten other European countries. Using the "ecology approach," a by-product of organizational theory, as a guide, (Hannan & Freeman, 1977; Baum, 1999; Kieser & Woywode, 2006), the EFESEIS project sees recently created SEs as a new "species" of entrepreneurial entities that produce goods and/or services. These new SEs occupy specific ecosystems in the countries under study. As several scholars have noted (Hannan & Freeman, 1977; Kieser & Woywode, 2006), the emergence, growth, maturation, and death of organizations is a dynamic process that is often influenced by a variety of factors—including, most prominently, the arrangement of the ecosystem and the availability or scarcity of resources. Although the ecology approach provides major insights into how new species emerge and why others are no longer capable of surviving, it focuses primarily on macro-level issues, outlining and describing the genesis, maturation, and shortcomings/difficulties of new organizations. We depart from the ecology approach by focusing on meso-level issues of organizational emergence and growth, rather than macro-level issues.

Data from the EESEIIS project was gathered via a mixed-methods approach that included reviews of the existing literature on SEs in Germany and other European nations. A total of thirteen in-depth expert interviews and five focus groups (involving thirty social entrepreneurs and diverse stakeholders) were held. A key component of the EFESEIIS project is the analysis of case studies that were identified by examining the scholarly literature and through expert interviews. Each of the cases are textbook examples of new generation SEs that managed to emerge and grow within a specific context. In order to analyze the case studies in accordance with current ideas on organizational analysis, we widened our methodological approach by also taking into account insights from the literature on "organizational fields," an approach that was inspired by both neo-institutionalism

(Powell & DiMaggio, 1991) and social movement or process theory (Fligstein & McAdam, 2015). However, we restricted the scope of our analysis by focusing exclusively on youth welfare, a field of study that has produced a wealth of new programs and activities in Germany in recent years (Grabbe & Obuch, 2017; Spiess-Knafl et al., 2013). We argue that several factors explain why youth welfare has become a fruitful area of interest for SEs. Scholars following the ecology approach claim that new enterprises have emerged in this field due to significant environmental changes, organizational slack caused by established routines, an inability to tackle new problems and challenges, new actors bringing untouched resources to the table, and social upheaval caused by environmental change (Kieser & Woywode, 2006).

We will present two case studies from 2015, placing special emphasis on the extent to which both organizations are embedded in the field of youth welfare. We selected SEs that address important social welfare issues and fulfill the following criteria:

- they were founded in the last 10–15 years;
- they make active use of ICT tools and try to diversify their sources of income;
- their success is defined by their sustainability levels (i.e. they have an effective scaling up process) and are recognized as such by their peers (i.e. they have received pertinent awards and fellowships).

Data gathering was carried out via background interviews with leaders and managerial staff, as well as observations in situ, shadowing, and informal talks. All of the interviews were transcribed and subjected to content analysis, which involves extracting relevant information according to ex-ante fixed analytical categories (Gläser & Laudel, 2008).

Terminology: social innovation and social enterprise

In recent years, social policy debates have turned away from stressing de-commodification in order to place greater emphasis on the idea of social investment (Morel et al., 2015). Instead of passively protecting people, this new paradigm aims at empowering and preparing people for social risks through innovation and entrepreneurial concepts. The scientific literature focuses on both social innovation (Brandsen et al., 2016; Moulaert et al., 2015a, 2015b; Nicholls et al., 2016) and SE (Dees & Anderson, 2006; Nicholls, 2008). Concepts and ideas are widespread, but a shared understanding of major terms is missing.

Social innovations often take the shape of actions, frames, models, systems, processes, services, rules, regulations, and organizational forms (Nicholls et al., 2016). They emerge when problems of poverty, social exclusion, deprivation, and inequality cannot be sufficiently addressed by the "institutionalized field of public or private action" (Moulaert et al., 2015, p. 2). Depending on the political and institutional context in which they are embedded, social innovations vary in terms of their goals and major characteristics (Brandsen et al., 2016). Indeed, an innovative practice can be judged differently depending on where it emerged, as well as its relationship to the institutions that operate in that specific jurisdiction. Indeed, researchers from the WILCO project claim that "social innovations are in a significant way, new and disruptive towards the routines and structures prevailing in a given (welfare) system or local setting" (Evers et al., 2014, p. 14). Furthermore, Brandsen et al. (2016) emphasize that no one can "predict, what comes out of even a very promising innovation in the course of its development" (p. 5). Thus, social innovation is a complex concept involving two intertwined qualities: new social processes and new social outputs (Brandsen et al., 2016; Nicholls et al., 2016). The former concept stipulates that social innovation brings about social inclusion and well-being by profoundly changing social relations (Moulaert et al., 2015). The latter concept, meanwhile, places emphasis on the capacity of social innovation to address market failures and provide necessary public goods (Nicholls et al., 2016).

Debates on social innovation are often connected to debates on SEs because they are both seen as "vehicle[s] for social innovation throughout Europe" (Defourny & Nyssens, 2015, p. 46) or "the organizational enactment of social innovation ideas and models" (Nicholls et al., 2016, p. 5). This perspective is a by-product of the Social Innovation approach, which identifies SEs as drivers of social innovation by highlighting the capacity of organizations to tackle social problems in an innovative way and develop new concepts, instruments, and services (Dees & Anderson, 2006; Mulgan et al., 2007). In recent years, newer start-ups are seen as being carriers of social innovation. Self-proclaimed "changemakers" try to address social challenges via traditional business practices (Zimmer & Obuch, 2017, p. 17). Nevertheless, social innovation is not only limited to new organizations but can also take place in established organizations, where it is often called "social intrapreneurship" (Fuchs, 2014, p. 90; Mair & Marti, 2006, p. 37). Social innovations are implemented by using alternative sources of financing (Schmitz & Scheuerle, 2013,), creating spin-off companies, or via content-oriented realignment (Spiess-Knafl et al., 2013).

The German context

Welfare structures

Germany has been a pioneer in the introduction of social allowances, enacting social policies based on monetary transfers as early as the 1870s (Schmid, 2010). Since then, Germany's insurance-based welfare allowances have constituted the core of its conservative welfare regime, which aims at safeguarding the status quo (Esping-Andersen, 1990). Still, support for the needy and provisions for public services have never been perceived as a prime duty of the federal government. Instead, municipalities and districts have always been in charge of caring for the poor and providing public services alongside private nonprofits and commercial providers (Wollmann, 2012). Many of these providers—particularly those affiliated with the churches—have been given a privileged status that is based on a neo-corporatist approach to welfare (Heinze & Olk, 1981). As a result, Germany has a "dual system" of social service provision (Sachße, 1995) that features close co-operation between "public" or "municipal" and private/nonprofit social service providers. Moreover, the majority of private/nonprofit social service providers are affiliated with one of the German welfare associations—"umbrella" organizations that are engaged in the provision of social services (Boeßenecker & Vilain, 2013).

For decades, organizations that were aligned with Germany's welfare associations were protected from both commercial competition and economic failure. In the 1990s, however, structural unemployment, demographic change, and the costs of German re-unification called for a policy adjustment. Whereas social policy in Germany had been based on the principles of "solidarity" and "subsidiarity" for decades, competition brought about by both the establishment of quasi-markets and the acceptance of commercial social providers was now seen as an efficient cost-cutting strategy. Accordingly, social service provision was de-regulated and made accessible to commercial providers. Organizations that had secured membership in the welfare associations were now treated on an almost equal footing with nonprofit or commercial competitors. Finally, due to increasing financial difficulties, many local governments had to introduce austerity measures that had a serious impact on the local infrastructure (Henriksen et al., 2012). It is against this background that the emergence of SEs has gained momentum in Germany in recent years.

The German SE sector

Although there is a long tradition of social entrepreneurship in Germany, the notion of SE has only recently entered public debate. As stated earlier, entrepreneurship and competition was first emphasized in the social services sector in the 1990s, as providers were encouraged to "rationalize" their activities. Deprived of their privileges and state protection, they had to compete with commercial providers and adapt their strategies, structures, and configurations. Moreover, in the past decade, with the emergence of private/business foundations and sweeping changes to the welfare system, greater emphasis has been placed on promoting individual social entrepreneurs, their personalities, and their role as "changemakers" (www.ashoka.org).

The SE sector is currently bifurcated: traditional, rationalized welfare providers stand next to an emerging generation of social enterpreneurs.

The new social entrepreneurs are often supported by private foundations or facilitators—such as Ashoka—that provide fiscal support and management know-how. Both modes of support have been embraced in Germany. For instance, grants provide seed money for the creation of new organizations, while counseling and networking enables the new generation of SEs to better adapt to the changed environment and become more competitive and businesslike. Built around their charismatic founders, many of these single-issue SEs stress entrepreneurial ideas and use traditional business expertise to address social issues (Zimmer & Obuch, 2017).

Given the fact that SEs in Germany have not been legally defined to any great extent, the estimates for the number of SEs operating in the country vary significantly (see Scheuerle et al., 2013). Of course, the majority of SEs operate in the social welfare domain (Jansen et al., 2013), which is a highly regulated area. However, powerful lobby groups and the welfare associations discussed earlier cannot be easily bypassed. New actors that enter the field are therefore confronted with an ecosystem marked by traditional alliances and strict laws regulating financial transfers and entitlements.

A policy field in transformation: youth welfare

Many new generation SEs have emerged in the field of youth welfare, often with a specific focus on education. They are chiefly active in the German rust belts, serving children from deprived families, many of whom are (or once were) migrants. The field of youth welfare—as defined in Book VIII of the German Social Code, SGB VIII: Welfare of children and young persons—draws upon established pathways of service provision that are based on the principle of subsidiarity (Fischer, 2011; Grohs et al., 2015). Public authorities have to cooperate with recognized youth welfare organizations and are obliged to support them financially. As a consequence, nearly two thirds of all youth welfare services in Germany are offered by independent organizations (Schmidt, 2012). Despite the fact that the law allows for a plurality of private providers, commercial organizations are rare. Instead, most private providers belong to the nonprofit sector, including youth associations, local initiatives, and sports federations (BMFSFJ, 2017; Hepp, 2011). Most of them, moreover, are affiliated with the Free Welfare Associations (Holtkamp & Grohs, 2012) or Protestant/Catholic churches. Since there is close cooperation between authorities and youth welfare organizations, the field is shaped in a "traditional corporatist manner" (Fischer, 2011, p. 124). Traditional private providers that are "highly embedded in networks and cooperative arrangements" hold a strong position (Grohs et al., 2015, p. 174), which of course prevents new providers from offering social services (Oberhuemer, 2015).

Youth welfare is marked by a high degree of legal regulation that often leads to standardized processes and decisions, many of which clash with the various problems, backgrounds, and lifestyles of the younger generation. The traditional options of school attendance, vocational training, professional life, and starting a family seem outdated in the face of the diversity of unforeseeable and inconsistent life cycles and the variety of options (Lützenkirchen, 2014). At least three factors have fostered the emergence of SEs in this field. First, youth welfare has developed into a key area for social investment (Schönert et al., 2016). Growing public investment and employment in this field (Meuth et al., 2014; Rauschenbach, 2014) reflect the need to promote public policies that prepare individuals, families, and communities to adapt to various social risks, instead of simply reacting after other policies prove insufficient (Morel et al., 2015). Supporting youngsters to become highly productive members of German society has moved to the top of the social policy agenda. Due to the scarcity of public resources—especially at the local level—many private organizations, including foundations and corporations, have started to invest in programs and initiatives that are earmarked for youngsters (Striebing, 2017; Vodafone Stiftung, 2017).

Second, well-established organizations that are already engaged in youth welfare are confronted with problems of addressing and getting close to their target groups. Many of the established organizations are either connected to the two major churches or they are part of a local community and working on a volunteer basis (e.g. sports clubs). Individualization (Gürlevik et al., 2016) and rising mobility (Dietz et al., 2015) work in favor of commercial alternatives, many of which are regarded as being more attractive for young people (Schäfer, 2013). This development has been strengthened by the expansion of formal education in the form of full-time schooling (Meuth et al., 2014; Schäfer, 2013). As a result, the share of young people engaging with traditional social organizations is declining (BMFSFJ, 2017), as their services are less appealing among youngsters who strive for self-organization and autonomy (Enquete Kommission, 2002). Likewise, established organizations are less able to address and integrate migrant children or children from low-income families, a target group of increasing importance. According to the 15th Children and Youth Service Report (BMFSFJ, 2017), although overall educational levels have increased, inequality has only intensified in recent decades. A link between educational/occupational success and the socioeconomic status of the family of origin has been documented (Hepp, 2011). Similarly, the problems associated with children from immigrant families—many of whom are struggling with poverty—are expanding (Autorengruppe Bildungsberichterstattung, 2016; Oberhuemer, 2015) and becoming even more acute due to an estimated half a million refugees under 25 who have come to Germany since 2015 (BMFSFJ, 2017, p. 144).

Third, many established youth welfare organizations have had problems competing for public and private grants in an environment in which the rhetoric and logic of business has replaced the language of social work. The New Public Management approach favors competitive tendering, which means that contract-based imbursements have replaced tradition fiscal relations that once relied exclusively on public support. This remodeling benefits SEs in two ways: on the one hand, it offers service recipients an opportunity to choose their own service provider (Dölle, 2011); on the other hand, SEs are better able to secure stable and customized sources of income, so long as there is a demand for their services (Boetticher & Münder, 2009).

The field of youth welfare is especially well-suited for social innovation because it is currently gaining political support under the new social investment paradigm. Traditional and well-established service providers no longer meet the demands of new target groups, which, in turn, creates niche areas where innovative concepts that are attractive to young people and can address inequalities in the German system can flourish.

Social enterprises as social innovators

The following section explains how German SEs working in the field of youth welfare have become successful drivers of social innovation by following a niche approach. We base our argument on the experiences of two SEs: RheinFlanke and Chancenwerk.

RheinFlanke

RheinFlanke, an SE that focuses on mobile youth employment, was founded as a private limited liability company with public benefit status (gGmbH) in 2006–2007. Its main goal is to reach deprived adolescents via open sports programs (football) and help them develop and enhance their social skills. The enterprise employs about 50 staff members, most of them social workers. A supervisory board and a board of trustees (the latter of which is made up mainly of notable figures from television, politics, and the local economy) support RheinFlanke with advice, and help forge new contacts with sponsors and lawmakers.

Idea and target group

Although it has roots in the city of Cologne, RheinFlanke currently operates in nine cities along the Rhine in North Rhine-Westphalia, Germany's most populous state (17 million inhabitants). Poverty rates in the region are above the national average, and inequality has steadily increased in the last ten years (www.der-paritaetische.de/armutsbericht/problemregionen/). RheinFlanke focuses on districts with socioeconomic problems and significant migrant populations. Poor and/or migrant youth often face difficulties when trying to enter the labor market. RheinFlanke employees approach adolescents on football grounds, playfields, or schoolyards, and then try to build mutual trust by offering them, free of charge, enrollment in various athletic programs. Although football is RheinFlanke's flagship activity, many adolescents take advantage of other services, including social work for individuals and groups, counseling, and training. All in all, RheinFlanke's services aim at helping youngsters manage the difficult transition from school to professional life. "The enterprise's sports-based programs offer a low threshold to establish relations with youth that providers find especially difficult to reach" (Brüntrup, 2017, p. 27).

Success story

RheinFlanke started as a local street football league in the city of Cologne in 2006. Encouraged by Germany's hosting of the World Cup in that same year, the two founders of the organization created projects that use football to enhance social skills and development in young people. The approach had already been tried out successfully in major cities such as Berlin, Hamburg, and Munich but had not yet been implemented in North Rhine-Westphalia. The two social entrepreneurs initiated the street football league—"Köln kickt"—using start-up funds (10,000 Euros) that were provided by the city of Cologne. The project soon received positive feedback and further inquiries from municipal authorities, which, in turn, led its founders to establish RheinFlanke as a nonprofit organization (gGmbH) in 2007.

RheinFlanke has successfully expanded into eight neighboring cities, increased the number of its employees sixtyfold, and enlarged its operational budget almost 180 times (Brüntrup, 2017, p. 17). RheinFlanke has established itself as a reliable partner for public authorities in districts that struggle with severe social tensions. It is considered an innovative service provider that can attract at-risk adolescents and react to the challenges that currently mark the field of youth welfare (Brüntrup 2017, 24ff). RheinFlanke has also received several awards for its work, including the German Engagement Award (Deutscher Engagementpreis), the PHINEO impact-label (Phineo-Wirk-Siegel), the German Child and Youth Welfare award (Deutscher Kinder und Jugendhilfepreis), and the Prize for Integration by the German Football Association (DFB).

Business model

RheinFlanke's annual budget is about 1.5 million Euros. Public authorities contribute the major share (70%), while private sponsors make up the remainder (30%). No income is generated through final users. Rheinflanke is currently sponsored by 11 public contractors, including the European Union and authorities at the federal, state, and municipal level. The European Integration Fund is the single biggest sponsor, providing about 450 million Euros annually (including 30% of its own resources), followed by municipalities. Since public authorities oblige contractors to contribute approximately 30% of their funding from their own resources—a matching-grant approach—the successful recruitment of private sponsors is crucial for

RheinFlanke. It is currently supported by 25 prominent individual sponsors and foundations, most of whom have regional ties. Some of the more prominent individual sponsors include the Lukas Podolski Foundation (an organization founded by former football player Lukas Podolski), the GO-FUs e.V. (a network of former and current professional football players), and the Dirk Nowitzki Foundation (an organization founded by professional basketball player Dirk Nowitzki).

Two important factors in securing funding and recruiting new sponsors are RheinFlanke's strong public relations capacities and dense regional networks. Over time, RheinFlanke has established a network of "big donors" and a Board of Trustees that is staffed with movie stars, businesspeople, and politicians. These people help expand existing networks, create the necessary publicity to raise funds, and secure donations.

Chancenwerk

Chancenwerk strives to open up opportunities for adolescents who come from poor or migrant families. It provides schools with a tutoring program called "Learning Cascade," in which high school seniors receive tutoring by university students, and in return supervise their younger colleagues. Chancenwerk is a registered association whose activities serve the public good and is therefore entitled to receive taxation privileges in accordance with the German Fiscal Code.

Idea and target group

Chancenwerk's goal is to address the lack of educational opportunities for children from migrant or poor families. Its main program—the "Learning Cascade"—uses the transfer of knowledge from older students to younger students to address integration issues among German youth. University students support senior class pupils by tutoring them in subjects that are problematic for them. They receive tutoring once a week for 90 minutes in groups of six. Working on a volunteer basis, senior students help younger pupils once a week for 90 minutes.

Chancenwerk was first established in 2004 in Castrop-Rauxel, a former coal-mining town in the Ruhr area of North Rhine-Westphalia that attracted immigrant workers after World War II drew to a close. Indeed, the number of migrants living in North Rhine-Westphalia has always been above the German average (Information und Technik NRW, 2015; Städte und Gemeindenbund NRW, 2014). Like most towns in this part of Germany, Castrop-Rauxel faces a severe budgetary crisis (Ruhr Nachrichten, 2014) and an unemployment rate of 10.7% that far outpaces the 6.3% found in the rest of Germany (Bundesagentur für Arbeit, 2015). Chancenwerk has managed to scale-up successfully. Today, it cooperates with partner schools in underprivileged urban areas all across Germany.

Success story

Chancenwerk's founders, Murat and Serife Vural, started Chancenwerk in response to their own personal experiences with the educational system. They were born in Germany to Turkish migrants. Since they couldn't speak German all that well, both of the founders attended the lowest form of secondary school and encountered many educational hurdles. Despite little support by their teachers, the Vurals managed to work their way through the educational system. Due to their personal difficulties with the educational system—while also noticing that many of their friends lacked the motivation and self-esteem to succeed in school—they started Chancenwerk during their time at university.

In 2006, two years after it was founded, Chancenwerk won the Startsocial competition,[1] and Murat Vural became an Ashoka fellow. According to Vural, these accolades came about because migration and education were pressing issues at that time. Regardless, Vural received a three-year scholarship from Ashoka, enabling him to quit his day job and fully dedicate himself to the organization (Chancenwerk, 2015). Chancenwerk was also lucky enough to receive counseling from McKinsey & Company, whose expertise led to the creation of a viable business plan. In 2009, Vural presented his "Learning Cascade" idea at the Vision Summit in Berlin, which increased the visibility of Chancenwerk and helped them secure financial support from a foundation that paved the way for Chancenwerk's scaling-up in subsequent years. Chancenwerk started as a voluntary project, but would soon transform itself into a business with salaried employees, including Murat Vural (Chancenwerk, 2015). From a small association teaching a dozen pupils in Castrop-Rauxel, Chancenwerk has developed into a successful SE that coaches more than 2,400 pupils all over the country. As of 2015, Chancenwerk was active in twenty-two cities and over forty schools. It has also witnessed a significant increase in popularity in recent years and has been awarded several prizes and awards (see www.chancenwerk. de/zahlen-daten-fakten/). Indeed, in 2010 Murat Vural was awarded the Federal Cross of Merit for his attempts to encourage social inclusion among disadvantaged people.

Business model

During its early years, Chancenwerk relied primarily on donations by foundations and firms. It would eventually secure income from membership fees and public compensation for services rendered, as it became an official provider of youth welfare services. It currently generates an annual revenue of about one million Euros via donations from foundations (70%), corporate social responsibility (CSR) funds from various firms (15%), membership fees (15%), and compensation by public authorities for services rendered (<1%).

Membership fees are paid by grade five and six students, all of whom have to pay 10 Euros per month to participate in the Learning Cascade program (Serife Vural, personal Interview, December 5, 2015). CSR funds from firms and private foundations are mostly regional in nature, as companies and private funders tend to support schools in their local communities. In addition, Chancenwerk receives material assistance and pro bono support from other individuals and institutions. For example, several firms provide office space for its various regional branches. Chancenwerk also relies heavily on the voluntary activities of university students who agree to work with high school students and has partnered up with several universities, including the University of Cologne, the University of Bochum, and Witten/Herdecke University. Finally, Chancenwerk receives financial support from the "educational package," a program funded by the Federal Ministry of Labor and Social Affairs that uses educational and cultural support for children from low-income families to prevent social exclusion. The funds are administered by local administrations. Among other services, this program finances 45 minutes of learning support per week if a child is at risk of repeating a school year (Bundesministerium für Arbeit und Soziales, 2015, p. 6). Ultimately, Chancenwerk does not rely to any great extent on market-based sources of income but has instead established a large and professional network of supporters and donors, including volunteers and private/business foundations. This innovative, hybrid approach to funding guarantees the survival and further expansion of the organization.

Discussion: social innovation in established organizational fields

Based on the information about our two case studies provided earlier, we will now analyze the common features that make these SEs simultaneously drivers of social innovation in the field of youth welfare as well as textbook examples for the new species of SEs. These SEs successfully made use of both a changed organizational environment and a window of opportunity in terms of untouched resources.

The first shared feature is the focus on vulnerable, neglected, and emerging target groups. Both SEs focus on adolescents from either poor or migrant families in underprivileged urban areas. Both groups are gaining attention as a result of societal transformations and diminishing opportunities (especially in the education system). Both SEs address social needs that have not been adequately addressed by traditional providers and other organizations in innovative ways.

The percentage of German children growing up in poverty has risen in the last ten years (Baader & Freytag, 2017), while success in the education system continues to depend on one's socioeconomic background (Becker, 2012; Berkemeyer & Neißer, 2017). Moreover, educational achievement remains pivotal for future success and social integration (Baader & Freytag,

2017). In this context, recent increases in forced migration and displacement due to conflict and humanitarian crises (particularly in the Middle East and Africa) are further exacerbating the social divide. The number of refugees has grown immensely since 2015, and Germany has received nearly 1.5 million applications for asylum, most of them submitted by children and adolescents (particularly young men) (BAMF, 2017, pp. 3, 7). Programs and measures that address at-risk children and young adults are gaining in importance (Hagmann, 2013). However, critics bemoan the fact that traditional "children and youth welfare reaches those least who would most benefit from it" (Olk, 2013, p. 16). The likelihood that children will use these services decreases as the education levels of parents decreases (Olk, 2013). Since society (rather than the family) is often held responsible for the well-being of youngsters—especially children from less privileged families (Rauschenbach, 2014)—it is not surprising to see that both SEs take advantage of growing political and social pressure urging local administrations to enlarge their provision of services for youth.

Another common feature of both RheinFlanke and Chancenwerk is their reliance on innovative approaches, concepts, and services that are tailored to their target groups. This includes RheinFlanke's emphasis on sports and mobile youth employment, as well as Chancenwerk's award-winning Learning Cascade concept. Both RheinFlanke and Chancenwerk are similarly skilled at reaching adolescents who are overlooked by traditional providers and programs. Because their founders were inspired by personal experience or earlier work in the fields of education and youth welfare, both organizations are able to develop custom-fit services that appeal to vulnerable target groups.

Another common feature of both SEs is their willingness to diversify their income streams, combining traditional compensation from public authorities with alternative sources. For instance, Chancenwerk generates market-based income by imposing modest fees on their users. By contrast, RheinFlanke is successful in marketing its concept to local sponsors and foundations. Both organizations have managed to build up donor networks with private/business foundations or enterprises with CSR funds. They also rely on voluntary work and pro bono support. According to Achleitner et al. (2013), SEs in Germany enjoy easier access to new financial opportunities than traditional nonprofit organizations and for-profit enterprises. This might explain why both SEs managed to tap into new resources and get help from new actors, such as foundations and companies. Emerging SEs may also rely on social investment funds, prize money, and scholarships from incubator organizations (e.g. Ashoka and the Impact Hub network), or even crowdfunding. They take advantage of new opportunities provided by private actors, while simultaneously nurturing partnerships with public institutions—especially local governments and schools.

In the end, our analysis points out how these new SEs have managed to become accepted members of their organizational field. This was done by

Table 10.1 Cases (overview)

	RheinFlanke	Chancenwerk
Foundation	2006	2004
Legal form	Private limited liability company with public benefit status (gGmbH)	Registered association (e.V.)
Aim	Social development through football	Creating opportunities for children from a weak socioeconomic background
Success story	• Continuous expansion of sites and workforce	• Growing number of participating students • Starting as a student initiative and ending up as a respected enterprise with nationwide impact
	• German Engagement Award • PHINEO impact-label • German Child and Youth Welfare award	• Ashoka fellow • Federal Cross of Merit for social inclusion of disadvantaged people
Niches for innovation	• Focus on emerging, neglected target groups • Diversification of funding • Innovative, tailored solutions and concepts	

addressing—in an innovative manner—severe problems that were not tackled by traditional actors and institutions, raising new funds and resources, and securing public support and legal recognition. The SEs under study still adopt a conservative approach to welfare, which is marked by close cooperation between local governments and private actors for the provision of social services. However, they also embrace the social investment approach, which aims at empowering and preparing people to take social risks. They are active in transforming the field of youth welfare, and they provide innovative solutions to emerging local problems. By creating "niches" in which social innovation can flourish, they have established themselves as alternative and complementary providers of social services in the German welfare system (Table 10.1).

Conclusion

Our research explains how SEs in a conservative context have managed to establish themselves in Germany's highly regulated welfare system. They act as drivers of social innovation, addressing and tackling unmet needs of children and youth at school and in their neighborhoods. They tend to operate in fields that are characterized by increasing demands, a need for transformation, new investments in terms of grants and programs by private donors, and relatively secure, legally regulated sources of public funding. They also distinguish themselves by offering alternative, flexible, and holistic solutions to social problems while also using innovative business models to address the failures of both the market and the state. By doing so, they meet the changing demands of welfare and social service production, which has been subject to a process of marketization in recent decades, resulting in the creation of a new and business-like culture. They manage to identify emerging target groups, develop tailored working concepts to reach these groups, and diversify their funding via professionally managed networks of support. This approach allows SEs to find success in a sector that features strong nonprofit providers that offer services in cooperation with public (especially local) authorities. Moreover, it transforms them into attractive partners for public authorities who seek out social innovation. SEs have to search for these windows of opportunity in order to become real drivers of social innovation.

Note

1 The Startsocial competition is an annual contest for civic engagement initiatives under the patronage of chancellor Angela Merkel. For further information, see https://startsocial.de/ueber-uns.

References

Achleitner, A. K., Mayer, J., & Spieß-Knafl, W. (2013). Sozialunternehmen und ihre Kapitalgeber. In S. A. Jansen, Heinze, G. Rolf, M. Beckmann, & R. Schües (Eds.), *Sozialunternehmen in Deutschland. Analysen, Trends und Handlungsempfehlungen* (pp. 153–165). Wiesbaden: Springer VS.

Autorengruppe Bildungsberichterstattung. (2016). *Bildung in Deutschland 2016*. Bielefeld: W. Bertelsmann Verlag.

Baader, M. S., & Freytag, T. (2017). *Bildung und Ungleichheit in Deutschland*. Wiesbaden: Springer.

BAMF, Bundesamt für Migration und Flüchtlinge. (2017). Aktuelle Zahlen zu Asyl. Retrieved from www.bamf.de/SharedDocs/Anlagen/DE/Downloads/Infothek/Statistik/Asyl/aktuelle-zahlen-zu-asyl-juli-2017.html?nn=7952222.

Baum, J. (1999). Organizational ecology. In St. Clegg, & C. Hardy (Eds.), *Studying organization* (pp. 71–108). London: Sage.

Becker, R. (2012). Bildung. Die wichtigste Investition in die Zukunft. In S. Hradil (Ed.), *Deutsche Verhältnisse. Eine Sozialkunde* (pp. 123–154). Bonn: BpB.

Berkemeyer, N., & Meißner, S. (2017). Soziale Ungleichheiten im Schulsystem und das Desiderat einer Soziologie der Schule. In M. S. Baader, & T. Freytag (Eds.), *Bildung und Ungleichheit in Deutschland* (pp. 229–254). Wiesbaden: Springer.

BMFSFJ, Bundesministerium für Familie, Senioren, Frauen und Jugend. (2017). *15. Kinder- und Jugendbericht. Bericht über die Lebenssituation junger Menschen und die Leistungen der Kinder- und Jugendhilfe in Deutschland*. Berlin.

Boeßenecker, K.-H., & Vilain, M. (2013). *Spitzenverbände der Freien Wohlfahrtspflege: Eine Einführung in die Organisationsstrukturen und Handlungsfelder der deutschen Wohlfahrtsverbände*. Weinheim/München: Juventus.

Boetticher, A. V., & Münder, J. (2009). *Kinder- und Jugendhilfe und europäischer Binnenmarkt*. Baden-Baden: Nomos.

Brandsen, T., Evers, A., Cattacin, S., & Zimmer, A. (2016). Social innovation: A sympathetic and critical interpretation. In T. Brandsen, A. Evers, S. Cattacin, & A. Zimmer (Eds.), *Social innovations in the urban context* (pp. 3–18). Heidelberg: Springer Open.

Brüntrup, M. (2017). *Let's work together? Innovative social entrepreneurship in the field of youth policy welcomed by German local governments – A case study of the social enterprise Rheinflanke.* Bachelor Thesis.

Bundesagentur für Arbeit. (2015). Statistik. Retrieved from https://statistik. arbeitsagentur.de/Navigation/Statistik/Statistik-nach-Regionen/Politische-Gebietsstruktur-Nav.html?year_month=201507.

Bundesministerium für Arbeit und Soziales. (2015). The Educational Package. A new start for taking part. Retrieved from www.bmas.de/SharedDocs/Downloads/ EN/PDF-Publikationen/A857be-educational-package-brochure.pdf?__blob= publicationFile&v=1.

Chancenwerk. (2015). *10 Jahre Chancenwerk – Eine Zeitreise -2004-2014.* Brochure.

Dees, G. J., & Anderson, B. B. (2006). Framing a theory of social entrepreneurship: Building on two schools of practice and thought. *ARNOVA Occasional Paper Series: Research on Social Entrepreneurship: Understanding and Contributing to an Emerging Field, 1*(3), 39–66.

Defourny, J., & Nyssens, M. (2015). Social innovation, social economy and social enterprise: What can the European debate tell us? In F. Moulaert, D. MacCallum, A. Mehmood, & A. Hamdouch (Eds.), *The international handbook on social innovation* (pp. 9–12). Cheltenham: Edward Elgar.

Dietz, B., Frevel B., & Toens, K. (2015). *Sozialpolitik kompakt.* Wiesbaden: Springer VS.

Dölle, D. (2011). Potentiale von Social Entrepreneurship für die Kinder- und Jugendhilfe. In H. Hackenberg, & S. Empter (Eds.), *Social entrepreneurship – social business: für die Gesellschaft unternehmen* (pp. 203–219). Wiesbaden: Springer VS.

Enquete Kommission. (2002). *Bericht. Bürgerschaftliches Engagement: auf dem Weg in eine zukunftsfähige Bürgergesellschaft.* Wiesbaden: Springer VS.

Esping-Andersen, G. (1990). *The three worlds of welfare capitalism.* Cambridge: Policy Press.

Evers, A., Ewert, B., & Brandsen T. (2014). *Social innovations for social cohesion. Transnational patters and approaches from 20 European cities.* Liege: EMES European Research Network asbl.

Fischer, J. (2011). Die doppelte Modernisierung – Politische Steuerung und Jugendhilfe im Wandel. In G. Flößer (Eds.), *Jugendhilfeforschung* (pp. 141–150). Wiesbaden: VS Verlag für Sozialwissenschaften.

Fligstein, N., & McAdam, D. (2015). *A theory of fields.* Oxford: Oxford University Press.

Fuchs, P. (2014). Soziale Innovationen durch Sozialunternehmen. Schlüssel zur Lösung gesellschaftlicher Probleme? *Forschungsjournal Soziale Bewegungen, 27*, 90–99.

Gläser, J., & Laudel, G. (2008). *Experteninterviews und qualitative Inhaltsanalyse.* Wiesbaden: VS Verlag.

Grohs, S., Katrin S., & Rolf G. H. (2015). Social entrepreneurship versus intrapreneurship in the German social welfare state: A study of old-age care and youth welfare services. *Nonprofit and Voluntary Sector Quarterly, 44*(1), 163–180.

Gürlevik, A., Hurrelmann, K., & Palentien, C. (2016). Jugend und Politik im Wandel? In A. Gürlevik, K. Hurrelmann, & C. Palentien (Eds.), *Jugend und Politik* (pp. 1–25). Wiesbaden: Springer VS.

Hagmann, G. (2013). Verlierer vermeiden. *DJI Impulse, 101*, 26–28.

Hannan, M., & Freeman, J. (1977). The population ecology of organizations. *American Journal of Sociology, 82*(5), 929–954.

Heinze, R. G., & Olk, T. (1981). Die Wohlfahrtsverbände im System sozialer Dienstleis-tungsproduktion. *Kölner Zeitschrift für Soziologie und Sozialpsychologie, 33*, 94–114.

Henriksen, L. S., Smith, S. R., & Zimmer, A. (2012). At the eve of convergence? Trans-formation of social service provision in Denmark, Germany, and the United States. *Voluntas, 23*(2), 458–501.

Hepp, G. F. (2011). *Bildungspolitik in Deutschland. Eine Einführung.* Wiesbaden: Springer VS.

Holtkamp, L., & Grohs S. (2012). Rahmenbedingungen kommunaler Jugendpolitik: Strukturmuster und Besonderheiten der kommunalen Ebene. In W. Lindner (Eds.), *Political (Re-)Turn? Impulse zu einem neuen Verhältnis von Jugendarbeit und Jugendpolitik* (pp. 177–192). Wiesbaden: VS Verlag für Sozialwissenschaften.

Information und Technik NRW. (2015). NRW: Ein Viertel aller Einwohner hat einen Migrationshintergrund. Retrieved from www.it.nrw.de/presse/pressemitteilungen/2014/pres_142_14.html.

Jansen, S. A., Heinze, R. G., Beckmann, M., & Schües, R. (2013). *Sozialunternehmen in Deutschland. Analysen, Trends und Handlungsempfehlungen.* Wiesbaden: Springer VS.

Kerlin, J. A. (2010). A comparative analysis of the global emergence of social enterprise. *Voluntas, 2*, 162–179.

Kieser, A., & Woywode, M. (2006). Evolutionstheoretische Ansätze. In A. Kieser & M. Ebers (Eds.), *Organisationstheorien (6. Auflage)* (pp. 309–351). Stuttgart: Verlag W. Kohlhammer.

Lützenkirchen, H.-G. (2014). *Fußball und Jugendhilfe. Das Modell der RheinFlanke Köln.* Köln: RheinFlanke.

Mair, J., & Marti, I. (2006). Social entrepreneurship research: A source of explanation, prediction and delight. *Journal of World Business, 41*, 36–44.

Meng, Z. (2016). Reinventing social enterprise in China. Language, institution and strategy. In Y. Chandra, & L. Wong (Eds.). *Social entrepreneurship in the Greater China region. Policy and cases* (pp. 1–18). London: Routledge.

Meuth, M., Warth, A., & Walther, A. (2014). No crisis but a paradigm shift? German youth policy between continuity and change. *International Journal of Adolescence and Youth, 19*, 79–92.

Morel, N., Palier, B., & Palme, J. (2015). Social investment: A paradigm in search of a new economic model and political mobilization. In N. Morel, B. Palier, & J. Palme (Eds.), *Towards a social investment welfare state. Ideas, policies and challenges* (pp. 353–376). Chicago, IL: Policy Press.

Moulaert, F., MacCallum, D., & Hillier, J. (2015a). Social innovation: Intuition, precept, concept, theory and practice. In F. Moulaert, D. MacCallum, A. Mehmood, & A. Hamdouch (Eds.), *The international handbook on social innovation* (pp. 13–24). Cheltenham: Edward Elgar.

Moulaert, F., MacCallum, D., Mehmood, A., & Hamdouch, A. (2015a). General introduction: The return of social innovation as a scientific concept and a social practice. In F. Moulaert, D. MacCallum, A. Mehmood, & A. Hamdouch (Eds.), *The international handbook on social innovation* (pp. 1–6). Cheltenham: Edward Elgar.

Mulgan, G., Tucker, S., Ali, R., & Sanders, B. (2007). *Social Innovation: What it is, why it matters and how it can be accelerated.* Oxford: Skoll Centre for Social Entrepreneurship.

Nicholls, A. (2008). *Social entrepreneurship. New models of sustainable social change.* Oxford: Oxford University Press.

Nicholls, A., Simon, J., & Gabriel, M. (2016). Introduction: Dimensions of social innovation. In A. Nicholls, J. Simon & M. Gabriel (Eds.), *New frontiers in social innovation research* (pp. 1–26). Basingstoke: Palgrave Macmillan.

Oberhuemer, P. (2015). Access and quality issues in early childhood education and care: The case of Germany. In L. Gambaro, K. Stewart, & J. Waldfogel (Eds.), *An equal start? Providing quality early education and care for disadvantaged children* (pp. 121–146). Bristol: Policy Press.

Olk, T. (2013). Alle Kinder gezielt fördern. *DJI Impulse, 101*, 16–18.

Powell, W., & DiMaggio, P. (1991). *The new institutionalism in organizational theory.* Chicago, IL: University of Chicago Press.

Rauschenbach, T. (2014). Wohin entwickelt sich die Kinder- und Jugendhilfe? Anmerkungen zu einem Praxisfeld im Wandel. In S. Faas & M. Zipperle (Eds.), *Sozialer Wandel* (pp. 173–186). Wiesbaden: Springer VS.

Ruhr Nachrichten. (2014, April, 2). Aufatmen bei der Stadt: Haushalt 2014 genehmigt(02.04.2014).RuhrNachrichten.Retrievedfromwww.ruhrnachrichten. de/staedte/castrop/Stadtfinanzen-Aufatmen-bei-der-Stadt-Haushalt-2014-genehmigt;art934,2323474.

Sachße, C. (1995). Verein, Verband und Wohlfahrtsstaat. Entstehung und Entwicklung der dualen Wohlfahrtspflege. In T. Rauschenbach, C. Sachße, and T. Olk (Eds.), *Von der Wertgemeinschaft zum Dienstleistungsunternehmen* (pp. 123–149). Frankfurt: Suhrkamp taschenbuch.

Schäfer, K. (2013). Jugendarbeit unter Druck. *DJI Impulse, 101*, 13–15.

Scheuerle, T., Glänzel, G., Knust, R., & Then, V. (2013). Social Entrepreneurship in Deutschland. Potentiale und Wachstumsproblematiken. Eine Studie im Auftrag der KfW, Centrum für Soziale Innovationen und Investitionen. Retrieved from www. kfw.de/PDF/Download-Center/Konzernthemen/Research/PDF-Dokumente-Studien-und-Materialien/Social-Entrepreneurship-in-Deutschland-LF.pdf.

Schmid, J. (2010). *Wohlfahrtsstaaten im Vergleich* (3rd ed.). Wiesbaden: VS Verlag.

Schmidt, C. (2012). *Kinder- und Jugendhilfeleistungen in deutschen kreisfreien Städten: Ausprägung und Erklärungsfaktoren.* Wiesbaden: Springer VS.

Schmitz, B., & Scheuerle, T. (2013). Social Intrapreneurship. Innovative und unternehmerische Aspekte in drei deutschen christlichen Wohlfahrtsträgern. In S. A. Jansen, R. G. Heinze, & M. Beckmann (Eds.). *Sozialunternehmen in Deutschland* (pp. 187–218). Wiesbaden: Springer VS Verlag.

Schönert, C., Freise, M., & Zimmer, A. (2016). *Social economy: Delivering social outcomes. A social investment perspective.* Münster. Retrieved from www. uni-muenster.de/imperia/md/content/ifpol/innosi/innosi-649189-d3_3.pdf.

Spiess-Knafl, W., Schües, R., Richter, S., Scheuerle, T., & Schmitz, B. (2013). Eine Vermessung der Landschaft deutscher Sozialunternehmen. In S. A. Jansen, R. G. Heinze, & M. Beckmann (Eds.), *Sozialunternehmen in Deutschland* (pp. 21–34). Wiesbaden: Springer VS Verlag.

Städte- und Gemeindebund Nordrhein-Westfalen. (2014). Jedes dritte Kind in NRW mit Migrationshintergrund. Retrieved from www.kommunen-in-nrw.de/mitgliederbereich/mitteilungen/detailansicht/dokument/jedes-dritte-kind-in-nrw-hatte-einen-migrationshintergrund.html?cHash=7d63d496 86dfb65a2cd230bedf0a2376.

Striebing, C. (2017). Fürsorge durch Wandel: Stiftungen im deutschen Schulwesen. In H. K. Anheier, S. Förster, J. Mangold, & C. Striebing (Eds.), *Stiftungen in Deutschland 2: Wirkungsfelder* (pp. 23–117). Wiesbaden: Springer VS Verlag.

Vodafone Stiftung Deutschland. (2015). Menschen und Ideen fördern. Die Arbeit der Vodafone Stiftung Deutschland zur Verbesserung der Chancen auf Bildung und sozialen Aufstieg. Retrieved from www.vodafone-stiftung.de/taetigkeitsberichte.html.

Wollmann, H. (2012). Entwicklung, Stand und Perspektive der deutschen kommunalen Selbstverwaltung im europäischen Vergleich. In B. Egner, M. Haus, & G. Terizakis (Eds.), *Regieren. Festschrift für Hubert Heinelt* (pp. 421–441). Wiesbaden: VS Verlag.

Zimmer, A., & Obuch, K. (2017). A matter of context? Understanding social enterprises in changing environments: The case of Germany. *Voluntas.* Published online July 2017. doi:10.1007/s11266-017-9893-6

11 The in-between space of new generation social enterprises

Mara Benadusi and Rosario Sapienza

Approach and methodology

Our main research objective is to verify the existence of a new generation of social enterprises (NGSEs) in Europe and identify its specific features at the transnational level. Fifty-five case studies from eleven countries—Albania, Austria, England, France, Germany, Italy, the Netherlands, Poland, Scotland, Serbia, and Sweden—have been examined in this study, using a multidisciplinary methodology that includes organizational life histories, narrative methods, in-depth interviews (with both individuals and groups), participatory exercises, desk analysis, and shadowing techniques (Czarniawska, 2007; McDonald, 2005; Quinlan, 2008). All of these cases cover several different sectors, including environmental and sustainable development, social integration, intermediate labor market initiatives for unemployed people, education, health care, and services for people with disabilities. We adopted a maximum variation sampling approach when deciding which social enterprises (SEs) would be included in our study. We ultimately opted for a broad approach that included micro- and macro-enterprises, small and large enterprises, local and national organizations, as well as community-based and internationally oriented enterprises. We also chose to adopt a diachronic approach in order to better identify the lifecycle of each organization (Thomas, 2011).

The remainder of this chapter is cut into three sections. A comparative overview of the structural features that characterize the SEs in our study is provided in the "Taxonomies" section, with a special focus on the age of the foundation, fields of operation, revenue size, and mission. The "Topographies" section discusses how settling in marginalized, expansive, or central areas can influence an SE's evolutionary pathways and expansion strategies, oftentimes shaping the organization's reaction to the most recent economic crisis while also determining enabling and disabling factors. The "Biographies" section, meanwhile, focuses on human factors—both individual and collective—such as personal background, business ideas, and the political/ideological origins of an entrepreneur's involvement in the social economy. The last section, "Physiologies," explores functioning and productive engines, highlighting the most innovative aspects of governance and decision-making processes, ICT and social media use, coping mechanisms, and collaborative work styles.

The fifty-five case studies included here are not necessarily representative, as our analysis avoids unilateral readings or simplifications. Our exploratory approach seeks to expand our knowledge of NGSEs, thus paving the way for more extensive investigations in the future, without resorting to some of the stale and tired views that are widespread in both public forums and the scholarly literature. Indeed, new generation social entrepreneurs are often portrayed as a heroic, unique group of people (Light, 2010), with unique personalities and traits, including strong ethical beliefs (Bornstein, 1998; Drayton, 2002), exceptional leadership skills (Thompson et al., 2000), and a passion to realize their visions (Bornstein, 2004). However, these studies are biased because they choose to analyze successful entrepreneurs (Mair and Martí, 2006). The social entrepreneur—especially in managerial studies—is often portrayed as an agent of change who is capable of using outstanding ideas to revolutionize ways of producing value and reducing expenses in times of crisis. Our research, however, does not aim to identify typologies of social entrepreneurs, but rather to assess whether certain NGSEs can actually be identified as such, adopting behavior—in terms of governance, use of networks, models of enterprise, values, motivations, and work styles—and needs that are different from previous conceptualizations.

Taxonomies

While selecting the NGSEs for our sample, we used their foundational periods as our main criterion, while all the other variables were treated as features that should be examined locally. We chose to focus on 2006 due to two interconnected phenomena. In 2006, Muhammad Yunus, the founder of the Grameen Bank, was awarded the Nobel Peace Prize, giving rise to initiatives meant to promote a host of activities associated with SEs in Europe, including training, research, evaluation, and consultation services. At the same time, the intensification of the economic crisis in Europe had serious repercussions on the SE sector as progressive cuts in welfare spending and a subsequent crisis of unmet social needs led to the emergence of new areas of expression for social businesses.

The fifty-five case studies included here reveal a fragmented and nonlinear developmental path. In some cases, the year in which an organization was founded merely represented a moment of formalization, the end of an incubation period for an idea that had originated in the past. In other cases, meanwhile, the founders' biographies reveal previous attempts to establish socially oriented initiatives. A significant shared feature of the SEs in our study involves their economic independence from the public system. In over two-thirds of the cases examined, less than one-third of their income came from public support, while at least one-third was paid directly by final users. The source of economic revenue varies considerably, as 80% of SEs relied on final users, 62% relied on project-based fundraising, donations, and/or other forms of sponsorship, and 30% relied on public procurement. One of the most difficult aspects of our research involved the formal/legal status of the SEs in our study. Almost half of these entities are small, traditional companies that are owned by one person—a sole proprietorship. Apart from their legal character, SEs seek to maintain a precarious balance between the need to make a positive social impact and create an economically sustainable organization.

It is not easy to summarize all areas of intervention and arrive at some useful generalizations. The main sectors—environmental and sustainable development, social integration, intermediate labor market initiatives for unemployed people, education, health care, and services for people with disabilities—include diverse subcategories of intervention that end up overlapping with each other. Likewise, areas of intervention tend to be adapted to the local context, particularly in terms of the role and presence of agencies and institutions at local, regional, and national levels. The public system serves as a primary decisive variable, although it is far from being the only one. In many cases, SEs seek to avoid competition from large third-sector associations by opting to work in a niche area or by choosing to take a supporting role. They often compensate for the gaps created by a weak, timeworn, and "lethargic" state apparatus (as some stakeholders have defined the social services sector). The same is true in relation to other organizations and response systems, such as churches, political parties, trade unions, philanthropic networks, and voluntary organizations.

The lower incomes associated with these companies are in line with their relatively small workforces. In fact, two-thirds of respondents claimed that their enterprise had fewer than ten full-time equivalents (FTEs). Work teams are often supplemented with occasional collaborators, partnership networks, and volunteer work. This kind of work is often found in the personal investment sector, which encourages self-employment and features a strong identification with the enterprise itself. Customers, supporters, volunteers, workers, and members sometimes overlap, a peculiar aspect of NGSEs that distinguishes them from both conventional companies and nonprofit or third-sector organizations. The circular pattern of internal growth is also interesting, as users of the SE sometimes go on to volunteer for the organization.

This phenomenon can be seen clearly in several case studies. A good example is WINDA,[1] an SE in Poland that provides young adults who were raised in foster families or orphanages with vocational and social reintegration programs. Long-term reintegration is combined with a social program that emphasizes volunteering, participating in projects, assuming positions within the organization, public work, and accepting external employment contracts. Indeed, the organization has set up several different organizational levels that participants can work their way through, oftentimes ending with integration in the labor market. Of course, while volunteers are still an important resource for NGSEs, these enterprises must create a harmonious environment in which different types of employees and volunteers can come together and have their needs met.

At Glasgow Wood Recycling (GWR),[2] a Scottish charity/limited by guarantee company, 19 full time employees work alongside 20 volunteers, 30% of whom have a disability. In order to create interest in the organization, volunteers are given opportunities to provide manual labor and/or take part in marketing and administration duties. In this case, it is clear that volunteers represent a fundamental part of the SE model, serving as both beneficiaries and contributors to the SE's social and economic outcomes.

In many instances, SE employees work for low rates of pay, and many SEs are only able to stay open and pursue their pathways due to individuals who are prepared to work free of charge. Volunteers can also be an important resource for SEs when facing skill shortages. Sometimes the individuals in question are young, well-trained, highly motivated, and empathize strongly with the enterprise. In many cases, moreover, there are also points of similarity between their activities within the company and the pathways of personal and/or professional growth they have undertaken. Whatchado[3] in Austria exemplifies this situation. During its start-up phase in particular, the company was made up of young, highly-engaged professionals from fourteen different nations, most of whom worked as volunteers due to financial constraints. As a result, many of the people who joined the organization in its early days were motivated by its social mission above all else. In other words, this type of situation is often marked by a personal investment among employees and volunteers that isn't based solely on financial compensation.

Non-pecuniary incentives are used in most cases to recruit and motivate both paid staff and unpaid workers (Bacchiega & Borzaga, 2001; Battilana & Dorado, 2010; Haugh, 2007; Thompson et al., 2000). At the same time, the SE's social mission has frequently been cited as a "motivating force that provides employees with the intrinsic rewards of job satisfaction" (Doherty et al., 2014, p. 425). Many of the cases examined here reveal a universe of meta-economic transactions, a series of exchanges that go beyond the mere dispersal of cash for hours worked. In addition, there is also an element of temporality in this transaction, in which these types of exchanges are spread out over time so that the team, regardless of its role, co-invests in the enterprise and shares/identifies with its business objectives. This trend is amplified when teams are made up of friends and/or family.

Topographies

Our research takes into consideration the working environments and territorial settings of several SEs. Indeed, an NGSE's location at the frontier, the center, or in an expansion area is an important variable because these types of issues can lead to distinct challenges and opportunities. Among our cases studies, we found social businesses headquartered in deprived or marginalized areas where people's expectations are lower, opportunities are fewer, and services are more difficult to access. In other cases, meanwhile, organizations prefer to be located in central areas because they enjoy greater institutional support, a more favorable ecosystem, and serve as political hotspots. Special attention has also been devoted to SEs operating in areas that are currently undergoing requalification or expansion. Organizations located in areas subject to urban renewal are typical examples of this. In fact, urban renewal can serve as a catalyst for social entrepreneurship and finding community-driven alternatives to failing private and public markets (Murtagh & McFerran, 2015). However, it is also possible for SEs to assume less virtuous—and more opportunistic—roles in these settings.

Some of the organizations we surveyed appear to run this risk, especially those that intercept resources earmarked for urban renewal and use them for residential or touristic purposes. One example is Le Court-Circuit,[4] a cafe/restaurant established in November 2010 in Lyon, France. The cafe offers homemade meals prepared with organic ingredients from regional producers and farmers. Le Court-Circuit's basic identity is also inseparable from the Guilllotière neighborhood, an important meeting place for migrants passing through Lyon. In recent years, the neighborhood has been characterized by a significant amount of Italian and African migrants. Since Guillotière is located close to the city center, new residents, artists, and enterprises have begun settling in areas of the city that were once abandoned. This change has provoked several different challenges and reactions. Some people have invoked gentrification and bemoaned a loss of identity, while others claim that Guillotière is the new place to be.

A similar situation emerged in Scotland with the Glad Café,[5] an eatery that was set up in south Glasgow. The founders of the Glad Café participate in wider discussions about local renewal and are seen as credible actors in efforts to regenerate the socioeconomic fabric of the area. This, in turn, has raised the profile of their business, thus encouraging local residents to spend money there.

Another important factor to take into consideration is the tendency among SEs to adapt to the various enabling/disabling factors found in the local ecosystem where they operate. The most frequently mentioned disabling factors in our sample are legal constraints, lack of institutional support, bureaucracy and increasing administrative efforts, dependence on private donations, dealing with the personalities and popularity of their founders, weak business engines, being too project-dependent, lack of reserves, and a lack of qualified personnel. As these examples illustrate, economic/financial weakness is an especially prominent issue. Due to their hybrid nature, SEs are called upon to emphasize social impact over profits, often to the latter's detriment. Thus, the most common problem among SEs seems to be a weak business engine.

A number of enabling factors also emerged in our sample, including informal networks, the role of donors and sponsors, the support of so-called business angels, the presence of incubators, mentoring and umbrella organizations, networking with celebrities and journalists, and greater access to awards/prizes.

Many NGSEs are by-products of the 2008 economic crisis, the subsequent decline in public spending on social policies, and a weakening of the European welfare system. NGSEs gain their energy—be it in a symbolic or economic sense—from the progressive withdrawal of the state and the related increase in unmet social needs. SEs are being called on to deal with worsening social exclusion, vulnerability, and poverty; the increasingly harsh bite of unemployment; a deteriorating quality of life in urban areas; and the myriad social and health problems that often emerge in tandem with economic privation. The crisis has created—in both a direct and indirect manner—an ideal environment in which new approaches to social entrepreneurship can gain momentum, thereby creating "niches" that allow SEs to grow even in situations where welfare services have been repealed and third-sector actors have encountered serious difficulties. All of these factors have created an atmosphere that emphasizes cooperation and solidarity, as ideas on mutual aid have been granted more leeway than in previous decades. The intrinsic value of offering goods and services while simultaneously taking into account their social and environmental impact has played an important role in the emergence of NGSEs in Europe.

Many of the case studies included in our research reinforce the idea that the 2008 financial crisis shaped the missions and activities of many NGSEs. For instance, it created an opportunity for Homes for Good[6] in Scotland to fill a gap in the market by providing low-income residents with quality accommodations. Indeed, the real estate market cratered during the 2008 economic crisis and property values in Glasgow tumbled accordingly. In short, it was the right time to buy these properties at a low cost, refurbish them, and make them available in the rental market. The crisis had a similarly positive impact on the Eco Social Farm[7] in Albania, leading previously donor-driven entities to search for new forms of income generation. Indeed, the reduction in available grants and funding led some conventional NGOs to consider using SEs as sustainability tools. The activities of Lanificio 159[8] in Italy also grew significantly (and became much more diverse) after the 2008 economic crisis because NGSEs enlarged their competitive power and attractiveness to the detriment of traditional, rooted enterprises. In the Netherlands, meanwhile, representatives from Dockt & EVHB[9] noted that people were more cautious about investing as a result of the crisis, which means that stakeholders and potential clients—especially smaller municipalities—were open to more efficient ideas and solutions.

At the same time, however, these developments reflect dynamics associated with neoliberal views on government, many of which have a pronounced hold on the sector during moments of crisis. Our research confirms the work of other scholars and practitioners who have found that SEs tend to reinforce neoliberal ideas on social welfare (Dey & Teasdale, 2013; Eikenberry, 2009; Garrow & Hasenfeld, 2014; Hogg & Baines, 2011; Kim, 2016; Park, 2011). The idea that embracing market solutions and privatizing social services challenges long-held views on social rights and obligations is also found among organizations that have survived this transition and are currently obliged to adapt to the forces that blur the boundaries between the market and the welfare state. Some of our case studies, however, point toward the presence of a "counter-narrative"—or at least signs that SEs are hesitant to embrace the dominant discourse on the role SEs ought to play in times of crisis. Oftentimes, these actors display a critical reflexivity that can sometimes translate into "everyday forms of resistance" (Scott, 1985) that are capable of eroding dominant paradigms from within, a phenomenon that has been noted in at least one other study (Dey & Teasdale, 2013).

Another element worth mentioning is the recent "green wave" that is currently spreading throughout NGSEs in response to negative economic trends, many of which focus on questions of consumption—especially energy consumption. However, this issue is marked by several diverging pathways, as some NGSEs are more inclined to align themselves with the dominant rhetoric of "green" policies in Europe, while others are more rooted in "deep green" versions of sustainability that stress "a radical reconceptualization of prosperity and wealth" (Vickers & Lyon, 2014, p. 452). This tension between new green trends and previous environmental engagement was clearly emphasized by Enercoop[10] in France. As the following interview excerpt suggests, the need to preserve the values and practices of the oppositional environmentalist movements that emerged in Europe in the 1970s and 1980s is often counterbalanced by the apolitical attitudes that have spread among second-generation social entrepreneurs:

> The first generation of activists, always present inside Enercoop, has been joined today by a number of second generation activists, who are less interested in proper political action because they are often suspicious of it. At the same time, this generation is sensitive to the development of equitable trade and energy economies. As Enercoop is growing, its sociological profile is also evolving. People with less political and militant experience continue to be interested in this organization because they think of an ecology by itself and not an ecology to accomplish political goal.
>
> (Chabanet & Cautrès, 2016)

Biographies

The human dimension is crucial in all types of SEs. On the one hand, NGSEs are often shaped by the various political/ideological features of the experiences and life stories of their founders. On the other hand, this variable essentially imbues the risks of founding an SE with a style, method, and energy that—in most cases—is based more on personal, human, and professional qualities than on purely technical aspects and/or consolidated business tools. When analyzed through its human component, NGSEs appear to be the products of competing motivations and intentions. Although founding an NGSE is often seen as a means for young people to secure their first meaningful job, it is more accurate to say that these types of activities tend to take place later in the life cycle. Indeed, the average age of founders in our sample is around 42 years, which questions the correlation between new generation SEs and the new generation as a whole.

Social business is also sometimes experienced as a stopover for managers of companies that are already active on the market, many of whom are disappointed by the values associated with traditional enterprises and are interested in using their skills in service of a good cause. It can also be a testing ground for third-sector business operators who are dissatisfied with the traditional formulas of the nonprofit sector or who are simply concerned about the decline in the public social policies. For others, meanwhile, NGSEs are spaces for sublimating and exorcizing personal traumas or pain, experiences of vulnerability, and marginalization, thereby turning a personal affliction into a virtuous and edifying story to experience and recount to others. NGSEs typically represent a meeting place in which people recognize and celebrate a shared purpose and put into practice a form of social engagement that goes well beyond the provision of wage labor in an enterprise that is fueled by common values, practices, and languages. Furthermore, NGSEs are also predominantly feminine spaces, especially among enterprises that were founded after 2006 and were eager to seize opportunities that aligned nicely with their founders' inclinations and ambitions. In fact, female founders make up approximately 50% of our sample, which is much higher than what is normally found in conventional businesses and older SEs.

Beyond the importance of individual career paths and/or civic commitment, the biographies of social entrepreneurs play a crucial role in determining the various decisions that often shape the life cycle of a company. Nonetheless, examining the personalities of founders is not the best way to accurately assess the basic identity of these organizations. Our investigation reveals the role of NGSEs, especially during the implementation phase. The ability to encourage teamwork and build a tight-knit group of collaborators is decisive in the long run. In fact, many of the anecdotes we collected show that the founder is often joined and aided by other actors—not only managers and people with specific know-how but also supporters, volunteers, collaborators, and other people who are tasked with managing daily operations. The business and social sides of these hybrid organizations help explain the climate of teamwork and synergy that often emerges within NGSEs. The majority of people who play key roles in NGSEs either come from the business/professional sector or the world of activism/politics. Indeed, it is safe to say that, although managers and activists often come from divergent backgrounds, SEs act as a middle ground where the two groups can work together.

The NGSEs in our study were more healthy and dynamic when business/professional groups cooperated with activist/political groups. For instance, Glasgow Wood Recycling features the strong social orientation of its founder Peter Lavelle, a trained social worker who specialized in disabilities, and several professionals with experience in wood production and manufacturing. Similarly, Whatchado in Austria wouldn't have been nearly as successful had Ali Mahlodji's childhood dream of helping marginalized young people find a professional vocation and "do[ing] something useful without commercial ambitions" not been aided by the professionalism of other staff members, all of whom were business administration and international business management graduates. The Youth Center ARKA[11] in Shkodra, Albania, was subject to similar trends, as its founders, Arta and Marjan, had strikingly different backgrounds. For instance, Arta graduated in business administration and has expertise in finance. Marian, meanwhile, has a background in social work and experience managing programs that focus on orderly migration and integrating returned émigrés.

There are many case studies illustrating teamwork—that is, individuals passing along responsibilities in the manner of a relay race or the coordination that is created between members of a cohesive family unit. In some cases the two metaphors—the SE as family and the SE as a relay race—end up complementing each other. For example, a representative from Wert-Voll gGmbH[12] in Germany used this metaphor to explain the role of project developer and executer in the organization. Like "the center position in a basketball game," he or she "passes the projects like balls to the best player on the court, i.e., established experts. Through this method it is possible to dunk the ball in the basket and hence reach the organization's goals." As a result, hierarchical and/or generational dependence gives way to coordination and the tendency to consult members of the group. To quote members of Panato[13] in Poland, "nobody is imposing any vision, we rather discuss"; "the existential message conveyed is everybody can do it." Other SEs expressed similar ideas: "we are all in the same ship together"; "we are all equals" (Kacprzyk-Murawska et al., 2016).

Physiologies

Our research on NGSEs explores the productive engine of SEs, highlighting their most innovative aspects, including (among other things) governance and decision-making processes, gender and/or age balance, the use of ICT and social media, coping mechanisms, and collaborative work styles. Social innovation appears to be an essential ingredient of NGSEs that affects an organization's tendency to turn problems into opportunities. For instance, several companies distinguish themselves through their use of space, both physical and virtual. Hotels, restaurants, and pubs discover new goods and services and become spaces of co-working and co-creation, thus contributing to the very spirit of the community. The same is true of websites that explore new dimensions of 2.0 sociality. However, reshaping space can also be understood in a broader sense, revealing a propensity for reinventing disruptive practices in relation to conventional codes that are often associated with the business world, nonprofits, and third-sector organizations. Unfortunately, less than half of the SEs in our study invested significantly in ICT and social media, which undermines clichés regarding the close ties between SEs, social innovation, technological innovation, and social media.

We noticed that several of the entrepreneurs we interviewed offered anecdotes emphasizing their desire to transform a problem into an opportunity. Indeed, it is rare for NGSEs to remain untouched by the ambition of their founders. Their effective and at times heroic narratives describe critical moments that required dramatic recoveries. This type of narrative often includes a more or less stable launch, the emergence of an unexpected problem, tension that erupts and reaches a dramatic climax, and then the development of an inventive response that allows the group to turn the corner and resolve the problem. One very common slogan among NGSEs is "always try to look for a solution," and actors in this sphere often express the idea that "some chances came by coincidence" and "a mistake is often a learning opportunity" (Blasco & Bauernfeind, 2016).

The resilience of people, as well as their ability to successfully navigate a complicated situation, is measured by the skill with which they manage to overcome obstacles and their propensity to help other people get back on their feet. If the various narratives featured in this study are any guide, adaptability and the ability to implement coping mechanisms are also crucial factors, especially when describing the "art of getting by," a prominent feature among social entrepreneurs who focus on innovation issues. Emily Rose Yates's narrative, for example, focuses on her own resilience and coping mechanisms in dealing with her handicap, attributes that she hopes to encourage in her potential beneficiaries.[14]

Some SEs tend to grow quickly and in an unbalanced way, venturing into risky terrains where traditional enterprises would not dream or exposing themselves without first consolidating their organizational structure and putting in place a solid business engine. In many cases, the urge to accelerate comes from the SE's desire to have a social impact rather than a desire to consolidate its business and revenue stream. A good example of this kind of rapid growth is Voisin Malin,[15] a French SE that promotes greater access to public services and social rights among disadvantaged urbanites. Voisin Malin employees met with 10,000 families (approximately 30,000 residents) via door-to-door visits between 2012 and 2014. It also plans on extending its operations to twenty cities by 2020, reaching 15% of residents in 200 high-priority neighborhoods. Its ultimate goal is to create 300 Voisin Malins over the next five years and become a national force. Kromkommer[16] in the Netherlands is another example of the same tendency. This SE, which unknowingly embarked on a process of rapid growth, focuses on food waste. Between 2010 and 2015, the number of German pupils affected by the training programs offered by Chancenwerk[17] nearly quintupled, going from 544 to 2,400. In Poland, the Pottery Village,[18] an SE in the village of Kamionka that serves the unemployed, started with approximately 1,000 clients when it first started out, reached two thousand clients shortly thereafter, and now serves 10,000 clients. Delivered Next Day Personally,[19] a courier and mail delivery service that was set up in Scotland to break down barriers preventing people with disabilities from working, has witnessed rapid development in terms of location, number of employees, fleet quality, and workload. Homes for Good, also in Scotland, started with about fifty properties but currently manages nearly two hundred properties. Some SEs view the process of acceleration as a target to aim for, no matter what the cost. For instance, Digital Mums,[20] an SE from the United Kingdom that offers support to mothers who are out of work, envisions a future marked by rapid growth and international trading.

This phenomenon can be explained, at least in part, by the fact that NGSEs combine a business idea with an ambitious value proposition. Balanced budgets and/or breaking even are seen as valid goals, but an SE's primary aim is to have an impact on various social issues, the environment, and the ecosystem in which it carries out its activities. While a low-profit approach is quite common, in some cases the SE is tempted to rapidly scale-up in order to both make ends meet and provide evidence of economic sustainability. However, many of the cases analyzed here risk losing control of their rapid growth. In an organization marked by uncertainty, a lack of economic strength is compensated for by seeking new arrangements and balances, a wider range of activities, and/or expanding the area being served. Unlike traditional for-profit enterprises, it seems that these developmental trajectories are not always devised on the basis of statistical analysis, estimates, or economic projections.

Conclusions

Despite the strength of various clichés associated with NGSEs, their human capital is not particularly youthful, nor is it dominated by groups that are often associated with so-called socially oriented start-ups. This feature deserves attention because it contradicts the idea that NGSEs are invariably characterized by age and are inclined to adopt expressive codes, attitudes, and work styles that are typical of the world of start-ups. NGSEs, in short, are not dominated by young people looking for their first job who, in times of crisis, refuse to accept their somewhat grim prospects and decide, instead, to harness their own resources in order to create an innovative enterprise. Indeed, the NGSEs discussed in this chapter are populated by middle-aged men and women who, for various personal and professional reasons, decided to invest new energy into their relatively advanced and mature life paths. Interestingly, the NGSEs in our study are predominantly feminine spaces, especially in enterprises that were founded after 2006. In fact, female founders, many of whom were eager to seize opportunities that mirror their own inclinations and ambitions, are quite common in our sample.

Another element that undermines some of the stereotypes associated with NGSEs is the emphasis on teamwork and the complementary backgrounds/skills of the workforce during the early stages of the SE's development. Our research suggests that the founder's charisma is often augmented by the collective efforts of multiple actors and that these types of endeavors cannot be reduced to the motivations and heroic actions of a single individual.

Our findings also point out that a strong neoliberal tendency can be found among NGSEs. The organizations we analyzed are a product of the 2008 economic crisis, a steep decline in public spending on social policies, and a weakening of the European welfare system. The tendency to exploit the social economy and use it in conservative (rather than transformative) ways is present in several cases. Indeed, by assuming control over services that were once overseen by public institutions, NGSEs may force local communities to manage their own welfare provisions. Organizations located in areas that were undergoing urban renewal served as vibrant examples of this tendency.

Many people working in the social economy also share the concern that embracing commercial approaches might undermine older views on social rights and obligations. In fact, some of our case studies show evidence of an emerging counter-narrative—or at least signs that SEs are hesitant to embrace the dominant discourse during times of crisis. Some of these counter narratives either manifest themselves in hidden areas of organizational life or take the form of "hidden transcripts" (Scott, 1985). This suggests that NGSEs are not simply docile entities that endorse the inherent norms and principles of neoliberalism. At times, these actors display a critical reflexivity that can translate into everyday forms of resistance, some of which are capable of challenging neoliberal orthodoxies from within.

Finally, we have shown that NGSEs are capable of producing new "evolutionary perspectives" (During, 2016) that can (re)generate social commitment among entrepreneurs and organizations. An interesting example of this involves how the workforce is often conceptualized. Many of the case studies discussed in this chapter reveal a universe of meta-economic transactions, a series of exchanges that redefine the spaces used by SEs and traditional businesses. Another innovative element refers to the attitude toward risk and the way SEs attend to growth and impact issues. NGSEs often venture into risky terrains that traditional enterprises would not dream of entering without first consolidating their organizational structure.

Our research intended to verify the existence of NGSEs and identify their specific features at the transnational level. Based on the transversal analysis of 55 case studies, we cannot unequivocally claim that a new generation of SEs—one that is distinct from previous generations—actually exists. Instead, our empirical evidence allows us to confidently state that there exists a broad "new-generation sphere" for SE—a hybrid space that hosts heterogeneous entities and brings together new and old actors who adopt approaches, languages, work styles, and tools that promote renewal in the sector. This new sphere is, in effect, a transitory space rather than a site of rebirth.

Notes

1 See www.lsswinda.pl/.
2 See http://glasgowwoodrecycling.org.uk/.
3 Whatchado is an online career platform tool based in Vienna that emphasizes the life stories of its users. See www.whatchado.com/en/.
4 See www.le-court-circuit.fr/.
5 The Glad Café is a licensed cafe in the Shawlands area of south Glasgow. See www.thegladcafe.co.uk/.
6 See www.homesforgood.org.uk/.
7 The Eco Social Farm for Social Integration in Oblika is an initiative associated with The Door, a nonprofit that focuses on the social inclusion and integration of vulnerable and excluded groups. See www.fp7-efeseiis.eu/eco-social-farm/.
8 Lanificio 159 is an enterprise out of Rome that has been working in the cultural/entertainment sector since 2007. See www.lanificio.com.
9 The Dutch group focuses on energy and other challenges associated with creating "an independent, honest and sustainable society." See www.energievan-hollandschebodem.nl/.
10 Enercoop is a renewable energy concern that was created in France in September 2005. See www.enercoop.fr/.
11 The Youth Center Arka focuses on youth employment through vocational training, cultural/artistic activities, and economic/social development. See www.fp7-efeseiis.eu/youth-center-arka/.
12 Wert-Voll gGmbH provides migrant children (and children from families with a migrant background) with better occupational and educational opportunities while also reconnecting them with their elders and the natural environment. See www.wert-voll.org/.
13 Panato is a handicraft workshop, café, and cultural/social center in the middle of the most disenfranchised and underfinanced part of Wroclaw. See http://panato.org/.
14 As a blogger and freelance consultant, Emily serves as an inspirational example for other people with disabilities who strive to realize their aspirations and overcome their limitations. See www.emilyroseyates.co.uk/.
15 See www.voisin-malin.fr/.
16 See www.kromkommer.com/english.
17 See www.chancenwerk.de/.
18 See http://garncarskawioska.pl/.
19 See www.dndp.co.uk/.
20 See https://digitalmums.com/.

References

Bacchiega, A., & Borzaga, C. (2001). Social enterprises as incentive structures: An economic analysis. In C. Borzaga, & J. Defourny (Eds.), *The Emergence of social enterprise* (pp. 273–294). London: Routledge.

Battilana, J., & Dorado, S. (2010). Building sustainable hybrid organizations: The case of commercial microfinance organizations. *Academy of Management Journal*, *53*, 1419–1440.

Blasco, E. M., & Bauernfeind, A. (2016). *The new generation of social entrepreneurs: Five case studies from the Austrian ecosystem.* EFESEIIS Internal Report, Impact Hub.

Bornstein, D. (1998). Changing the world on a shoestring. *The Atlantic Monthly*, *281*(1), 34–39.

Bornstein, D. (2004). *How to change the World: Social entrepreneurs and the power of new ideas.* Oxford: Oxford University Press.

Chabanet, D., & Cautrès, B. (2016). *The new generation of social entrepreneurs: Five case studies from the French ecosystem.* EFESEIIS Internal Report, Sciences Po – Cevipof.

Czarniawska, B. (2007). *Shadowing: And other techniques for doing fieldwork in modern societies.* Copenhagen: Copenhagen Business School Press.

Dey, P., & Teasdale, S. (2013). Social enterprise and dis/identification: The politics of identity work in the English third sector. *Administrative Theory & Praxis*, *35*(2), 248–270.

Doherty, B., Haugh, H., & Lyon, F. (2014). Social enterprise as hybrid organizations: A review and research agenda. *International Journal of Management Reviews*, *16*(4), 417–436.

Drayton, W. (2002). The citizen sector: Becoming as entrepreneurial and competitive as business. *California Management Review*, *44*(3), 120–133.

During, R. (2016). *Understanding evolutionary pathways and societal embedding – evolutionary theory of the social enterprise.* Alterra Wageningen UR, Retrieved from http://www.fp7-efeseiis.eu/evolutionary-theory/.

Eikenberry, A. M. (2009). Refusing the market: A democratic discourse for voluntary and nonprofit organizations. *Nonprofit and Voluntary Sector Quarterly*, *38*(4), 582–596.

Garrow, E. E., & Hasenfeld, Y. (2014). Social enterprises as an embodiment of a neoliberal welfare logic. *American Behavioral Scientist*, *58*(11), 1475–1493.

Haugh, H. (2007). Community-led social venture creation. *Entrepreneurship Theory and Practice*, *31*, 161–182.

Hogg, E., & Baines, S. (2011). Changing responsibilities and roles of the voluntary references PART 1 NGSEs and community sector in the welfare mix: A review. *Social Policy and Society*, *10*(3), 341–352.

Kacprzyk-Murawska, M., Józwik, E., & Praszkier, R. (2016). *The new generation of social entrepreneurs: Five case studies from the polish ecosystem.* EFESEIIS Internal Report, University of Warsaw.

Kim, J. H. (2016). *Neoliberalism and the politics of social enterprises in South Korea: The dynamics of neoliberal governmentality and hegemony.* Sociology Dissertations. Retrieved from http://scholarworks.gsu.edu/cgi/viewcontent.cgi?article=1085&context=sociology_diss.

Light, P. C. (2008). *The search for social entrepreneurship.* Washington, DC: Brookings Institution Press.

Mair, J., & Martí, I. (2006). Social entrepreneurship research: A source of explanation, prediction, and delight. *Journal of World Business, 41*(1), 36–44.

McDonald, S. (2005). Studying actions in context: A qualitative shadowing method for organizational research. *Qualitative Research, 5*(4), 455–473.

Murtagh, B., & McFerran, K. (2015). Adaptive utilitarianism, social enterprises and urban regeneration. *Environment and Planning C: Government and Policy, 33*, 1585–1599.

Park, M.-J. (2011). *The birth of social heroes.* Seoul: Imagine.

Quinlan, E. (2008). Conspicuous invisibility: Shadowing as a data collection strategy. *Qualitative Inquiry, 14*, 1480–1499.

Scott, J. C. (1985). *Weapons of the weak: Everyday forms of peasant resistance.* New Haven, CT: Yale University Press.

Thomas, G. (2011). A typology for the case study in social science following a review of definition. *Discourse, and Structure, Qualitative Inquiry, 17*(6), 511–521.

Thompson, J., Alvy, G., & Lees, A. (2000). Social entrepreneurship – A new look at people and potential. *Management Decision, 38*, 328–338.

Vickers, I., & Lyon, F. (2014). Beyond green niches? Growth strategies of environmentally-motivated social enterprises. *International Small Business Journal.* Retrieved from http://isb.sagepub.com/content/early/2012/12/04/0266242612457700.full.pdf+html.

12 A framework to understand enabling ecosystems for social enterprises

Mario Biggeri, Enrico Testi, and Andrea Ferrannini

Introduction

In recent years, the attention given by international organizations and governments to social enterprises (SEs) has led scholars to place greater emphasis on the environment in which SEs are set. In her seminal paper on creating a research agenda for SE, Helen Haugh (2005) argues that the environmental context in which SEs operate is an increasingly important topic that needs to be addressed. The contextual environment in which SEs operate is also considered a key issue by Peattie and Morley (2008), while Munoz (2010) stresses the importance of highlighting the connections between the socio-economic and political localities and the processes underlying the emergence, successes, failures, and impacts of SEs.

Several studies show that SEs have grown in number, influence, and political-economic importance over the past twenty years by basically affirming their role as providers of public services that had once been handled by the state (Angroff & McGuire, 2003; Bornstein, 2004; Harding, 2004; Defourny & Nyssens, 2008; Manetti, 2012). Policy makers developed the understanding that SEs stemming from the private and third sector or as spin-offs of the public sector (Hall et al., 2012; Hazenberg & Hall, 2016), and their flourishing in a country or in a locality, have a positive impact on society. SEs are in fact seen as serving the needs of the community, creating job opportunities for disadvantaged people (Birkhölzer, 2009). This "positive" understanding of SEs has been amplified due to the 2008 economic crisis while also influencing research on the relationship between SEs and the system. In fact, since SEs are seen as having a positive impact on society, most studies and analyzes focus on which parts of the system enable or hamper SEs. Academics and policy makers have used a plethora of terms to define the context or system in which SEs operate. For instance, Scotland's First Minister, Alex Salmond, talked about the "supportive environment" (Ainsworth, 2012, p. 1), the (EU Commission, 2015) about "ecosystems," others such as the Organisation for Economic Co-operation and Development (OECD) about "enabling ecosystem" (OECD-LEED, 2016) stressing the role that the system has in supporting the birth and growth of SEs.

Works from Smith and Stevens (2010), Zafeiropoulou and Koufopoulos (2013), and Qureshi et al. (2016) have underlined the role of the network relations and of the embeddedness of SEs in the ecosystem in their development and the social value they are able to create. It is therefore of paramount importance to create an analytical framework that allows us to analyze these relations and the (positive) contributions that SEs bring to the ecosystem. This chapter will propose an analytical framework that explains the complex relationship between SEs and their ecosystem. We argue that an enabling ecosystem gives SEs the power, means, opportunities, and authority to pursue their goals, and that the general objective of SEs is to contribute to Sustainable Human Development (SHD).

The framework we propose is based on the Sustainable Territorial Evolution for Human Development (STEHD) analytical framework elaborated by Biggeri and Ferrannini (2014). The STEHD features a people-centred focus (i.e., the idea that SEs ought to improve the quality of life of the people and communities they serve) that merges the Capability Approach of Amartya Sen (Sen, 1999) with the meso-economic perspective and the extant literature on local development. The STEHD framework stresses the importance of multidimensionality at both an individual and a local level. The framework places the concepts of freedom and agency at the heart of dynamic processes of territorial transformation and individual and collective human development and empowerment. Since the STEHD framework adopts a people-centred focus based largely on individual capabilities, we use literature on entrepreneurship and social entrepreneurship to complement the SE literature, especially when discussing the motivations and choices made by the people leading SEs.

The second section highlights the connections between the capability approach and the enabling ecosystem concept. The third section offers a revised version of the STEHD framework that can be applied to SEs and used to analyze the relationship between SEs and their ecosystem. The fourth section focuses on such relationships. The "Conclusions" section identifies the preliminary policy implications of using such a framework to analyze SE ecosystems.

Background: social enterprises, ecosystem, and the capability approach

The terms "system," "ecosystems" (EU Commission, 2015), "enabling ecosystem" (OECD-LEED, 2016), and "supportive environment" (Ainsworth, 2012, p. 1) have been used to describe the relationship between SEs and the locality in which they are set.

Choosing between the terms "system," "ecosystem," or "environment" in order to analyze the relationship between SEs and their locality involves adopting a different perspective and focusing on specific features of the relationship. However, doing so would broaden considerably the scope of this work. We will therefore focus only on the enabling ecosystem concept, as we believe it has two important implications in terms of how we analyze the relationship between SEs and their locality. For if SEs are considered part of an ecosystem, then a strong relationship, in some cases even dependency, between SEs and other parts of the ecosystem is implied. Many authors have tackled the strong relationship between SEs and the local system. For example, Pasetto (2010) says that SEs tend to preserve strong ties with the local area. Evers and Schulze-Boeing (2001) point out that SEs provide services that depend on close relationships in a local cultural context. Hynes (2009) shows that local networks are crucial for SEs, as they allow organizations to access different types of resources, most notably voluntary labour. Meanwhile, Eversole et al. (2013) stress the extent to which SEs are embedded in rural communities, while Di Domenico et al. (2010) show how SEs are able to achieve social impact by successfully harnessing different resources of the locality.

The second implication of the word "ecosystem" revolves around the idea that our analysis should go beyond the relationship between SEs and the locality they serve and embrace all the different parts of the ecosystem, some of which might not be set in the same locality. It means broadening the casual chain of (reciprocal) influence between SEs and the different parts of the ecosystem considering that changes in one part of the ecosystem, even those not directly related to SEs, might affect them. If we use it to analyze the relations between SEs and the ecosystem over a period of several years, this perspective will help us understand which features of the ecosystem at the macro, meso, and micro level led to the evolution and co-evolution of SEs and the ecosystem. These two implications speak to the need to understand how economic, social, cultural, and institutional processes, involving a plethora of actors, contributed to the emergence of SEs.

The word "enabling" is used here to denote the power, means, opportunity, or authority to allow someone to do something. Therefore, talking about enabling ecosystems for SEs means assessing how the ecosystem provides SEs with the power, means, opportunity, or authority to meet their objectives, be they solving environmental issues, aiding people who have been excluded from the job market, or providing homecare for sick and/or elderly people. By solving society's most pressing social problems, SEs can have a positive effect on local development (Borzaga & Tortia, 2009; Birkhölzer, 2009) and improve the quality of life of both individuals and the community as a whole. These effects can be assessed in terms of SHD through the capability approach of Amartya Sen (1985, 1999). For example, Roy et al. (2014) suggest that the capability approach can be used with other frameworks to build a chain of causality from the trading activity of the SE to the health and well-being of individuals and communities. Cornelius and Wallace (2013) use the capability approach to evaluate the contribution of SEs in building community capabilities and enabling social inclusion. Yujuico (2008) employs the capability approach as a means of understanding the concept of social entrepreneurship. Lastly, Scarlato (2012) was the first to connect the capability approach of Amartya Sen with the extant literature on SEs by building a theoretical framework that examines the relationship between SEs and human development.

According to Scarlato (2012, p. 31), SEs directly increase capabilities, encourage the accumulation of relational goods and social capital, facilitate the conversion of potential capabilities into functionings, implement the principle of subsidiarity, and stimulate the demand of citizens for a progressive improvement in institution efficiency. The enabling ecosystem concept therefore offers us a good theoretical background—i.e., the capability approach of Amartya Sen (1985, 1999)—in which to highlight how the system provides to SEs the power, means, opportunity, or authority to pursue their objectives as well as how SEs contribute to SHD in any given locality.

However, while human development and the capability approach have been used to highlight some of the effects SEs have had on the system, the capability approach has not yet been used as a theoretical framework to assess the effects the ecosystem has on SEs and other organizations. This is because the capability approach originally focused on individuals and communities rather than on larger organizations such as local governments and SEs. Thus, a dynamic and analytical framework that can analyze how SEs relate to their ecosystem and the process through which they contribute (or do not contribute) to Sustainable Human Development is still needed. The next section of this chapter will attempt to create such a framework by building on the STEHD framework offered by Biggeri and Ferrannini (2014). The rationale for using the STEHD framework is based on the following arguments, all of which derive from the two implications of using the word "ecosystem" mentioned earlier in this section.

First, a framework to analyze the SEs' ecosystem should explain how the ecosystem and its parts co-evolve and influence each other. Borzaga and Defourny (2001), Kerlin (2009, 2010), and Doherty et al. (2009) have shown that SEs have developed along different pathways as a result of historical, cultural, and social processes specific to different countries. The conditions that helped SEs flourish in some countries were connected to how their economy and welfare systems evolved alongside each other over time. Therefore, in order to better understand the SEs' ecosystem we need to take into account all parts of the ecosystem and address how these influence each other and co-evolve, and this is provided by the STEHD framework.

Second, the framework should unveil the processes through which SEs can have a positive or a negative effect on the system. SEs make an important contribution to society by employing disadvantaged people and providing access to services and products of collective interest. SEs are seen as useful tools to promote SHD since, according to Scarlato (2012), they enlarge the citizenry's capabilities. When SEs have positive effects in the local ecosystems, they contribute to social cohesion and reinforce territorial functionings. The role of SEs and the degree of usefulness they have in the system are the result of the evolution of social needs, the welfare state, and civil society. There is, in short, a positive relationship between social needs that have gone unmet by the welfare state, third-sector organizations, or the for-profit sector and the degree of usefulness and social impact of SEs in the ecosystem. SEs not only provide services that are not usually provided by other actors in the locality but also encourage public authorities to be more innovative. For example, SEs might ask public authorities to modify some public services by adopting innovative policies that received positive feedback from their beneficiaries.

Nonetheless, the assumption that SEs have only a positive influence on the ecosystem might be reductive. SEs might be subject to mission drift and sacrifice social objectives to achieve financial sustainability (Brandsen & Karré, 2011; Carroll & Stater, 2009; Eikenberry & Kluver, 2004; Jones, 2007; Pache & Santos, 2010). In extreme cases, SEs might even engage in criminal behaviour to win public tenders. Moreover, some organizations might claim to be SEs in order to take advantage of dedicated funds and other fiscal incentives (Dey & Teasdale, 2015). The positive or negative effect that SEs have on the ecosystem can be the result of both the choices that SEs make (e.g. choosing not to engage in criminal behaviour in order to win public tenders) and the relationships they build with the ecosystem (e.g., being totally dependent on public tenders). It is therefore important to adopt a framework that highlights the processes through which SEs affect the different parts of the ecosystem while also focusing on which parts of the ecosystem influence the decision-making processes inside the SE and how they co-evolve over time.

Third, the framework should take into account the main dimensions of SEs. SEs vary in terms of the activities they perform, the resources they use, their basic objectives, and the sector in which they operate (Pinch & Sunley, 2015). SEs with the same objectives that operate in the same sector might differ due to the different capacities their employees have in terms of transforming material and immaterial resources into products or services. The differences that emerge among SEs (e.g., sources of funding and the capacities of human resources and management) are influenced by the ecosystem in which they are set. For instance, in those ecosystems where an agglomeration of SEs was formed as a consequence of an outsourcing of services from the public sector, we might expect a greater presence of SEs that rely on public tenders as a main source of revenue.

Therefore, a framework that tries to analyze an enabling ecosystem for SEs should take into account the main areas in which SEs differ and be able to highlight the processes through which SEs transform resources, both material and immaterial, into potential achievements (capabilities) and achieved functionings (the goals they value). Taking into account the main dimensions allows us to assess the main typologies of SEs in a locality, the kind of relationships SEs have with the ecosystem, as well as identify the barriers to their development. For example, if most SEs in a locality have a lot of employees and work through public tenders, we might want to ascertain the degree in which SEs influence policy makers through their collective action, or how much they are free to innovate in service delivery by respecting the rules set down by public authorities. Assessing these differences is also necessary when drafting policies aimed at promoting SEs. For example, social impact bonds might not be appropriate to promote the growth of small, lightly structured SEs.

In the next section we will offer a framework that will allow us to answer the needs identified in the aforementioned arguments.

A framework to analyze social enterprises in the ecosystem

In order to analyze SEs and their ecosystem, we need to include in the framework components that are capable of explaining the processes through which SEs relate to the ecosystem. This will be accomplished by referring to previous research on SEs, social entrepreneurship, entrepreneurship, local development, the CA approach, and behavioural economics. The framework is divided into two main parts: the local level, on the left, that has been modified from the STEHD framework to take into account the role of the market, and the SE on the right. Some elements associated with the local level are influenced by elements outside the local system; these have been identified as extra-local level and placed at the bottom of Figure 12.1.

The local level

The local level consists of seven blocks, four of which are central to our analysis: territorial achieved functionings (A), the socio institutional context (H), collective agency (P), and demand for goods and services (M).

A. Territorial achieved functionings

Territorial achieved functionings (A) are the results achieved by the local area and its community. These might be assets such as infrastructure or power plants, as well as the physical and natural endowment of the locality. Component (A) has a direct influence on component (B)—"goods and services at the local level"—including public goods and specific public goods (Bellandi, 2009) that can be converted by the SE in capabilities and in functionings. However, (A) also influences another component of the framework: the socio-institutional context (H). For example, (A) can influence the development of social networks by affecting the likelihood of interaction between actors (Sorenson, 2003) while also creating/removing spatial/temporal constraints. Territorial achieved functionings that reduce

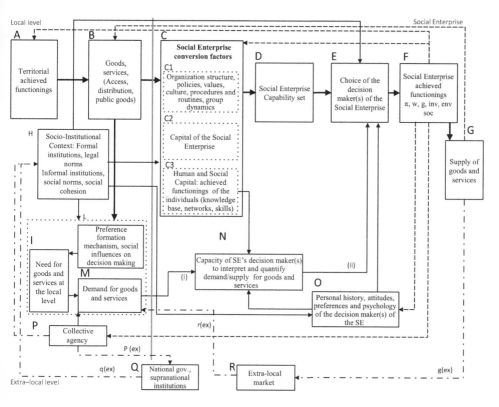

Figure 12.1 A framework to analyze social enterprises in the ecosystem.
Source: Adapted from Testi, E. (2017).

the time needed by agents to interact (e.g., a fast transport system), or that provide spaces that create interaction (e.g., community centres or public squares), positively influence social cohesion and social capital at the local level. SE achieved functionings (F) contribute, through a feedback loop, to (A) and by reflex to (B). The feedback loop is important because it is connected to the idea that different parts of the ecosystem are connected and influence each other.

H. The socio-institutional context

Borzaga and Defourny (2001) and Kerlin (2009, 2010) have focused on how the socio-institutional context (H) affects the emergence and development of SEs. The socio-institutional context represents one of the most important blocks of our framework. (H) includes formal institutions, legal norms, informal institutions, social norms, social cohesion, and the demographic, economic, and social composition of the community. (H) therefore accounts for all parts of the system that were not included in the figure. (H) at the local level is influenced by q(ex)—most notably the government and supranational organizations indicated in the STEHD framework.

The socio-institutional context (H) has a direct influence on the preference formation mechanism at the local level (L). As Taylor-Gooby has argued, "individual rational choices can be directed at short-term or longer-term outcomes, and selection of goals seems to be influenced by the context in which the choice is made" (Taylor-Gooby, 2008, p. 173). For example, preferences could be influenced, as shown in the work of Carreira da Silva and Valadez Martinez (2015), by a preexisting understanding of social rights among the population that leads to a preference for a specific type of welfare system.

(H) has also a direct influence on the preferences of those who manage SEs (O). Due to their embeddedness in the local area, individuals that work in the SE are subject to the same laws, social pressures, and social reward mechanisms that formal and informal institutions are required to abide by. (H) also influences the conversion factors of the SE by defining the boundaries of how (and which) resources can be converted. The best example of this is a law that does not foresee the use of a residential building for production purposes.

P. Collective agency

Collective agency (P) in the form of social movements can alter the environment in which organizations operate. For example, (P) can influence the preference formation mechanism of the local community (L); create a need for certain goods and services (I); and, in turn, influence the demand for goods and services (M). For instance, if a campaign against pollution was created by a group of citizens, their fellow citizens could start demanding products that respect certain ecological standards. Collective agency at the local level (P) might also influence the national government or supranational institutions p(ex). The links between the SE's achieved functionings (F), collective agency (P) and its feedback q(ex) to the national government and supranational institutions (Q) can also be used to explain the rise of a specific type of social entrepreneur: the social engineer (Zahra et al. 2007). Social engineers have a profound influence on society by fracturing existing institutions and replacing them with more efficient ones. An example of a social engineer is Prof. Muhammas Yunus, who, by founding the Grameen Bank (a de facto SE), promoted collective action among poor people and changed formal and informal institutions at both the local level and across the globe.

M. Demand for goods and services

When SEs sell products and services, they have two main markets. Public tenders usually regulate the public market. Therefore, the public authority issuing the tender decides the quantities and the quality of the goods or services. However, the private market also needs to be analyzed and understood in order to decide which goods or services need to be provided. In our framework, the demand for goods and services, at both the public and private level, is indicated by (M) "demand for goods and services at local and non-local level." (M) is also influenced by r(ex), which represents both the demand for goods and services produced at the local level (but demanded by actors operating at an extra-local level) and the provision of goods and services to the local level by actors operating at the extra-local level. (M) is also the expression of local needs (I) which emerge from the preferences (L) of the people and organizations in the local area. (I), (L), and (M) are influenced by (H). The demand side, and its connection with the extra-local level, represents an advancement of the STEHD framework.

The social enterprise

The part of the framework that identifies the processes within the SE takes the representation of a person's capability set and the social/personal context built by Robeyns (2005, p. 98) and connects it to the SE's capability set. SEs in this framework are treated as organized groups of individuals in which the results to be achieved and expressed by their choice (E) are those considered worthy by the decision maker(s) of the SE. Our use of the term "decision maker(s)" refers to founders, managers, and other members who take part in the different governance structures among SEs. We also include cooperatives in this framework, a type of SE in which all members have the right to vote and make decisions. SEs are therefore conceived as a place in which the achieved functionings (C3) of the individuals (e.g., their knowledge, their networks, and their skills) combine with the resources of the SE (C2) and its organization structure, policies, values, culture, procedures, and routines (C1). The combination of (C1), (C2), and (C3) are used to convert resources of the locality (B) to reach, as an organization, a set of capabilities (D) and achieved functionings (F), namely profit redistribution (π), wages (w), working conditions (g), investments (inv), environmental effects (env), social effects on the community (soc), and the supply of products and services (G). The management or members of the SE choose (E) which capabilities should become achieved functionings (F) based on their preferences (O).

The blocks in the SE framework that need to be further explained are (N) "Capacity of SE's decision maker(s) to interpret and quantify demand/supply of goods and services" and (O) "Personal history, attitudes, preferences, and psychology of the decision maker(s) of the SE." Blocks (N), (O), and (C3) refer to the characteristics, skills, and capacities possessed by the individuals who work in the SE. This involves broadening the literature on SEs to include social entrepreneurship and social entrepreneurs. Even though the literature on social entrepreneurship is broader than the literature on SE—because it refers to a process or behaviour (Mair & Martí, 2006) that can be adopted by any person—some of the research could also be applied to SEs, especially when referring to the behaviour or features of the entrepreneurs who work for SEs.

In explaining blocks (N) and its connections with blocks (C3) and (O), we will draw upon the literature on organizational learning and innovation in firms. Moreover, while discussing block (O) we will also briefly refer to the literature on entrepreneurial behaviour and strategic decision-making.

N. Capacity of SEs' decision maker(s) to interpret and quantify demand/supply of goods and services

The evidence that SEs usually serve local markets (Seelos et al., 2010) might suggest that the knowledge of the local market and its particular features are of paramount importance for SEs. The capacity of SEs' management and members to interpret and quantify the market is influenced by many different factors. One of them is the mental models, that in the framework are set in (O) and that are used by the decision makers to interpret market information (i) (Day & Nedungadi, 1994). The effectiveness of market information processing depends on the degree to which the mental models that are used to interpret information are adequate representations of reality (Sinkula, 1994). The extent to which mental models are an adequate representation of reality is influenced by (C3) "Human and social capital of the members of the SE," particularly their embeddedness in local social networks and their knowledge base and personal skills. Many authors have shown the importance of information flows in social networks. Granovetter (1973) argued that job information passes through social networks. Coval and Moskovits (2001) claim that investors who invest locally have better returns, which might be due to having greater access to information through local networks. The more the decision makers of the SE are embedded in local social networks, the more their mental models will interpret local information correctly.

However, it is important to note that not all information can be understood, processed, and learned. The capacity of the SE to assimilate new knowledge—in this case the information coming from (i)—depends on the absorptive capacity (Cohen & Levinthal, 1990) of the SE, which is determined by the prior knowledge of its members (C3) as well as the cognitive distance (Nooteboom, 2000) between prior knowledge and (i). For example, an SE active in the field of support services for disabled people might have the type of knowledge that is useful understanding related problems in the community—for example, the problems of non-self-sufficient elders. However, this knowledge might not be enough to understand issues and identify opportunities that are cognitively distant, such as waste disposal or renewable energy.

SEs can increase their capacity to interpret (i) by promoting internal values and policies (C1) that create a favourable learning environment inside the organization or by adopting a multi-stakeholder model in which decision-making is shared with different stakeholders, including public authorities, volunteers, workers, and sometimes even beneficiaries (Depedri,

2007). The presence of different stakeholders increases the knowledge base, draws attention to a wider array of issues, and encourages organizations to make use of more information in the decision-making process. The inclusion of beneficiaries and their families provides SEs with a competitive advantage in understanding and learning the needs of the locality. Moreover, a multi-stakeholder model can lead to the co-creation of products and services (Needham, 2008; Durose & Richardson, 2015) tailored to the specific needs of the locality.

For Lee et al. (1992) the organizational learning process is cyclical. An individual's actions lead to organizational interactions with the environment. Outcomes are interpreted by individuals who learn by updating their beliefs about cause and effect relationships. This process is revealed in the framework whenever it is noted that (N) leads to (E), which then leads to the achieved functionings of the SE (F). From (F) a feedback loop develops in which (O)—the personal history, attitudes, and psychology of the individuals involved in the SE—influences both (N) and (E).

O. *"Personal history, attitudes preferences, and psychology of the decision makers of the SE"*

This block is central to the proposed framework because it influences the choices (E) taken by the decision makers in the SE. It is not our intention to clearly define what factors influence the choices of decision makers in SEs, as this is beyond the scope of this paper. However, it is important to note at least some of the main factors individuals consider when a decision is being made. For instance, risk aversion, time discounting, trust, altruism, and positive and negative reciprocity (Falk et al., 2016) can influence choices in multifarious domains, including financial decision-making, educational choices, labour market behaviour, charitable giving, social norm enforcement, and health outcomes (see, e.g., Dohmen et al., 2009, 2011; Fehr et al., 2003; Kirby et al., 1999; Komlos et al., 2004; Rose-Ackerman, 1996; Smith et al., 2005; Tanaka et al., 2010). Decision-making might also be swayed by gender, age (Ackert et al. 2009, Croson & Gneezy, 2009), personal history (Alesina & Giuliano 2009; Giuliano & Spilimbergo 2008; Piketty, 1995), attitudes and personality (Ben-Ner & Halldorsson, 2010; Brocklebank et al., 2011; Dohmen et al., 2008; Lönnqvist et al., 2011; Volk et al., 2012), social identity (Benjamin et al., 2007), religion (Orbell et al., 1992; Tan, 2006), and education (Ackert et al., 2009; Jakiela et al., 2010).

E. *"Choice of the decision maker(s) in a social enterprise"*

(E) "Choice of the decision maker(s) in a SE" refers to what the SE achieves in terms of profit redistribution (π), wages (w), working conditions (g), investments (inv), environmental effects (env), social effects on the community (soc), and the supply of products and services (G). The choice of the decision maker(s) in a SE (E) is influenced by (O) "Personal history, attitudes preferences, and psychology of the decision makers of the SE"; (H) the socio-institutional context of formal and informal institutions, social norms (Bowles, 1998, 2009; Huck, 1998; Rodriguez-Sickert et al., 2008), culture, and social cohesion/conflict levels (Kranton et al., 2012); (ii) information that is influenced by the capacity of the decision makers (N) to interpret information (i) coming from the market (M).

Since SEs are different and operate in different institutional contexts (H), it is not possible to generalize the choices common to all SEs. Based on the definition of SE used in this book we hypothesize that SEs that produce (G) might make choices that have a positive (soc), whenever (π) is positive or equal to 0. In some countries, the maximum amount of (π) as well as the minimum level of (w), (g), and (env) are set by laws that SEs must comply with. (inv) is based on the information coming from the market (ii).

An under-researched topic in the SE literature concerns the choices of decision makers in SEs and what influences them. Using our framework the question would be which element of the framework between (O), (H), or (ii) influences more the choices of decision makers in SEs? And under which conditions does a decision maker is taking choices? For example, even if a decision maker has preferences for taking more prosocial choices and increase (soc), the conditions under which he is taking the choice, might prevent him/her to take them. This could be the case when the decision maker has information (ii) that other companies, not concerned with social issues, will take part to a tender. If the tender doesn't value the social aspects of the goods and services required, the decision maker of the SE might be prevented to take prosocial choices if these entail not being competitive on the market and losing the tender. Therefore, the decision maker could, for instance, reduce (w) or (g) to be competitive. This example speaks to the idea that decisions are based on context and time. This has important implications at the ecosystem level. For instance, the presence of several SEs in an ecosystem that exacerbates competition between SEs and other types of enterprises might force some organizations to compress (soc), (w), and (g), and disregard (env) to survive. This hinders the potential benefit that the ecosystem could draw from SEs' presence.

Effect of SEs in the ecosystem and the various features of an enabling ecosystem

The achieved functionings (F) of the SE influence through a feedback loop the territorial achieved functionings at the local level (A). For example, environmental effects (env) might create pollution that decreases the resources available in the local area (the final result of all the processes of the STEHD framework on the local system) or negatively affect infrastructure. (F) also influences the personal history, attitudes, and psychology (O) of the people who work for the SE, as well as their achieved functionings (C3). For example, an SE could train its employees, increase their achieved functionings, and influence their attitudes and psychology by increasing their wages (w) or by providing a pleasant working environment (g). The SE's achieved functionings also influence (C2)—especially when the SE decides to invest (inv) in machinery and buildings—and (C1) when a particular policy or organizational structure is implemented.

The goods and services (G) provided by the SE have a direct effect on the goods and services available and accessible at the local level (B). This, in turn, increases the capabilities of the individuals in the STEHD framework as well as the capabilities of SEs. The availability and accessibility of goods and services (B) has a direct influence on local needs (I) and the demand for goods and services (M).

The various effects of SEs in the ecosystem are shaped by the choices made by decision makers among all the possible choices available (D). The more prosocial these choices are, the more beneficial the effect on the ecosystem. The focus on choices, and what influences them, brings us to the understanding that it is not enough to have SEs in an ecosystem if this is not "enabling" in the sense of "giving to SEs the possibility to fully pursue their final end – benefiting society."

The analytical framework described earlier to organize data that was culled from the interviews and focus groups involving 164 stakeholders (from 11 European countries) who participated in the European Research project "Enabling the Flourishing and Evolution of Social Entrepreneurship for Innovative and Inclusive Societies" (EFESEIIS).[1] The results of such organization are presented in Table 12.1. 107 stakeholders took part to the focus groups, while the remaining 57 took part to interviews. Project partners transcribed the results of the interviews and focus groups. The method employed to analyze the transcripts was the "Constant Comparative Method" (Glaser & Strauss, 1967; Lincoln & Guba, 1985). Each country wrote a report of the results. We analyzed the reports, isolating the parts that referred to the ecosystem and assessing to which block of the framework (e.g., "B-Goods and services) they belonged. The table shows the elements most frequently cited by stakeholders as those creating an enabling ecosystem. The list does not pretend to be exhaustive and considers ecosystem features that are common to the countries that took part in this project. The first column shows the block in which the various enabling features have been placed. The second column displays the enabling features identified by the stakeholders, while the third column shows its effect on the other parts of the framework.

The presence of many of these features, in tandem with the positive effects they have on the other parts of the framework and the ecosystem as a whole, might create, according to some of the stakeholders we interviewed, enabling conditions for SEs. The enabling ecosystem is mainly dependent on socio-institutional context (H), the resources present at the local level (B), the presence of a market characterized by the preference for, need, and

Table 12.1 The main features of an enabling ecosystem

Block in the framework	Enabling feature	Effect on other parts of the framework
B—Goods and services	• Access to diverse sources of funding corresponding to the different needs and maturity stages of the SE (grants, microcredit, and bank credit) • Access to business support services (legal and fiscal) • Training and support services cover all stages of the SEs' development • Widespread trust in SEs (social capital) and access to trust-based resources (such as volunteers or donations)	• Expansion of the SEs' Capability Set (D)
	• Access to training specific to the SEs' sectors of activity	• Conversion factor of the SE C) and expansion of the SEs' Capability Set (D) • Capacity of decision makers to quantify demand for goods and services (N) • Increased quality of (G)
H—Socio-institutional context	• Presence of a legal framework that defines features of SE without being too strict in regards to requirements, modes, and sectors of activity, thereby promoting hybridization of forms and innovations • Presence of fiscal incentives for SEs • Social acceptance of SEs' work and their role in society • Social reward mechanisms for those who work in SEs	• Conversion factor of the SE (C) and expansion of the SEs' Capability Set (D) • Better human resources and increases in C3 with positive effects on (N) and expansion of the SEs' Capability Set (D)
	• The education system promotes attention to social issues and entrepreneurship • Presence of a thriving third sector • Knowledge of SEs by public authorities, citizens, and the business community • SEs are included in decision-making processes at the local level, especially on matters relating to the provision of public services • Presence of control mechanisms (including impact evaluation) to promote virtuous SEs and sanction SEs' misbehaviour or fake SEs	• Positive effect on preference formation mechanism (L), which highlights the demand (M) for goods and services with a social component

Block in the framework	Enabling feature	Effect on other parts of the framework
L—Preference formation mechanism, social influences on decision-making	• The community aims to reach a higher level of Social and Human development • The community supports the inclusion of disadvantaged people	• Effect on (I) for the emergence of new needs in order to reach the desired level of Social and Human Development; similar effect on the demand (M) for goods and services with a social component
I—need for goods and services	• Existence of widespread needs that can constitute a market for SEs • Public or private actors are willing to pay to fulfil the demand for goods and services that can be provided by SEs	• Effect on the demand (M) for goods and services provided by SEs
M—Demand for goods and services	• The demand for goods and services is significant enough to constitute a market for SEs • Demand, both public and private, is geared towards goods and services that have a social component (e.g. public tenders that contain social clauses) • The demand, especially from public authorities, is accessible to most, if not all, SEs • Information on the severity of needs (potential demand) are freely accessible	• Effect on the information coming from the market (i), which, in turn, influences the decision-making process of SEs
—Collective agency	• Collective agency advocates for the recognition of needs (I) that can be fulfilled by SEs and promotes socially oriented preferences (L).	• Effect on the demand (M) for goods and services with a social component • Effect on the socio-institutional context (H) to provide specific public goods for SEs

Source: Author's own elaboration.

demand of certain services (L, I, M), and the effect that collective agency has on them. The market in such an ecosystem promotes competition but does not exacerbate it because it recognizes and values the social component of goods and services. In such an ecosystem, SEs are incentivized to provide (G), increase (soc), (w), and (g), and reduce (env), all of which will benefit society in meaningful ways. Policy makers can use the framework to check for the presence/absence of these features in their territory and understand which parts they should address in order to create an enabling ecosystem that supports SEs.

Conclusions

The framework for SE ecosystems depicted in Figure 12.1 represents a first step in trying to disentangle and systematize the relations between SEs and the ecosystem. Even if it might not account for all the possible relationships that can develop between the different parts of an ecosystem, the framework allows us to explain the main relationships via the different chains of causality, effects, and feedbacks. It also gives us the possibility to appreciate the co-evolution of the SE at the local and extra-local level by dynamically connecting them. The framework also reveals the processes through which SEs can have a positive or negative effect on the system via the chain (E) and (F) while also enlarging this understanding by taking into account the socio-institutional context (H), the personal history and attitudes of the decision makers (O), and the information coming from the local area (i).

The framework, per se, does not tell us what constitutes an enabling ecosystem for SE, but, as Table 12.1 illustrates, it can be useful in building analytical tools that can organize information related to ecosystems and appreciate how different aspects are related to each other. It can also inform policy makers on how to foster SEs in a certain area—for instance, by addressing with targeted policies the blocks in the framework that are seen as hindering the development of SEs (e.g., human capital or access to certain services) or by improving their capacity to understand local needs (e.g., by providing access to data from social services or by financing specific researches).

Table 12.1 is a useful starting point in building a diagnostic tool that can assess how much the ecosystem is enabling the development of SEs, thereby informing policies on how to create or maintain them. The framework has at least three implications for policy makers:

1   It enlarges our understanding of how different elements are often interconnected. This means drafting policies that do not focus on one single factor—e.g., financing—above all others.
2   The idea that not all SEs are the same and differ in relevant dimensions, including (C1), (C2), (C3), (O), and (N). This involves drafting policies that are transversal, that take into consideration some of these differences, and do not exclude some types of SEs.
3   The focus on the socio-institutional context (H) is of utmost importance in terms of addressing the sustainability of an ecosystem. In fact, the social component provides a setting in which the demand for goods and services with a social value emerges, creating a favourable market situation in which SEs can operate.

(H) also has an effect on how SEs are perceived in society and how socially rewarding it is to work in an SE while also helping to create a culture that focuses on social problems and incentives entrepreneurship. These factors, in turn, create the conditions that might convince people to use SEs to solve social problems.

By adopting the framework elaborated in this paper, policy makers might be able to adopt a more holistic approach, by consider the different features of the ecosystem, when planning and implementing policies for SEs.

Note

1 EFESEIIS stands for "Enabling the flourishing and the evolution of Social Entrepreneurship for Innovative and Inclusive Societies." It is a EU funded research project. For more information, see www.fp7-efeseiis.eu.

References

Ackert, L. F., Gillette, A. B., Martinez-Vazquez, J., & Rider, M. (2009). *Risk tolerance, self-interest, and social preferences*. Andrew Young School of Policy Studies Research Paper Series, (11-03).

Ainsworth, D. (2012, 24 August). *Scotland's social enterprises seem to have it made, Third Sector*, 28 March. Retrieved from http://thirdsector.thirdsector.co.uk/2012/03/28/scotlands-social-enterprises-seemto-have-it-made/.

Alesina, A. F., & Giuliano, P. (2009). *Preferences for redistribution* (No. w14825). National Bureau of Economic Research.

Angroff, R., & McGuire, M. (2003). *Collaborative public management: New strategies for local governments*, Washington, DC: Georgetown University Press.

Bellandi, M. (2009). Industrial districts and specific public goods. In G. Becattini, M. Bellandi, & L. De Propris (Eds.), *The handbook of industrial districts*. Cheltenham: Edward Elgar Publisher, 712–725

Ben-Ner, A., & Halldorsson, F. (2010). Trusting and trustworthiness: What are they, how to measure them, and what affects them. *Journal of Economic Psychology, 31*(1), 64–79.

Benjamin, D. J., Choi, J. J., & Strickland, A. J. (2007). *Social identity and preferences*. National Bureau of Economic Research Working Paper No. 13309.

Biggeri, M., & Ferrannini, A. (2014). The sustainable territorial evolution for human development (STEHD) framework. In M. Biggeri, & A. Ferrannini, (Eds.), *Sustainable human development* (pp. 39–68). Palgrave Macmillan, New York and Basingstoke.

Birkhölzer, K. (2009). The role of social enterprise in local economic development. In *2nd EMES International Conference on Social Enterprise, Trento (Italy)* – July 1–4.

Bornstein, D. (2004). *How to change the world: Social entrepreneurs and the power of new ideas*. New York: Oxford University Press.

Borzaga, C., & Defourny, J. (2001). *The emergence of social enterprises*. London: Routledge.

Borzaga, C., & Tortia, E. (2009). Social enterprises and local economic development. In E. Clarence, & A. Noya (Eds.), *The changing boundaries of social enterprises* (pp. 195–228). Paris: OECD Publishing.

Bowles, S. (1998). Endogenous preferences: The cultural consequences of markets and other economic institutions. *Journal of Economic Literature, 36*(1), 75–111.

Brandsen, T., & Karré, P. M. (2011). Hybrid organizations: No cause for concern. *International Journal of Public Administration, 34*, 827–836.

Brocklebank, S., Lewis, G. J., & Bates, T. C. (2011). Personality accounts for stable preferences and expectations across a range of simple games. *Personality and Individual Differences, 51*(8), 881–886.

Carreira da Silva, F., & Valadez Martinez, L. (2015). Sophie's choice: Social attitudes to welfare state retrenchment in bailed-out Portugal. *European Societies, 17*(3), 351–371.

Carroll, D. A. & Stater, K. J. (2009). Revenue diversification in non-profit organizations: Does it lead to financial stability? *Journal of Public Administration Research and Theory, 19*, 947–966.

Cohen, W. M., & Levinthal, D. A. (1990). Absorptive capacity: A new perspective on learning and innovation. *Administrative Science Quarterly, 3*, 128–152.

Cornelius, N., & Wallace, J. (2013). Capabilities, urban unrest and social enterprise: Limits of the actions of third sector organisations. *International Journal of Public Sector Management, 26*(3), 232–249.

Coval, J. D., & Moskowitz, T. J. (2001). The geography of investment: Informed trading and asset prices. *Journal of Political Economy, 109*(4), 811–841.

Croson, R., & Gneezy, U. (2009). Gender differences in preferences. *Journal of Economic Literature, 47*(2), 448–474.

Day, G. S., & Nedungadi, P. (1994). Managerial representations of competitive advantage. *The Journal of Marketing, 58*, 31–44.

Defourny, J., & Nyssens, M. (2008). Social enterprise in Europe: Recent trends and developments. *Social Enterprise Journal, 4*(3), 202–228.

Depedri, S. (2007). *Speaking on the job: Incentives, preferences and complementarities in working relationships* (Doctoral dissertation, PhD Thesis). University of Siena.

Dey, P., & Teasdale, S. (2016). The tactical mimicry of social enterprise strategies: Acting 'as if' in the everyday life of third sector organizations. *Organization, 23*(4), 485–504.

Di Domenico, M., Haugh, H., & Tracey, P. (2010). Social bricolage: Theorizing social value creation in social enterprises. *Entrepreneurship Theory and Practice, 34*(4), 681–703.

Dohmen, T., Falk, A., Huffman, D., & Sunde, U. (2008). Representative trust and reciprocity: Prevalence and determinants. *Economic Inquiry, 46*(1), 84–90.

Dohmen, T., Falk, A., Huffman, D., & Sunde, U. (2009). Homo reciprocans: Survey evidence on behavioural outcomes. *The Economic Journal, 119*(536), 592–612.

Dohmen, T., Falk, A., Huffman, D., & Sunde, U. (2011). The intergenerational transmission of risk and trust attitudes. *The Review of Economic Studies, 79*(2), 645–677.

Doherty, B., Haugh, H., & Lyon, F. (2014). Social enterprises as hybrid organizations: A review and research agenda. *International Journal of Management Reviews, 16*, 417–436. doi:10.1111/ijmr.12028.

Durose, C., & Richardson, L. (2015). *Rethinking public policy-making: Why co-production matters.* Bristol: Policy Press.

Eikenberry, A. M., & Kluver, J. D. (2004). The marketization of the non-profit sector: Civil society at risk. *Public Administration Review, 64*, 132–140.

European Commission. (2015). *A map of social enterprises and their ecosystems in Europe,* Directorate-General for Employment, Social Affairs and Inclusion.

Evers, A., & Schulze-Boeing, M. (2001). Germany: Social enterprises and transitional employment. In C. Borzaga, & J. Defourney (Eds.), *The emergence of social enterprise* (pp. 120–35). London: Routledge.

Eversole, R., Barraket, J., & Luke, B. (2013). Social enterprises in rural community development. *Community Development Journal, 49*(2), 245–261.

Falk, A., Becker, A., Dohmen, T. J., Huffman, D., & Sunde, U. (2016). *The preference survey module: A validated instrument for measuring risk, time, and social preferences*. IZA Discussion Papers 9674, Bonn.

Fehr, E., Fischbacher, U., Von Rosenbladt, B., Schupp, J., & Wagner, G. G. (2003). *A nation-wide laboratory: Examining trust and trustworthiness by integrating behavioral experiments into representative survey*. CESifo Working Paper Series No. 866, Munich.

Giuliano, P., & Spilimbergo, A. (2008). *Growing up in bad times: Macroeconomic volatility and the formation of beliefs*. UCLA, Los Angeles.

Glaser, B., & Strauss, A. (1967). Grounded theory: The discovery of grounded theory. *Sociology the Journal of the British Sociological Association, 12*, 27–49.

Granovetter, M. S. (1973). The strength of weak ties. *American Journal of Sociology, 78*(6), 1360–1380.

Hall, K., Miller, R., & Millar, R. (2012). Jumped or pushed: What motivates NHS staff to set up a social enterprise? *Social Enterprise Journal, 8*(1), 49–62.

Harding, R. (2004). Social enterprise: The new economic engine?, *Business Strategy Review, 15*(4), 39–43.

Haugh, H. (2005). A research agenda for social entrepreneurship? *Social Enterprise Journal, 2*, 346–357.

Hazenberg, R., & Hall, K. (2016). Public service mutuals: Towards a theoretical understanding of the spin-out process. *Policy & Politics, 44*(3), 441–463.

Huck, S. (1998). Trust, treason, and trials: An example of how the evolution of preferences can be driven by legal institutions. *Journal of Law, Economics, & Organization*, 44–60.

Hynes, B. (2009). Growing the social enterprise–Issues and challenges. *Social Enterprise Journal, 5*(2), 114–125.

Jakiela, P., Miguel, E., & Te Velde, V. L. (2010). *You've earned it: Combining field and lab experiments to estimate the impact of human capital on social preferences*. National Bureau of Economic Research Working Paper No. 16449.

Jones, M. B. (2007). The multiple sources of mission drift. *Nonprofit and Voluntary Sector Quarterly, 36*, 299–307.

Kerlin, J. A. (2009). *Social enterprise: A global comparison*. Lebanon, NH: Tufts University Press.

Kerlin, J. A. (2010). A comparative analysis of the global emergence of social enterprise. *Voluntas, 21*, 162–179.

Kirby, K. N., Petry, N. M., & Bickel, W. K. (1999). Heroin addicts have higher discount rates for delayed rewards than non-drug-using controls. *Journal of Experimental Psychology: General, 128*(1), 78.

Komlos, J., Smith, P. K., & Bogin, B. (2004). Obesity and the rate of time preference: Is there a connection? *Journal of Biosocial Science, 36*(2), 209–219.

Kranton, R., Pease, M., Sanders, S., & Huettel, S. (2012). *Identity, group conflict, and social preferences*. Working paper, University of Chicago, Chicago.

Lee, S., Courtney, J. F., & O'Keefe, R. M. (1992). A system for organizational learning using cognitive maps. *Omega, 20*(1), 23–36.

Lincoln, Y. S., & Guba, E. G. (1985). *Naturalistic inquiry* (Vol. 75). Sage, Beverly Hills, CA.

Lönnqvist, J. E., Verkasalo, M., & Walkowitz, G. (2011). It pays to pay–Big. Five personality influences on co-operative behaviour in an incentivized and hypothetical prisoner's dilemma game. *Personality and Individual Differences*, 50(2), 300–304.

Mair, J., & Marti, I. (2006). Social entrepreneurship research: A source of explanation, prediction, and delight. *Journal of World Business*, 41(1), 36–44.

Manetti, G. (2012). The role of blended value Accounting in the evaluation of socio-economic impact of social enterprises. *VOLUNTAS: International Journal of Voluntary and Nonprofit Organizations*, doi:10.1007/s11266-012-9346-1.

Muñoz, S. A. (2010). Towards a geographical research agenda for social enterprise. *Area*, 42(3), 302–312.

Needham, C. (2008). Realising the potential of co-production: Negotiating improvements in public services. *Social Policy and Society*, 7(2), 221–231.

Nooteboom, B. (2000). Learning by interaction: Absorptive capacity, cognitive distance and governance. *Journal of Management and Governance*, 4(1–2), 69–92.

OECD-LEED. (2016). *Building enabling ecosystems for social enterprises.* Capacity Building Seminar, 17–18 February 2016, Brussels. Retrieved from www.oecd.org/employment/leed/social-oecd-eu-cbs.htm.

Orbell, J., Goldman, M., Mulford, M., & Dawes, R. (1992). Religion, context, and constraint toward strangers. *Rationality and Society*, 4(3), 291–307.

Pache, A.C., & Santos, F. (2010). When worlds collide: The internal dynamics of organizational responses to conflicting institutional demands. *Academy of Management Review*, 35, 455–476.

Pasetto, A., (2010). *Imprese Sociali e sistemi produttivi locali.* Paper discussed at IV Colloquio Sull'Impresa Sociale.

Peattie, K., & Morley, A. (2008). *Social enterprises: diversity and dynamics, contexts and contributions.* Retrieved from http://orca.cf.ac.uk/30775/.

Piketty, T. (1995). Social mobility and redistributive politics. *The Quarterly Journal of Economics, 110,* 551–584.

Pinch, S., & Sunley, P. (2015). Social enterprise and neoinstitutional theory: An evaluation of the organizational logics of SE in the UK. *Social Enterprise Journal, 11*(3), 303–320.

Qureshi, I., Kistruck, G. M., & Bhatt, B. (2016). The enabling and constraining effects of social ties in the process of institutional entrepreneurship. *Organization Studies, 37*(3), 425–447.

Robeyns, I. (2005). The capability approach: A theoretical survey. *Journal of Human Development*, 6(1), 93–117.

Rodriguez-Sickert, C., Guzmán, R. A., & Cárdenas, J. C. (2008). Institutions influence preferences: Evidence from a common pool resource experiment. *Journal of Economic Behavior & Organization*, 67(1), 215–227.

Rose-Ackerman, S. (1996). Altruism, nonprofits, and economic theory. *Journal of Economic Literature*, 34(2), 701–728.

Roy, M. J., Donaldson, C., Baker, R., & Kerr, S. (2014). The potential of social enterprise to enhance health and well-being: A model and systematic review. *Social Science & Medicine, 123,* 182–193.

Scarlato, M. (2012). Social enterprise and development policy: Evidence from Italy. *Journal of Social Entrepreneurship*, 3(1), 24–49.

Schumpeter, J. A. (2001), *Capitalismo, Socialismo e Democrazia (1942).* Milano: ETAS.

Schumpeter, J. A. (2002), *Teoria dello sviluppo economico (1911).* Milano: ETAS.

Seelos, C., Mair, J., Battlana, J., & Dacin, M. T. (2010). *The embeddedness of social entrepreneurship: Understanding variation across local communities.* IESE Business School, University of Navarra, Working Paper No. 858, Navarra

Sen, A. (1985). Well-being, agency and freedom: The Dewey lectures 1984. *The Journal of Philosophy, 82*(4), 169–221.

Sen, A. (1998). Mortality as an indicator of economic success and failure. *The Economic Journal, 108*(446), 1–25.

Sen Amartya, K. (1999). *Development as freedom.* New York: Knopf.

Sinkula, J. M. (1994). Market information processing and organizational learning. *The Journal of Marketing,* 35–45.

Smith, B. R., Matthews, C. H., & Schenkel, M. T. (2005). The search for and discovery of different types of entrepreneurial opportunities: The effects of tacitness and codification. *Frontiers of Entrepreneurship Research,* 283–293.

Smith, B. R., & Stevens, C. E. (2010). Different types of social entrepreneurship: The role of geography and embeddedness on the measurement and scaling of social value. *Entrepreneurship and Regional Development, 22*(6), 575–598.

Sorenson, O. (2003). Interdependence and adaptability: Organizational learning and the long-term effect of integration. *Management Science, 49*(4), 446–463.

Tan, J. H. (2006). Religion and social preferences: An experimental study. *Economics Letters, 90*(1), 60–67.

Tanaka, T., Camerer, C. F., & Nguyen, Q. (2010). Risk and time preferences: Linking experimental and household survey data from Vietnam. *American Economic Review, 100*(1), 557–571.

Taylor-Gooby, P. (2008). Choice and values: Individualised rational action and social goals. *Journal of Social Policy, 37,* 167–185. doi:10.1017/S00472794070 01699.

Testi, E. (2017). *Analysing social enterprises and their ecosystem* (PhD Thesis PhD in Economics) Curriculum Economia e Gestione dello Sviluppo Locale, University of Florence, Italy.

Volk, S., Thöni, C., & Ruigrok, W. (2012). Temporal stability and psychological foundations of cooperation preferences. *Journal of Economic Behavior & Organization, 81*(2), 664–676.

Yujuico, E. (2008). Connecting the dots in social entrepreneurship through the capabilities approach. *Socio-Economic Review, 6*(3), 493–513.

Zafeiropoulou, F. A., & Koufopoulos, D. N. (2013). The influence of relational embeddedness on the formation and performance of social franchising. *Journal of Marketing Channels, 20*(1–2), 73–98.

Zahra, S. A., Gedajlovic, E., Neubaum, D. O., & Shulman, J. M. (2009). A typology of social entrepreneurs: Motives, search processes and ethical challenges. *Journal of Business Venturing, 24*(5), 519–532.

13 Concluding remarks on social entrepreneurship in Europe

H. Thomas R. Persson, Mario Biggeri,
Enrico Testi, Marco Bellucci, and Roel During

Introduction

The three-year long EFESEIIS (Enabling the Flourishing and Evolution of Social Entrepreneurship for Innovative and Inclusive Societies) project allowed us to produce a detailed and wide-ranging, book-length study of social entrepreneurship in Europe. The authors set out to capture and to share the knowledge gathered by the EFESEIIS project, which, in turn, will enhance our understanding of the various ecosystems that lead to functioning social enterprises (SEs). The terms "system," "ecosystems" (EC, 2015), "enabling ecosystem" (OECD-LEED, 2016), and "supportive environment" (Ainsworth, 2012) have been used to describe the relationship between SEs and the jurisdiction in which they are set. Some chapters in this study have discussed social entrepreneurship in Europe, as well as the research background, theoretical frameworks, and methodologies of the EFESEIIS project. Other chapters, meanwhile, have examined the rise and main features of social entrepreneurship in Europe, the diversity of the SE sector, and the behavior of decision-makers working in SEs. Furthermore, social capital and the role of stakeholder networks in shaping the development of SEs have been discussed, while attempts have also been made to understand the innovative behavior of SEs, niches of social innovation, the new generation of SEs, and enabling ecosystems.

Given the vast number of topics and perspectives discussed in this book, it is no small task to write a concluding chapter that provides a clear picture of the research offered in each chapter. Nevertheless, this chapter briefly summarizes and compares the development of SEs and their ecosystems in Europe. This will be done by recapturing the nature of social entrepreneurship and SEs; examining some of the main findings presented in this work; touching upon some of the policy implications of this research; and offering suggestions on how to improve the study of social entrepreneurship, SEs, and social innovation.

Main findings

Capturing the main findings of a three-year-long research project is not a particularly straightforward process. For starters, in order to determine what the main findings are, one needs to put aside one's own biases (e.g. recognizing that established trends in one jurisdiction may be seen as new developments in other jurisdictions). For example, early on in the EFESEIIS project it became clear that settling on a definition of social entrepreneurship that can be applied to all of the case studies and schools of thought discussed in the EFESEIIS project was going to be a difficult task. While some European countries have adopted legal categories for SE, others have not. Moreover, even when legal categories do exist, they often differ from country to country. Consequently, an organization that is listed as an SE in one context might not be considered an SE in another. Fortunately, a working definition of social entrepreneurship has been provided by the European Commission, one that offers researchers from the EFESEIIS project the means to better assess SEs in a wide variety of contexts. The European Commission defined social entrepreneurship as an activity whose primary purpose is to pursue social goals; produce goods and services in a highly entrepreneurial, innovative, and efficient manner to generate benefits for society and citizens; use surpluses mainly to achieve social goals; and accomplish its mission through the way in which it involves workers, customers, and stakeholders affected by its business activity. The prime objective of social entrepreneurship, therefore, is to generate and maximize social value while remaining economically profitable (EC, 2012, p. 23).

Researchers from the EFESEIIS project understood early on that most of the variations found in our case studies were brought about due to the nature and level of development of the national and regional ecosystems in which SEs are often situated (see Chapters 4 and 8). SEs operate in different sectors, they take on different legal forms, their capacity to remain and stay compatible in the market differ, and they are often dependent (to varying degrees) on external funding. While they widely differ in terms of income sources, profitability levels, and the size of their labor force (including both employees and volunteers), most SE activities tend to focus on social welfare, a phenomenon that has been confirmed by other researchers (Hazenberg et al., 2016; Savio & Righetti, 1993). While early versions of SEs—many of which stemmed from popular movements and related societal transformations—helped give birth to modern welfare institutions, SEs became more prominent players during the 1970s, 1980s, and 1990s—especially Work Integration Social Enterprises (WISEs) (Defourny & Nyssens, 2008). SEs came to be seen as quick and inexpensive means of curbing escalating costs in the welfare sector, a way of thinking that remains popular to this day.

The neoliberal turn initiated during the 1980s still shapes the manner in which many European welfare regimes try to reinvent themselves. By attempting to either replace or complement existing public services, the SE sector (and the private sector as whole) is now involved in policy design and implementation, assuming a management role alongside traditional public authorities. As a result, the discourse surrounding SEs has shifted away from an emphasis on altruism towards one that stresses entrepreneurs and entrepreneurship (Evers, 2005). Indeed, this phenomenon has been noted in all of the case studies included in the EFESEIIS project. As a result, social entrepreneurs are injecting business logic into the SE discourse in an ever-expanding manner. Of course, this trend creates several challenges—from both within and without—that SEs are compelled to address. For instance, staying true to one's mission is difficult to maintain when management systems and legal forms are being challenged. Moreover, stakeholders tend to express disapproval whenever a social venture starts to become too business-like (Hlady-Rispal & Servantie, 2018).

Given the rather heterogeneous nature of welfare regimes in Europe, it should come as no surprise to find that the history of SEs is far from uniform. While some historical trends may point in a certain direction, the circumstances tend to differ greatly. This becomes clear when looking at the evolutionary aspects of social entrepreneurship (Chapter 4), the managerial aspects of social entrepreneurship (Chapter 5), the extent to which stakeholder networks shape the development of ecosystems (Chapter 8), and various aspects of social innovation (Chapters 9 and 10). Nevertheless, different types of social capital seem to be of great importance for all social entrepreneurs. For instance, Zablocka et al. (Chapter 7) found that most SEs combine bonding social capital—e.g., the creation of common goals, culture, and group-specific practices—with bridging social capital—e.g., networking with local stakeholders (Bellucci & Manetti, 2017). This phenomenon is also discussed in Chapter 5.

Social entrepreneurs and their enterprises

Looking at the managerial aspects of SEs—including organizational objectives, financial and human resources, governance, and stakeholder influence—Bellucci and his colleagues (Chapter 5) stress that the differences that emerge at the national level make it almost impossible to adopt a comparative approach or propose a standardized model of intervention that can be used by policy-makers. Nevertheless, some shared aspects are apparent, many of which are capable of both strengthening and weakening social entrepreneurship in Europe. While local embeddedness—i.e., trying to deliver solutions to problems that are unique to a specific locality—is thought to strengthen SEs, market constraints, low public awareness, excessive bureaucracy, unclear legal frameworks, and a lack of funding that is geared specifically towards SEs often act as significant obstacles. Although this may put constraints on policymaking efforts at the EU level, it is worth noting that policymaking at the local, regional, and national levels is much more important to SEs anyway, as smaller, localized policy initiatives help standardize and rationalize social entrepreneurship at all levels.

SEs, many of which are driven by ideals and values rather than profits, have been identified as valuable tools for solving societal problems (Borzaga & Defourny, 2001; Defourny & Nyssens, 2006). The primary objective of SEs (as noted earlier) is to solve social or environmental problems. This is in stark contrast to traditional companies that see social goals as being secondary to profit maximization. Nevertheless, as Testi and his colleagues argued in Chapter 6, social entrepreneurs and decision-makers in traditional enterprises tend to make a similar amount of pro-social choices. While decision-makers from SEs seem to be more socially aware—and therefore more likely to make more pro-social choices—some social entrepreneurs tend to make less pro-social choices when faced with competitive pressures and shrinking resources. Although this finding may be hard to accept among scholars who study SEs, Testi and company have shown that representatives from SEs and traditional enterprises are perhaps more alike than they'd care to admit. Thus, if SEs are meant to provide as much social value as possible, then it is safe to say that much work needs to be done in order to produce procurement processes that are based on quality, innovation, and social value rather than fiscal concerns alone. Interestingly enough, policy-makers ought to favor these types of measures because they will most likely produce similar results among for-profit enterprises.

Ecosystems and an evolutionary theory in the making

No organization comes to life, develops, and exists in a vacuum; rather, organizations are shaped by historic, current, and future trends. In Chapter 8, Hazenberg et al. explores the development of SE ecosystems across Europe by creating a stakeholder typology based on each region's historical and cultural context, socioeconomic and political factors, and social/stakeholder networks. Four classifications—statist-micro, statist-macro, private-micro, and private-macro—were developed by taking into consideration three factors: the dominant stakeholder types found in an ecosystem, the extent to which local factors are emphasized (rather than national or supranational factors), and the involvement of other economic sectors in a specific ecosystem.

The authors found that Albania, Austria, France, Poland, and Serbia have statist-macro ecosystems, due to the predominance of state institutions in delivering support to the SE ecosystem. Scotland and Sweden, both of which use public sector bodies to deliver support to SEs, have statist-micro ecosystems, due to their greater focus on regional and local institutions (even though both nations receive support from supranational entities). Both private-macro and private-micro ecosystems are characterized by a lack of state funding and a focus on marketization. However, while the type of marketization seen in private-macro systems (e.g. England and Germany) is often driven by a centralized state, marketization in private-micro systems (e.g. Italy and the Netherlands) is usually driven by disparate third/private-sector organizations at the local level. Although this typology can help us understand the diversity of SE ecosystems, it is important to understand that the boundaries between different ecosystem types are both distorted and fluid as the basic makeup of an ecosystem is constantly shifting.

Biggeri et al. (2017) developed a framework for assessing SE ecosystems that allows us to explain the causal relationships, effects, and feedback that emerge between SEs and their ecosystems. This framework helps us chart the coevolution of SEs and their ecosystems at the local level and beyond while also revealing the processes through which SEs produce positive or negative effects on the system. This was accomplished by taking into account socio-institutional context, the personal history and attitudes of key decision-makers, and information that emerges in the ecosystem itself. Although this framework will not tell us what constitutes an enabling ecosystem, the authors suggest that it can be used for building analytical tools that can both process relevant information and inform policy-makers on aspects of the ecosystem that need to be addressed. It does so by explaining how different elements are interconnected, assessing the diverse needs of SEs, and emphasizing the importance of socio-institutional factors in contributing to the sustainability of any given ecosystem. We believe that this new framework encourages a more holistic approach to policymaking.

While the typology and framework discussed in Chapters 8 and 12 will help researchers and policy-makers better understand how to influence local, regional, and national ecosystems, explaining how an ecosystem arrived at its current state is much more difficult to determine. Since the EFESEIIS project emphasizes how social entrepreneurship has evolved over the years, we decided during the early stages of our research that an evolutionary perspective was required. During and van Dam do just that in Chapter 4, offering up a theoretical tool that can help explain how different institutional contexts produce different SEs. During and van Dam's contribution is basically an attempt to understand how SEs can both emerge from nothing and take an active part in reshaping their specific institutional context. Unlike earlier approaches, in which the future of an enterprise was thought to be determined solely by its intuitional context, this new evolutionary perspective acknowledges a greater degree of agency on behalf of SEs.

During and van Dam's approach borrows heavily from the works of Charles Darwin, particularly his concepts of variation, selection, and heredity. The authors point towards five different examples of variation that can help us assess the development of SEs while also stressing that these five variations won't necessarily lead to a well-functioning SE (During et al., 2016).

Ideas migrate easily from one context to another. Moreover, the diversity and quality of ideas are enhanced in cities or regions that have creative reputations (van Dam et al., 2015). Determining which ideas survive, however, is a matter of selection, which, in turn, is often determined by the quality of the ideas in question. If the environment is not ready for an idea (or is even hostile to it), there is little chance of success.

How the SE perceives itself and its environment is key, which leads to an important question: what determines the basic attitude of an environment towards an SE? Heredity defines how traits that are important for survival and adaptability are passed from one generation to the next—or in the case of SEs, from one generation of enterprises to the next. This is clear from the number of serial entrepreneurs who become involved with SEs and other related sectors. Similarly, one can see that the ecosystem itself also undergoes a process of learning that influences the next generation's traits. The fact that both entrepreneurs and the ecosystem can learn should be seen as a sign of coevolution. The evolutionary path is not always straight or unambiguous. Environments can be enabling, disabling, or both and are often shaped by public opinion, reactions to current events, history and traditions, defensive moves from established institutions, and political/ideological debates. Nevertheless, managing this type of ambiguity is an integral part of social learning and oftentimes serves as a catalyst for social innovation.

Social innovation

Social innovation, another context-dependent phenomenon, often involves actions, frameworks, models, systems, processes, services, rules, organizational forms, and sometimes products (Nicholls et al., 2016). The idea that innovations and development go hand in hand is not particularly new (Backhaus, 2002) and applies just as well to welfare systems, social entrepreneurs, and SEs. The construction of European welfare systems—including health-care systems, schools, and social services—was the result of social innovation but resulted in several different types of welfare regimes (Esping-Andersen, 1993). Indeed, what is considered a social innovation in one context will not necessarily be considered as such in another context. Nonetheless, it is still possible to arrive at a consensus in terms of determining what qualifies as an innovation. European welfare systems, like the economy in general, are going through "profound shifts" that can be characterized as examples of "creative destruction" (Harvey et al., 2010, p. 528). Social innovations play a part in this process and will most likely be appropriated by current welfare regimes, resulting in innovations that promise to solve problems that traditional approaches are simply unable to address.

As Chapter 9 explains, the majority of SEs we surveyed regard social innovation as being central to social entrepreneurship. The new generation of social entrepreneurs, discussed by Grabbe et al. in Chapter 6, is part of an ongoing process of creative destruction in which managerial welfare strategies are replaced by entrepreneurial approaches. This is what is happening in Germany, as social entrepreneurs attempt to address severe social problems that established welfare entities were unable to solve. Their somewhat novel approach is based on raising funds and resources from individuals and organizations that had not previously invested in social welfare projects, while simultaneously making efforts to build public support for their efforts. In the German context, then, these types of activities are firmly linked to NGSEs. However, as Hazenberg et al. argue in Chapter 8, these activities might not be considered novel in another national context.

Future research and policy implications

This book has established that SEs, most of which are driven by ideals and values rather than profit, have been identified as valuable tools for solving societal problems. And yet decision-makers in SEs are not necessarily more likely to make pro-social choices. This could be because their differences with decision-makers in traditional enterprises are, in the grand scheme of things, not all that vast, or because they tend to mimic the behavior of others when faced with similar constraints and choices (Dey & Teasdale, 2015; Parkinson & Howorth, 2008). Does this undermine the activities of SEs? The answer is no. As Chapter 6 illustrates, those who self-identify as social entrepreneurs often make pro-social choices, regardless of whether they work for an SE or a traditional for-profit enterprise. This implies that SEs are more important than ever, and that policy that emphasizes social value ought to be encouraged. Ultimately, it is a question of whether market forces should prevail over social goals. The easiest way of achieving the latter is to make sure that procurements include elements favoring social value, an argument that has been noted often by social entrepreneurs. And of course it perhaps goes without saying that for-profit enterprises would be forced to mimic the behavior of SEs.

There are also significant methodological issues that need to be overcome, as the most viable and effective methods for measuring social impact have not yet been clearly delineated (Manetti et al., 2015). However, as Bellucci and company stress in Chapter 5, though local embeddedness and stakeholder engagement often strengthens SEs, they often face innumerable market constraints, low public awareness, excessive bureaucracy, an unclear legal framework, and a lack of funds that are geared towards their specific activities—all of which make it difficult for SEs to compete with larger and well-established for-profit enterprises.

If we can agree that the goal of this project is to "enable the flourishing and evolution of social entrepreneurship for innovative and inclusive societies," then we can also conclude that much still needs to be done by policy-makers at the local, regional, and national level. Successful social entrepreneurs will not be limited to people who come up with the next big idea, but rather people who can navigate local ecosystems. Thus, being aware of the political, social, and cultural factors that inform and restrict managerial strategies within a variable and unpredictable environment will only help encourage successful social entrepreneurship in the years to come.

References

Ainsworth, D. (2012). *Scotland's social enterprises seem to have it made.* Third Sector. Retrieved from http://thirdsector.thirdsector.co.uk/2012/03/28/scotlands-social-enterprises-seem-to-have-it-made/.

Backhaus, U. (2002). Seventh chapter of the theory of economic development. *Industry and Innovation, 9*(1–2), 93–145.

Bellucci, M., & Manetti, G. (2017). Facebook as a tool for supporting dialogic accounting? Evidence from large philanthropic foundations in the United States. *Accounting, Auditing & Accountability Journal, 30*(4), 874–905.

Bellucci, M., & Manetti, G. (2018). *Stakeholder engagement and sustainability reporting.* London: Routledge.

Biggeri, M., Testi, E., & Bellucci, M. (2017). Enabling ecosystems for social enterprises and social innovation: A capability approach perspective. *Journal of Human Development and Capabilities, 18*(2). doi:10.1080/19452829.2017.1306690.

Borzaga, C., & Defourny, J. (Eds.). (2001). *The emergence of social enterprises.* London: Routledge.

Defourny, J., & Nyssens, M. (2006). Defining social enterprise. In M. Nyssens (Ed.), *Social enterprise: at the crossroads of market, public policies and civil society* (pp. 3–26). London: Routledge.

Defourny, J., & Nyssens, M. (2008). Social enterprise in Europe: Recent trends and developments. *Social Enterprise Journal, 4*(3), 202–228.

Dey, P., & Teasdale, S. (2015). The tactical mimicry of social enterprise strategies: Acting 'as if' in the everyday life of third sector organizations. *Organization, 2*(34), 485–504.

During, R., van Dam, R. I., & Salverda, I. E. (2016). *Using evolutionary theory for pluralism in social policies.* Paper presented at the 2016 Social Policy Association Annual Conference: Radical, Resistant, Resolute, Symposium: Social Innovation and Social Policy: A Solution or Surrender to Welfare Austerity? Lost in Translation? Reconciling Social Innovation Discourse with Policy Implementation, Belfast.

EC. (2012). *Work programme 2013 (Revision) Theme 8 Socio-economic sciences and humanities (European Commission C(2012) 9371 of 14 December).* Retrieved from http://ec.europa.eu/research/participants/data/ref/fp7/154030/h-wp-201302_en.pdf.

EC. (2015). *A map of social enterprises and their ecosystems in Europe, Directorate-General for Employment, Social Affairs and Inclusion.* Retrieved from ec.europa. eu/social/BlobServlet?docId=12987&langId=en.

Esping-Andersen, G. (1993). *The three worlds of welfare capitalism.* Princeton, NJ: Princeton University Press.

Evers, A. (2005). Mixed welfare systems and hybrid organizations: Changes in the governance and provision of social services. *International Journal of Public Administration, 28*(9–10), 737–748.

Harvey, M., Kiessling, T., & Moeller, M. (2010). A view of entrepreneurship and innovation from the economist "for all seasons": Joseph S. Schumpeter. *Journal of Management History, 16*(4), 527–531.

Hazenberg, R., Bajwa-Patel, M., Mazzei, M., Roy, M. J., & Baglioni, S. (2016). The role of institutional and stakeholder networks in shaping social enterprise ecosystems in Europe. *Social Enterprise Journal, 12*(3), 302–321.

Hlady-Rispal, M., & Servantie, V. (2018). Deconstructing the way in which value is created in the context of social entrepreneurship. *International Journal of Management Reviews, 20*(1), 62–80.

Manetti, G., Bellucci, M., Como, E., & Bagnoli, L. (2015). Investing in volunteering: Measuring social returns of volunteer recruitment, training and management. *VOLUNTAS: International Journal of Voluntary and Nonprofit Organizations*, 26(5), 2104–2129.

Nicholls, A., Simon, J., & Gabriel, M. (2016). Introduction: Dimensions of social innovation. In A. Nicholls, J. Simon, & M. Gabriel (Eds.), *New frontiers in social innovation research* (pp. 1–26). Basingstoke: Palgrave Macmillan.

OECD-LEED. (2016). *Building enabling ecosystems for social enterprises*. Capacity Building Seminar, 17th–18th February 2016, Brussels. Retrieved from www. oecd.org/employment/leed/social-oecd-eu-cbs.htm.

Parkinson, C., & Howorth, C. (2008). The language of social entrepreneurs. *Entrepreneurship & Regional Development: An International Journal*, 20(3), 285–309.

Savio, M., & Righetti, A. (1993). Cooperatives as a social enterprise in Italy: A place for social integration and rehabilitation. *Acta Psychiatrica Scandinavica*, 88(4), 238–242.

van Dam, R. I., During, R., Glad, T., & De Sena, N. (2015). *Enabling social entrepreneurship for social innovation. Report of city Level Focus Groups with social entrepreneurs and stakeholders in Amsterdam The Netherlands*. Working document EFESEIIS.

Index

Note: page numbers in **bold** refer to tables, those in *italics* refer to figures and references with 'n' denote notes section respectively.

Alterra 16
Ashoka International 28

Barroso Commission 32
Becker, Gary 28
Biggeri, M. 182
Bird, B. 72
Bornstein, David 54
Borzaga, C. 56, 61, 182, 185
Butterfield, K. D. 75

Cameron, David 31
capability approach 182
Carreira da Silva, F. 186
Chancenwerk 154, **158**; business model 155–6; idea and target group 154; success story 155
Clipici, E. 33
Coalition for Social Enterprise 28
Coleman, J. S. 97
collective agency 186
The Constant Comparative Method (CCM) 115
Cools, E. 72
cooperation, social capital and 100, 104–5, *105*
cooperative social movement 42–3
coordination mechanism 3
Cornelius, N. 181–2
corporate governance 58
Coval, J. D. 188
Cowling, M. 72

Darwin, Charles 40
data-gathering process 114–15; *see also* stakeholder typology

decision makers in social enterprises (DSE) 69–70, 187, 189–90; ecosystem perspective 70; hypothesis 75; interpretative framework 73–5; literature review 70–3; *see also* Tuscany, DSE research study
Defourny, J. 182, 185
Delivered Next Day Personally 174
Digital Mums 174
Dockt & EVHB 169–70
Drayton, Bill 28
Drucker, Piter 128
The Dutch group 176n9

economic innovation 13
The Eco Social Farm 169, 176n7
ecosystems 179–84, *185*; collective agency 186; decision makers 189–90; effect of SEs 190–1, 193; features of 192–3; goods and services 186–9, **192**; implications for policy makers 194–5; socio institutional context 185–6, **192**; territorial achieved functioning 184–5
education and innovation 134–6, **135**
EESC *see* European Economic and Social Committee (EESC)
embeddedness 112
Emergence of Social Enterprises in Europe (EMES) 28, 29
Enabling the Flourishing and Evolution of Social Entrepreneurship for Innovative and Inclusive Societies (EFESEIIS) project 3–5, 14, 21, 32, 54, 98, 146, 191, 200, 201, 204; ambivalences 18–19; Causal Process

Tracing in 39, 50; convergences 19–20; divergences 19; European social enterprises 56, 66n1; mixed methods and multi-disciplinary approach 16–17, 22; participants in 39; partnership structure 15–16; unifying concepts 20–1; work packages **17**
Enercoop 170, 176n10
England, supportive ecosystem in 44
enterprises 1
epigenetics factor 112
Erste Bank 42
Esping-Andersen, G. 25, 145
established organizations 151
European Alliance for Corporate Social Responsibility 28
European Commission 98; "Guide to Social Innovation" 6; Social Economy Unit 31; social initiatives 28, 31; social innovation 2
European Economic and Social Committee (EESC) 31
European Parliament 31
European social enterprises 38–9, 54–6; attitudes toward 45; challenges and obstacles 63–5; corporate governance 58; and Darwin's evolutionary theory 40–2, **41**, 46–50; decision-making processes of 58; drivers of innovation 61–3; EFESEIIS data on 56, 66n1; market constraints 64; motives and aspirations 57–8; negative environment 46; nepotistic structures 46; pathways of evolution 42–5; policy implications 65–6; primary objectives 56; recruitment process 64; service sectors 56–7; social benefits of 59; stakeholder engagement practices 58–61, 66; younger generation 58
European social policy 2, 13
European Union 30
European welfare system 13
Europe social entrepreneurship 200; ecosystems and evolutionary theory 203–5; main findings 200–2; policy implications 206; SEs and traditional enterprises 202–3; social innovation 205–6
Europe 2020 initiative 31
evolutionary pathways *49*, 49–50

evolutionary theory 3, 20–1, 38–9, 111–12, *113*; Darwin, Charles 40; in EFESEIIS project 39; heredity 48; selection 40, 47–8; and social enterprises 40–2, **41**; succession 48–9; variation 40, 46–7
Expert Group on Social Entrepreneurship (GECES) 31, 32
external environmental forces and innovation **138**, 138–9, **139**

Ferrannini, A. 182
for-profit enterprises 33, 98
France: "mutuelles" system 25; social enterprises in 44
Friedman, Milton 28

Galera, G. 56
genetic factor 111
Germany: Bismarck's reforms in 43; civil society organizations 44
Germany social enterprises 148–52
The Glad Café 168, 176n5
Glasgow Caledonian University (GCU) 15
Glasgow Wood Recycling (GWR) 167, 172
Global Entrepreneurship Monitor (GEM) 72
goods and services 186–9, **192**
Granovetter, M. 112
Granovetter, M. S. 99, 101, 188
grounded theory 39, 45, 50
G8 Task Force 31
"Guide to Social Innovation" 6

Harding, R. 72
Harvard Business School 28
Haugh, Helen 2, 179
How to Change the World: Social Entrepreneurs and the Power of New Ideas (Bornstein) 54
Hynes, B. 181

Impact HUB 15
industrial innovation 13
innovation 2, 141–2, **141–2**, 147–8; education 134–6, **135**; external environmental forces **138**, 138–9, **139**; key actors 139–40, **140**; methodology 130–1; motivations 136, **137**; organizational life cycle 132, **132**, **133**; organizational size

133, 133–4, 134; overview 127; previous experience 136, 136; professional satisfaction 136, 137; social awareness 131, 132; social enterprises and 61–3; staff and team characteristics 137, 138; theoretical background 128–30; *see also* social enterprises (SEs)
Institute for Social Innovation and Impact (ISII) 16
internal logics 111–12
ISII *see* Institute for Social Innovation and Impact (ISII)
Italian social cooperatives 42, 44, 62

Juncker Commission 32

Kerlin, J. A. 182, 185
key actors and innovation 139–40, 140
Klette, T. J. 130
Kortum, S. 130
Koufopoulos, D. N. 180
Kromkommer 174
Kropp, F. 72, 75
Krueger, N. 72

Lanificio 159 169, 176n8
Le Court-Circuit 168
Leech, N. L. 77
Liberal Reform Era 43
Lucas, Robert E. 28

Magazzino di previdenza 42
Mair, J. 6, 70, 72
marketization 118
Marti, I. 6, 70
memetic theory 40
Milosevic, Slobodan 43
mixed method approach 16–17
Montgomery, T. 111, 114, 119, 120
Morley, A. 2, 179
Moskowitz, T. J. 188
motivations and innovation 136, 137
Mulgan, G. 128
multi-disciplinary approach 16–17, 22
multi-stakeholder governance 58–61
Mumford, M. D. 128
Munoz, S. A. 179

Netherlands supportive ecosystems 44–5
new generation of social enterprises (NGSEs) 4; approach and methodology

164–5; biographies 171–2; physiologies 172–4; taxonomies 165–7; topographies 168–70; *see also* social enterprises (SEs)
Nga, J. K. H. 72
niche approach 145–6; Chancenwerk 154–8, 158; methodology 146–7; RheinFlanke 152–4, 157–8, 158; SE sector 149–50; social innovation and social enterprise 147–8; welfare structures 148–9; youth welfare 150–2
Noboa, E. 72
non-social enterprises (NSEs), decision makers in 75, 77, 78

O'Fallon, M. J. 75
Onwuegbuzie, A. J. 77
organizational life cycle and innovation 132, 132, 133
organizational size and innovation 133, 133–4, 134

paid employment 29, 29
Panato 172, 176n13
partnership 15–16
Pasetto, A. 181
Peattie, K. 2, 179
phenotype factor 111
PIN Polo Universitario Città di Prato 15
Pirvu, D. 33
pluralism 121–2
Poland: social enterprises in 43; Solidarity movement 27, 43
Pol, E. 61
Pottery Village 174
power, role of 113–14
Prabhu, G. N. 71
previous experience and innovation 136, 136
private-macro ecosystems 118–19
private-micro ecosystems 119–20
professional satisfaction and innovation 136, 137
Promoting Social Business 15
Putnam, R. D. 97

Reagan, Ronald 28
Renko, M. 72, 75
RheinFlanke 152, 157–8, 158; business model 153–4; idea and target group 152–3; success story 153
Rochdale Pioneers 42

SBI *see* Social Business Initiative (SBI)
Scarlato, M. 182–3
Schulze-Boeing, M. 181
Schumpeter, J. 128
Schumpeter, J. A. 6
Schwab Foundation for Social
    Entrepreneurship 28
Scottish and English ecosystems
    112, *113*
Scottish social enterprises 26
Sen, Amartya 180–2
sense of support, social capital and
    100–1, 103–4
Serbian social enterprises 44
Shamuganathan, G. 72
Sharma, A. 129
Smith, B. R. 180
social awareness and innovation 131, **132**
Social Business Initiative (SBI) 2, 31
social capital 20, 96; cooperation 100,
    104–5; definition of 96–7; EFESEIIS
    research results 101–5; future
    research on 105–6; positive impact of
    97–8; sense of support 100–1, 103–4;
    and social enterprises 98; strong ties
    99, 101; trust 100, 102–3; weak-ties
    concept 98–9
social cooperatives 42–3, 62
social economy 98; legislation 30; paid
    employment in 29, **29**
social enterprises (SEs) 1–2, 7, 13–14,
    69, 145–6; Chancenwerk 154–8, **158**;
    city development 45; coevolution 42;
    conceptions 27; definition of 5–6.
    28–29, 70–1; economic development
    18–19; ecosystems for *see* ecosystems;
    evolutionary theory and social
    networks 111–12, *113*; evolutionary
    theory of *see* evolutionary theory;
    Germany 148–52; institutional
    context 18, 21; methodology 114–15,
    146–7; pluralism in 121–2; power,
    role of 113–14; RheinFlanke 152–4,
    157–8, **158**; social capital and 98;
    and social innovation 2–3; social
    innovation and 147–8; social scientific
    perspective 18; stakeholder *see*
    stakeholder typology; succession 42;
    see also innovation; new generation
    of social enterprises (NGSEs)
social entrepreneurs 4, 33, 45, 49, 54, 72
social entrepreneurship 1, 7; definition
    of 6, 27, 70; in Europe 2020 initiative

31; fitness in 47–8, *48*; literature
    review 71–2; partnership in 15–16
social innovation 1, 7; definition of 6,
    61; European Commission on 2, 6;
    "Guide to Social Innovation" 6; *see
    also* innovation
Social Investment Package 13
social networks 111–12, *113*
socio institutional context 185–6, **192**
Solidarity movement 27, 43
staff and team characteristics and
    innovation 137, **138**
stakeholder engagement practices
    58–61, 66
stakeholder typology 120–1, *121*;
    private-macro ecosystems 118–19;
    private-micro ecosystems 119–20;
    statist-macro ecosystems 115–16;
    statist-micro ecosystems 116–17
statist-macro ecosystems 115–16
statist-micro ecosystems 116–17
Stevens, C. E. 180
strong ties 99, 101
survival of the fittest 40
Sustainable Human Development
    (SHD) 180, 182
Sustainable Territorial Evolution for
    Human Development (STEHD)
    180, 182
Swedish supportive ecosystems 44

Taylor-Gooby, P. 186
territorial achieved functionings 184–5
Testi, E. 203
Thatcher, Margaret 28
"trente glorieuses" 24
trust, social capital and 100, 102–3
Tuscany, DSE research study 75–6;
    data collection and management
    79, **80**; interpretation of results
    86–8; interpretative framework
    and variables 79; mixed method
    approach 76; qualitative
    methodology 76–7; quantitative
    methodology 77–8; questionnaires
    78–9, 88–93; regression analysis
    81–6
2008 economic crisis 1, 30

United Kingdom, social
    entrepreneurship in 28
United Nations 31
University of Northampton 16

Valadez Martinez, L. 186
van Dam, R. I. 204
Venturi, P. 61
Vermeulen, S. 72
Ville, S. 61
Voisin Malin 173–4

Wallace, J. 181–2
weak-ties concept 98–9
Weber, M. 6, 113–14, 122
welfare associations 148–9
Wert-Voll gGmbH 172, 176n12
Western European social enterprises 24, 34; customers in 33; evolution during 1980 27–9; and for-profit enterprises 33; historical evolution 25–7; market-driven approach 32–4; national, international, and supranational institutions 30–2;

semantic shift in 24; welfare state 24–6
Whatchado 167, 172, 176n3
WINDA case study 166–7
work integration social enterprises (WISEs) 32, 201

Yitshaki, R. 72, 75
The Youth Center ARKA 172, 176n11
youth welfare 150–2
Yujuico, E. 182
Yunus Centre for Social Business and Health 15
Yunus, M. 165, 186
Yunus, Muhammad 1, 15, 43
Yunus Social Business Centre 15

Zafeiropoulou, F. A. 180
Zandonai, F. 61

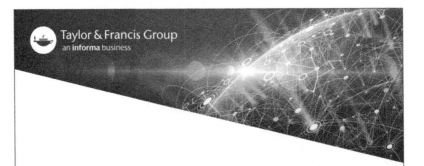

For Product Safety Concerns and Information please contact our EU
representative GPSR@taylorandfrancis.com Taylor & Francis Verlag GmbH,
Kaufingerstraße 24, 80331 München, Germany

Printed and bound by CPI Group (UK) Ltd, Croydon, CR0 4YY

01/05/2025

01858450-0003